The Gilbert Islands in World War Two

Peter McQuarrie

Masalai Press
2012

The Gilbert Islands in World War Two
© 2012 Peter McQuarrie

Cover design by George Taulealeausumai

ISBN 0-9714127-8-2

Published by:
Masalai Press
368 Capricorn Avenue
Oakland, CA 94611 USA

masalaipress@gmail.com
All rights reserved. No part of this publication may be reproduced or transmitted in any form or by any means, electronic or mechanical, including photocopy, recording, or any information storage or retrieval system, without permission in writing from the publisher.

Also by Peter McQuarrie

Tuvalu: A Celebration of 10 Years' Independence (photographs)
Strategic Atolls: Tuvalu and the Second World War
Conflict in Kiribati: A History of the Second World War
Tokelau: People, Atolls and History
A Floating World: Images of the Tuvalu Environment (photographs)

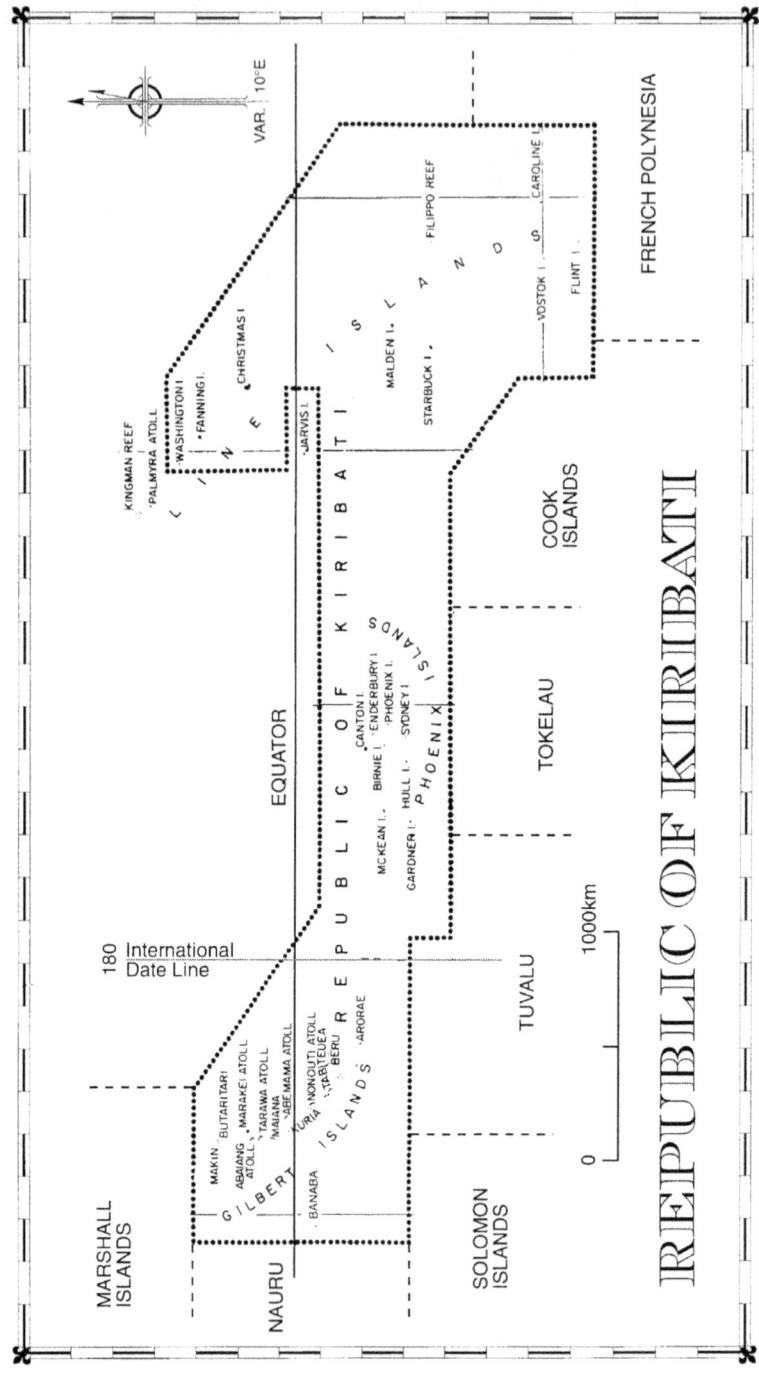

Map 1. The Republic of Kiribati in the Central Pacific

Contents

Preface i
Acknowledgements iii
List of abbreviations v
Glossary vi
Introduction vii

PART I THE DAWNING

1. The arrival of the German-Marshallese 3
2. Airfield surveys in the Phoenix and Line Islands 9
3. Fanning Island garrison 25
4. Coast-watching 33
5. German raiders 45

PART II THE RISING SUN

6. After Pearl Harbor—Tarawa and Ocean Island 55
7. Butaritari captured 67
8. Launch escape 77
9. Carlson's raid and the bombing of Keuea 91
10. Occupation of Ocean Island and Abemama 101
11. Occupation of Tarawa and fortification of Betio 115

PART III THE SETTING SUN

12. Bombing 127
13. Operation Galvanic 137
14. US occupation 165
15. Surrender on Ocean Island 187
16. Conclusion 197
17. Epilogue—dealing with the dead 209

Appendices:
A. Contributors 219
B. Coast-watchers in the Gilbert Islands 220
C. Chinese in the Gilbert Islands 222
D. Victims of the bombing at Keuea, 18 August 1942 228
E. Memorials 229
F. Japanese dead on Abemama 236
G. Honours and awards 237
H. Chronology 241
I. Abbreviations 244

Notes 245
Bibliography 261
Index 265

Maps:
1. The Gilbert Islands (Republic of Kiribati)
   in the Pacific .... preceding table of contents
2. The Gilbert Islands 2
3. Christmas Island, Northern Line Islands 10
4. Fanning Island, Northern Line Islands 24
5. Ocean Island, also known as Banaba 47
6. Tarawa Atoll 54
7. Japanese Intelligence map of the main settlement on Butaritari 68
8. Butaritari Atoll 92
9. Betio Islet, Tarawa, showing Japanese air field and fortification 116
10. American intelligence map of the Japanese defence area of
    Butaritari 159

Figures

Frontispiece: Gilbertese family on Abemama, with two Marine Corps sergeants, 20 December 1943.
1. Surveying gang, Christmas Island, June 1941.
2. New Zealand survey team between London and Paris, Christmas Island, 1941.
3. British flag flies at Christmas Island, 1941.
4. Fanning Island. Unloading supplies for the New Zealand Army garrison from *HMS Leander*, 5 September 1939.
5. Coast-watchers' stores are unloaded at Tamana Island, 13 August 1941.
6. First parade in uniform of the Ocean Island Defence Force, on the cricket ground, Ocean Island, July 1940.
7. *RCS Nimanoa,* in Tarawa lagoon. August 1941.
8. Japanese photograph of the three captured New Zealand radio operators from the Northern Gilberts.
9. Coast-watcher John Jones and Iabeta Tarakai meet again at Bikati, 51 years after the coast-watchers were captured there.
10. Thank you letter presented to Captain Webster of *Degei.*
11. Memorial at Keuea, Butaritari to the people who died when the village was bombed by Japanese planes on 18 August 1942.
12. Na Buariki of Keuea, survivor of the bombing.
13. A happy moment on Ocean Island in 1942 before the period of famine and disease.
14. Two of the British eight-inch guns installed by the Japanese at Betio.
15. Memorial on Betio to the 22 Europeans massacred there by the Japanese.
16. 'Softening up' bombing of Betio in preparation for the American invasion, 11 November 1943.
17. Marines wade ashore at Betio, Tarawa, 20–23 November 1943.
18. Assault on a Japanese bomb-proof shelter opposite Burns Philp pier, Betio, 20 November 1943.
19. Admiral Shibasaki's command centre, Betio, 1997.

20. Interior of Shibasaki's command centre.
21. Memorial to Japanese dead at Naa, North Tarawa.
22. American landing craft at Abemama.
23. Bishop Terrienne and priests liberated at Butaritari, November 1943.
24. Site of Shinto temple on Betio.
25. Arrival of Resident Commissioner Vivian Fox-Strangways and senior local administrative officers at Tarawa, soon after the battle.
26. Barracks of the Gilbert and Ellice Islands Labour Corps, Betio.
27. Labour corps workers on the wharf at Betio, November 1944.
28. Gilbertese girls pose with US Marine officers at Tarawa.
29. Change of dress from traditional—to American sponsored.
30. Many women and girls were busily engaged in laundry work for the Americans.
31. The first aircraft to land on the airfield at Abemama arouses much local interest.
32. Surrender leaflets dropped at Ocean Island early in 1944.
33. A well on Butaritari incorporates part of a WWII aircraft as its lining.
34. Amphibious landing craft (LVT) uncovered in 1974.
35. John Carter Bing (left) and an Ellice Islands crewman, *RCS Viti,* 1940.
36. John M. Jones at coast-watcher memorial.
37. Maria-Kannon monument at Betio Peace Park.
38. Korean monument at Betio Peace Park.

PREFACE

This book records the story of World War Two in the Gilbert Islands, which now form a part of the Republic of Kiribati. Previous accounts on this subject have been few in number; nearly all books in English have American authors and they have dealt almost exclusively with a single event—the Battle of Tarawa, with a focus on its effects on the American and Japanese combatants.

This present work documents the bigger picture, encompassing other dimensions of the war. It begins with the arrival of people of German descent who were fleeing from a harsh Japanese rule in Micronesia in the 1920s and 1930s; tells of the early days of the war, of coast-watching and German raiders; and deals with the periods of Japanese and American occupations. It is a history of a time and place and of the people involved: the indigenous Gilbertese (I-Kiribati), Ellice Islanders (Tuvaluans), German-Marshallese, New Zealanders, British, Chinese, American and Japanese. The book ends after the Japanese surrender in August 1945 by discussing the after-effects of the war, including how it shaped subsequent developments. The epilogue discusses the war dead and what became of their remains.

Sources used include oral and written accounts of the people who were personally involved. Other information comes from official records found in archives in Kiribati, Fiji, Tuvalu, New Zealand, the United States of America and Australia, and some translated Japanese material.

During World War Two, the people of the Gilbert and Ellice Islands were known as 'Gilbertese' and 'Ellice Islanders' and those are terms used to refer to them herein. Today they are known as 'I-Kiribati' and 'Tuvaluans' respectively.

The two northernmost atolls of the Gilbert Islands are herein given their correct names, Makin and Butaritari. It should be noted that during World War Two, the atoll of Butaritari was known to the Americans as Makin, while Makin was referred to as Little Makin.

i

A Note on Units of Measurement Used in this Book

The standard international system of measurement, the Metric System, is the basic standard used for this book. However, in most cases is seems appropriate to use the units which were actually used at the time and are those used in the primary sources. These generally use the Imperial System. In some cases where it appears useful for clarity, I have included the metric equivalent in brackets after the Imperial units.

In other cases there are current international standards which are not metric and so the units used during World War Two are still appropriate today. For example, aircraft still fly at attitudes measured in "feet" above the ground and the "nautical mile" is still the measurement of distance used in navigation. Ships still measure their speed in "knots" (nautical miles per hour). In these cases no conversions to other units are required.

ACKNOWLEDGEMENTS

Much of the work for this book was undertaken in 1997 under a research fellowship from the Macmillan Brown Centre for Pacific Studies, University of Canterbury, Christchurch, New Zealand. A shorter version of this book was published by the Macmillan Brown Centre in 2000, under the title *Conflict in Kiribati*. I am very grateful for permission to reuse the material here.

Many people provided first-hand information of their war experiences in the Gilbert Islands. Their names are listed in Appendix A. In this regard I am particularly indebted to ex coast-watcher, John M. Jones, who has been generous in sharing his time and recollections. Yuichi Nagura was extremely helpful in tracking down Japanese sources of information and translating material into English. Hiroshi Nakajima, President of the Pacific Society, also provided Japanese material, as did Takeo Kasahara and Yoshinori Kori.

I acknowledge the assistance of the following organisations in my research: Australian Archives, Archives New Zealand, and the National Archives of: Fiji, Tuvalu (Ellice Islands) and the United States of America. The staff of the Kiribati (Gilbert Islands) National Archives—Tarawa Nataua, Nei Temabine Iateru and Mereki Evii—were all tremendously helpful and efficient. Tanya Tremewan did a wonderful job in editing this book.

The following people helped me in various ways: Robert Austin, William H. Bartsch, Makurita Bauro, Dr Judith A. Bennett, Dr Niko Besnier, Sharon and Ellen Bing, Dr Alexandra Brewis, Cmdr Stan Brown, Fr Camilo, Dr Keith Chambers, Michael Claringbould, Margaret Cleary, James M Conway, Ralls Clotfelter, Rick Gillespie, Murray Grigg, Peter Foon, Sarbane Foon, Doug Hunt, Tangitangi and Faapusi Kaureata, Prof. Henry Lundsgaarde, Dr Barrie Macdonald, Allan McCarthy, Fuafua McQuarrie, Reg Motion, Mark Noah, Rosa Muller Norman, Jack Paton, Bruce M. Petty, John Ragg, Moira Reiher, Dr Jonathan Willis-Richards, Bob Rivers-Smith, Dr Kerry Rodgers, Joe Russell,

Gerry Sinclair, Inatio Teanako, Winston and Queenie Thompson, Sir Len Usher and Prof Bill Willmott.

Peter McQuarrie
Waitakere
New Zealand
February 2012

LIST OF ABBREVIATIONS

APO	Army Post Office
BPC	British Phosphate Commission
EEZ	Exclusive Economic Zone
GEIC	Gilbert and Ellice Islands Colony
HMFS	His Majesty's Fiji Ship
HMS	His Majesty's Ship
JPAC	Joint POW/MIA Accounting Command
JICA	Japan International Cooperation Agency
KGV	King George V
LMS	London Missionary Society
LORAN	Long Range Radio Aid to Navigation
MHLW	Ministry of Health, Labour and Welfare, Government of Japan
MV	Motor Vessel
NBK	Nanyo Boyeki Kabushiki Kaisha
NCO	Noncommissioned Officer
RCS	Resident Commissioner's Ship
RNZAF	Royal New Zealand Air Force
RNZNR	Royal New Zealand Naval Reserve
SS	Steam Ship
USCG	United States Coast Guard
USS	United States Ship
WPHC	Western Pacific High Commission

GLOSSARY

ba, coconut frond midrib

babai, giant swamp taro (*Cyrtosperma chamissonis*)

Banaban, Ocean Islander

be, loin cloth, lavalava

I-Matang, white-skinned person (European)

inai, a mat woven from a coconut frond

Kaubure, local government elder

Kiritimati, Christmas Island

maneaba, communal meeting house

Manra, Sydney Island

Nikumaroro, Gardner Island

non, a tree (*Norinda citrofolia*)

Orona, Hull Island

ren, a tree (*Messerschmidia messerschmidia*)

ruku, a creeping plant (*Convolvulus*)

Tabuaeran, Fanning Island

Teraina, Washington Island

Uea, High Chief

Photo Credits

1 – 3, Jack Paton; 4 Auckland Institute and Museum, neg C15, 424, from material donated by Merv Walker of Waiheke Is.; 5,7,8,9, 16 and 36 donated by John M. Jones; 6 by Paddy Orr; 10 Copy of letter supplied by Doug Hunt of Auckland and also held in the Sinclair family archive; 13 & 22 Archives N.Z. Phosphate Commission of N.Z. Records, A689, boxes 37 & 38; frontispiece and 17,18,23,24,26,27,28,31 NARA Record Group 80, US Navy photographs, 25 Smithsonian Institution, National Air & Space Museum, Washington D.C., 29&30 anon. donated by Prof. Henry P Lundsgaarde, 32 leaflets donated by Ralls C Clotfelter, US Navy Bombing Squadron VB-142; 34 Tony Falkland; 35 collection of Mrs Ellen Bing, Suva, Fiji. All other photographs by the author.

INTRODUCTION

The Gilbert Islands are now a part of the Republic of Kiribati which forms part of the huge archipelago of tiny gem-like islands and atolls known as Micronesia, covering approximately half of the Central Pacific Ocean between the Philippines and Hawai'i. Kiribati alone occupies an immense portion of the Central Pacific Ocean and no nation is more 'central' in the Pacific as the country straddles both the Equator and the 180th meridian. The 33 atolls and islands that make up the Republic all cluster about the Equator, 12 are north and 21 south. There are 16 islands to the east of the international dateline and 17 to the west. In an east–west direction the distance between the furthermost islands is 4000 kilometres and from north to south the furthermost islands lie 1800 kilometres apart. The limits of the Exclusive Economic Zone (EEZ) of Kiribati extend even beyond this over a distance greater than that across the continent of Australia. The EEZ of Kiribati actually borders on those of seven other Pacific islands countries or territories, namely French Polynesia, Cook Islands, Solomon Islands, Tokelau, Tuvalu, Nauru, Marshall Islands, and the US territories of Palmyra, Howland and Baker Islands.

The name Kiribati is a local corruption of the word 'Gilbert', reflecting the history of the Republic of Kiribati when its islands were part of the British Crown Colony—the Gilbert and Ellice Islands—created in 1916. The English name Gilbert came from Captain Thomas Gilbert of the British vessel *Charlotte*, who passed through the group in 1788. Prior to that the Gilbert Islands were known by the indigenous name Tungaru. The *Charlotte* was accompanied by the *HMS Scarborough* under command of Captain John Marshall and the ships were two of the first convict transports to travel from England to Australia. Gilbert and Marshall became the first Europeans to see the islands of Abemama, Aranuka, Kuria, Tarawa, Abaiang, Butaritari and Makin. During this voyage the group of islands to the north of the Gilberts were named the Marshall Islands after Captain Marshall.

The Ellice Islands broke away from the Gilberts as a separate British colony, 'Tuvalu', in 1975. The remaining island groups which have formed the

Republic of Kiribati since it became an independent country in 1979 are the Gilbert Islands, Line Islands, Phoenix Islands and the single isolated island of Ocean Island (also known as Banaba). Not all the islands in the Line and Phoenix groups are permanently inhabited but of those that are, the populations are comprised almost totally of Gilbertese (I-Kiribati) people, the indigenous people of the Gilbert Islands.

Ocean Island is the westernmost island in the country and also holds its highest point above the sea—80 metres. Like Nauru, its nearest neighbour, Ocean Island is a raised limestone island which once contained rich phosphate rock deposits. These were mined out over the first 80 years of last century. All other islands in Kiribati are low-lying, only four or five metres above sea level; most are flat atolls with central lagoons, or single coral rock islands. The Gilbert Group comprises 16 islands west of the dateline, which are evenly distributed north and south of the Equator. The eight Phoenix Islands in the next group eastwards, all slightly south of the Equator, lie north of the Samoas and Tokelau and are largely uninhabited. An additional two islands forming part of the Phoenix Group, Howland and Baker, are US possessions and not part of Kiribati. Further to the east again the eight Line Islands lie between Hawai'i and Tahiti. Christmas Island (Kiritimati) is in this final group and, in terms of land area, is the largest atoll in the world accounting for half the total land area of the country.

The total land area of Kiribati is only approximately 800 square kilometres while the sea area formed by the 200 nautical mile EEZ around each island totals more than three million square kilometres. This gives the country the highest ratio of sea-to-land of any country on earth. Apart from Ocean Island all the islands have sandy coralline soil which is of poor quality and affected by drought and high salinity. In general such soil supports only coconut palms, pandanus and breadfruit trees which, with *babai* (giant swamp taro), form the chief subsistence agricultural crops. The sea, however, supplies a greater abundance of food resources, both from the coral reefs and the deep ocean that surrounds them.

The Gilbertese people are Micronesians with links to other Micronesian peoples to their north and also with influences from their Polynesian neighbours to the south. The people speak one language, Gilbertese, which is an Austronesian language related to other Pacific languages and with little variation throughout the different islands of the country. The dialect originally spoken by the Banabans had some differences but was still easily understood by all other Gilbertese speakers.

The islands of the Gilbert Group are home to the majority of the population with about half the total living on South Tarawa, the capital. The Line and Phoenix Islands were never permanently inhabited and people have only lived on some of them since the beginning of the British administration era. At the start of World War Two the total population of all the islands was approximately 30,000 but in the 60 years since the war ended the number has more than trebled to over 100,000.

These little-known islands came into prominence when the Japanese entered the war and captured the Northern Gilbert Islands, two days after their attack on Pearl Harbor in Hawai'i. The British had made no attempt at defence. Most British expatriates had departed months earlier when Japanese occupation of the islands seemed imminent. The British colony, the Empire's orphan, was then left to the local people, the Japanese, New Zealanders at Fanning Island and on coast-watching duties, the US Army at Christmas and Canton Islands, and whoever else might have wanted to grab parts of it.

The level of involvement of the individual islands of Kiribati and their peoples in the war was varied. On some islands the war meant only greater isolation from the outside world. For others their first contact with war was through New Zealand coast-watchers stationed on many islands in 1941 and who brought the first radio communications and current news of the world. The New Zealand Army also maintained a garrison on Fanning Island, protecting the submarine cable communications station there. Other islands in the Line and Phoenix Groups became US air bases and those in the Gilbert Group and Ocean Island were bombed and then occupied, first by Japanese and then by American forces.

Ultimately three of the atolls in the Gilbert Islands formed the stage for the first major conflict in the Central Pacific, Operation Galvanic, of which the Battle of Tarawa played the major part. During this period, hundreds of ships and aircraft and thousands of troops were on or around the atolls. Tarawa became the scene of one of the bloodiest battles of the Pacific War. Although extremely costly in human lives, this first great amphibious landing against heavily fortified positions provided the Americans with valuable lessons for later island battles as they fought their way across the Pacific towards Japan. Subsequently US bases in the Gilbert Islands supported operations farther north in the Marshall Islands as the US Navy continued its island hopping campaign.

Some of the atolls and islands of Kiribati were severely affected by the influx of military personnel and hardware and by the way the occupying forces treated the indigenous people. On Tarawa and other Gilbert Islands, islanders were forced to work as slave labour for the Japanese or were later recruited by US forces and shipped off to work on other islands in the Pacific. Employment that was paid in western currency and food rations brought new affluence and changed values and lifestyle for some, while others were dying of malnutrition and disease or were executed by the Japanese on isolated Ocean Island. All told, some 750 Gilbertese people lost their lives as a direct result of the war. This represents approximately 2–3 per cent of the population, a figure which appears high considering that they were non-combatants and should have been evacuated to safe locations.

The fragile ecologies of the atolls experienced their first major environmental changes when occupying forces built fortifications, airfields and roads, and blasted and dredged coral reefs within lagoons. The war also brought changes that affected post-war political developments. Some islanders who had worked with the American forces wanted an end to British rule and for the Americans to take control over their lives. This idea was never realised but the British were forced to allow the people more say in the running of their affairs after the war. The war was a turning point after which the people moved more rapidly along a new road of increased education, training and self-determination.

Part I

THE DAWNING

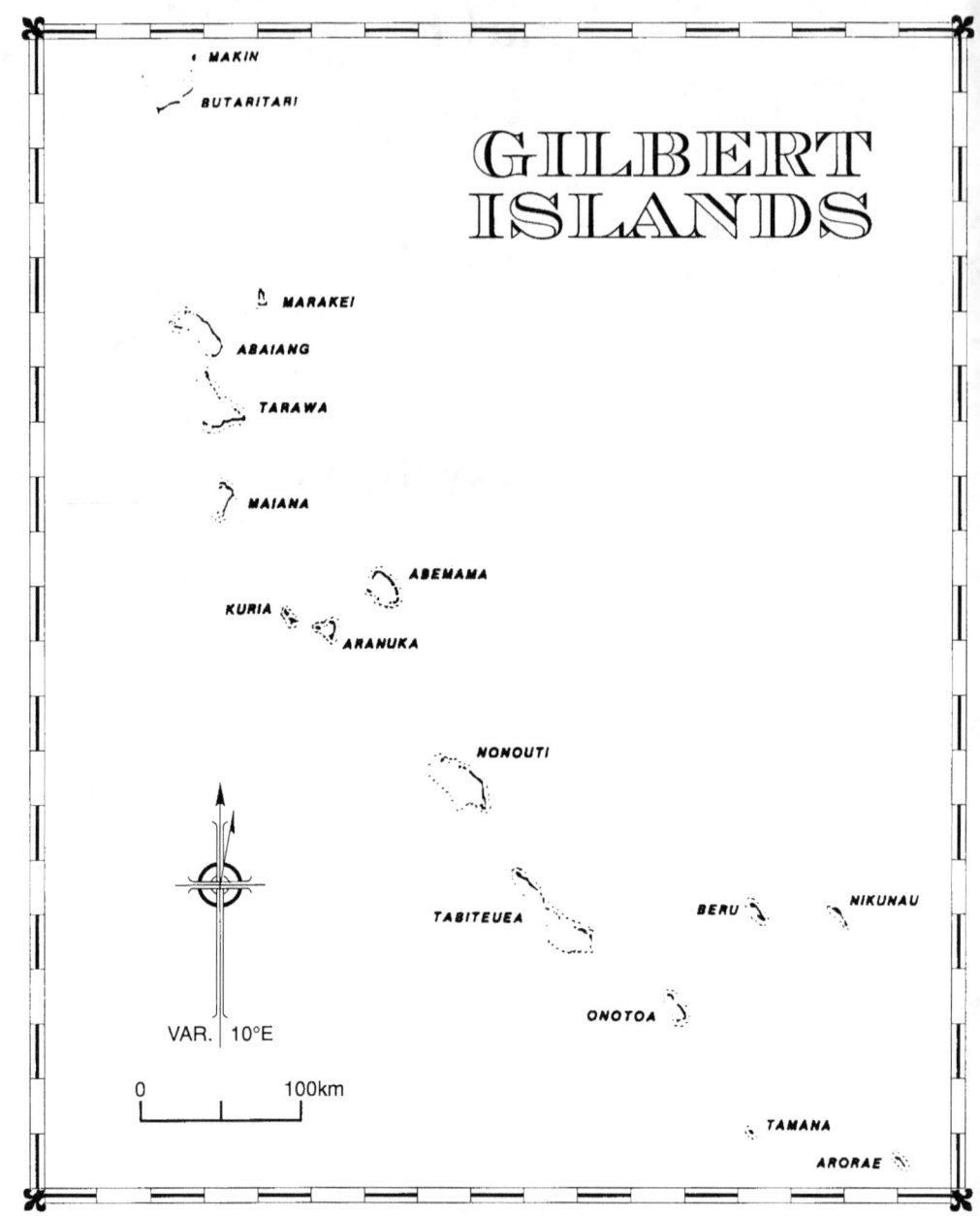

Map 2. The Gilbert Islands

1
The Arrival of the German-Marshallese

Perhaps it was in the 1920s that the Gilbertese received the first omen of the conflict to come between the Japanese and the Allies in the Gilbert Islands. At that time, people of German descent began to arrive in the northern Gilberts from the Marshall Islands, where Japanese rule had been making their lives increasingly difficult. At the southernmost perimeter of Japan's South Sea Empire, the Marshall Islands were to become a staging area for the invasion of the Gilbert Islands in 1941.

Why the migration?

In 1914, at the start of World War One, Japan had taken possession of all German Micronesian colonies north of the Equator. Unlike the previous colonisers of Micronesia (the Spaniards and the Germans), the Japanese then began developing the islands and resettling their own people there, thus relieving the pressure of the burgeoning population at home. The Japanese introduced strict rules along with harsh punishments to enforce them. Under this regime, Micronesians became third class citizens in their own islands (after the Japanese and the Koreans/Okinawans). The Japanese regarded the people of German descent as a class of still lower status, and treated them accordingly.[1]

Thus several German-Marshallese families who had been content under German rule left the Marshall Islands seeking better lives in the Gilbert Islands. In the Gilberts, they could expect Catholic schools with German and French priests. Their children would have the opportunity to learn the English language and European culture and religion, rather than the Japanese language, Buddhism and Shintoism taught in schools in the Marshall Islands.[2]

Butaritari in the Gilberts was a popular destination for German-Marshallese. It had become the headquarters of the Catholic Church in the Gilbert Islands in 1900 when Bishop Leray, the first bishop, moved there from Nonouti. With him came Mother Isabelle, two sisters and nine Gilbertese girls, to start a secondary school. Overseas traders based at Butaritari had married young local women and Mother Isabelle actually opened two separate schools, one for Gilbertese and another for half-caste European girls.[3]

Furthermore, due to its northern position, Butaritari has a much higher rainfall and does not suffer the droughts experienced in the southern and central Gilberts. Lush and green in comparison with some of the more desolate southern islands, it is more attractive to new arrivals in the islands. As a result, Butaritari has had a long history of contact with European and Chinese traders,[4] some of whom later moved on or branched out to other Gilbert Islands. Its closeness to the Marshall Islands encouraged shipping and trade in that direction.

Thus in 1925 a very popular and respected Catholic teacher, Brother Engelhardt, transferred from the Marshalls to the boarding school on Butaritari. Some of his Marshallese pupils and their families followed him there, and he soon started a boys' school.

A Question of Loyalties

Among all the German families who emigrated to Butaritari, there were members who became involved in World War Two in some way. Some were of special assistance to the Allies because they knew the topography and languages of the Gilbert and Marshall Islands. Although all were loyal to the Allied cause, the Allies regarded the German people in the Gilberts with suspicion after the Japanese took control of the Gilberts in 1941 and 1942. The Allies were uncertain about where the German loyalties lay or whether they had collaborated with the Japanese.[5] The Japanese too were unsure and suspicious of the German families, even after September 1940 when Japan, Germany and Italy signed the Tripartite Pact—an agreement for mutual military and economic assistance.

The situation was certainly complicated. Some of the German immigrants had been born in Micronesia when it was under German rule and so held German nationality; others had become naturalised British; while the younger ones were British because they had been born in the Gilberts. Some had married Gilbertese, settled down and now have many descendants living in Gilbert Islands. Other families stayed for only a short time because of the war; their descendants live in Fiji, the Marshall Islands and other parts of the world, but not in Gilbert Islands.[6]

Yet although they were sympathetic to Germany because of their ancestry, the German families were in the midst of a Pacific war between the Allies and Japan. In this context, the overriding factor that directed their loyalties was their dislike and mistrust of the Japanese. The Narruhn family, for example, held particularly bitter attitudes towards the Japanese after they confiscated all the family land holdings in Micronesia.

German-Marshallese in the Pacific War

Members of the following German-Marshallese families figure prominently in this account of World War Two in the Gilbert Islands.[7]

First, Robert Narruhn (born in Ponape) and his wife Rosa de Brum (born in Likiep, Marshall Islands) moved to Butaritari around 1920, when Robert was 31 years old. Bringing five children with them, they had a further four children on Butaritari before the outbreak of the war. Robert worked as manager of the Butaritari trading station of Burns Philp South Seas Limited, buying copra and selling trade goods. One of their sons, Frederick, was destined to work with the US Army as a guide and interpreter in the recapture of Butaritari. Another son, Robert, became a radio operator and worked for the coast-watching service on Tarawa before escaping to Fiji and joining the Fiji Navy (see Chapters 6, 8 and 13).

Another well-known German name in Gilbert Islands is Reiher. It can be traced back to a sea captain from Hamburg, Christopher Reiher, who married a Caroline Island woman, Mary, and settled in Jaluit (the headquarters of the

Marshall Islands). One of their sons, Fritz, sent all his children to the Catholic boarding school on Butaritari in the 1920s, then moved to the Gilberts with his wife, his brothers Henry and William and their families in about 1930. Based on Tarawa, Fritz and Henry were reputed to be expert sailors and boat builders (Chapter 8), maintaining a closeness to the sea, like their father.

The third brother, William Reiher, lived on Abemama and was also well respected as a person of character and for his skills as a sailor and boat builder. From 1931 to 1937, he built the concrete Protestant church at Tamana Island in the southern Gilberts and the largest vessel in the colony, the 41-tonne wooden ship *Santa Teretia*, for the Sacred Heart Mission at Abemama. After commanding this ship in the Gilbert Islands for about three years, in 1940 he was given command of the government auxiliary ketch *Kiakia* until August 1941. Thereafter, he retired to Abemama due to poor health.[8] He had applied for British naturalisation, which he would have obtained if the war had not disrupted the processing of the necessary paperwork. Later, in 1943, he helped pilot US ships into Abemama lagoon.

The Muller family was another based on Butaritari. Some branches had lived there since the late 19th century. Henry Muller (Heinrich Jelske Muller) arrived in 1889 with his wife who was from the de Brum family of Likiep in the Marshalls. Their son Fritz married Nei Reibo of Ukiangang, Butaritari in 1912 and worked as a carpenter for the Chinese trading firm of On Chong. Fritz's son Rudolph Keakea Muller worked on the On Chong ship *Macquarie* and assisted the US Army in the recapture of Butaritari in November 1943. Henry's other sons Herman and William married Nei Mangarita from Butaritari and Nei Ruta from Makin respectively. One member of the Muller family, Joseph, won commendation for assisting Carlson's marine raiders when they attacked the Japanese seaplane base on Butaritari in August 1942 (Chapter 9). Yet after December 1941, when the Japanese occupied Butaritari, the British were particularly suspicious of the Muller family as several family members worked for the only Japanese company operating in Gilbert Islands at the time, Nanyo Boyeki Kabushiki Kaisha (NBK).

Based in the Marshall Islands, in 1915 NBK gained a licence to operate a branch on Butaritari but nowhere else in the Gilbert and Ellice Islands. It had a small 220-tonne ship *Seikai Maru* with a crew of around 15, which operated between Jaluit and Butaritari, bringing trade goods and buying copra. The Japanese manager of NBK Butaritari, Chosito Kanzaki, married Lina Muller (Helen Lina Muller) daughter of Henry, on Butaritari in 1919. At the outbreak of World War Two, he and his assistant Suzuki were the only Japanese nationals in the Gilbert Islands. It seems that he was also a Japanese spy in the months leading up to the Japanese invasion. The *Seikai Maru* had radio communications which Kanzaki could have used to make reports to Jaluit. Certainly he became a Japanese intelligence and liaison officer during the occupation.

Born in Vienna, Austria, Captain Moritz von Reymond had a life at sea before marrying and settling in the Marshall Islands long before World War Two. His second wife, Maria Mitchell, was from Nonouti in the Gilbert Islands. Some of their children were born in the Marshall Islands, others on the Gilbert Islands of Marakei, Maiana and Nikunau, before Moritz and Maria finally settled on Butaritari. Moritz was 78 years old when the Japanese invaded Butaritari in 1941.

Following in his father's footsteps, Bruno von Reymond joined the merchant marine. When war broke out, he joined the Royal Australian Navy. For the recapture of Butaritari, he was seconded to the US Navy as a special member of the intelligence staff. In this role, he proved to be of great assistance with his local knowledge (Chapter 13). Both he and Fred Narruhn served with distinction and were later awarded honours by the Americans.[9]

Paul Schutz, a German trader for the Marshall Islands firm of Jaluit Gesellschaft, had been on Abaiang since 1892. His son William was born on Abaiang, then spent part of his youth at school in the Marshall Islands before returning to work in the Gilberts. After 16 years of employment with Burns Philp, he formed the first cooperative society in the colony, the Tangitang Cooperative Society on Abaiang. This later developed into a chain of cooperative trading stores dealing in copra and trade items, with branches on Butaritari, Makin, Marakei, Tarawa, Maiana and Abemama.

William had two sons, Willie and Henry, both of whom became involved in the war. Willie Schutz trained as a wireless operator and joined the government service in September 1941 at the Tarawa radio station. He was later responsible for sending out the 'LLLL' message, signifying that Japanese troops had landed on Tarawa (Chapter 6). During the war, Henry became involved with the Japanese and later the Americans on Tarawa.[10]

Finally, the large Brechtefeld family of Abemama descended from W Maximilliam Brechtefeld, who was on Nonouti in 1885 and then moved to Abemama. He had at least three wives and, reputedly, 50 known children. He traded for the Jaluit Gesellschaft company and died on Abemama in 1934. Chapter 8 covers the story of how George Brechtefeld risked his life to take a launch with supplies for coast-watchers on islands either occupied by Japanese or under their surveillance. Stephen Brechtefeld was a radio operator at Beru in the coast-watching radio service.

2

Airfield Surveys in the Phoenix and Line Islands

Lying between Fiji and Hawai'i, the Phoenix Islands were well-positioned for development as fuel stopovers for trans-Pacific air routes. As early as 1937 Amelia Earhart planned to use Howland Island in the Phoenix Group as a fuel stop in her well-publicised attempt to be the first woman pilot to circle the globe. However, it was somewhere in the vicinity of the Phoenix Group that she went missing on the long flight (4000 kilometres) between Papua New Guinea and Howland.

Initially the interest in the Phoenix Group focused primarily on its potential for commercial air services from Hawai'i to Australia, New Zealand and Fiji. Pan American World Airways established the first commercial air base in the Central Pacific. During 1938 and 1939 it developed a seaplane base in the lagoon at Canton Island, and used it as one stopover in its service to New Zealand. The first Pan American trans-Pacific flight to land on Canton, a Boeing 314 clipper, touched down in the lagoon on 24 August 1939. However, in the Pacific War, the bases of the Phoenix and Line Groups were to become a vital military link in the aircraft grave routes across the Pacific to Australia and the southwest Pacific. As the war drew closer, British, New Zealand and US governments grew increasingly interested in using the air bases as staging points for military aircraft.

Initial Surveys and Island-Grabbing

In August 1935 the British warship *HMS Wellington* made an investigative voyage to Hull (Orona), Sydney (Manra) and Gardner (Nikumaroro) Islands, and found all were uninhabited. On Hull, however, a large, corrugated-iron shed

Map 3. Christmas Island, northern Line Islands

contained tools and a Union Jack, left from an earlier British settlement of copra cutters from Tokelau who had worked there in the 1920s.[1]

Not to be excluded from island-grabbing in the Central Pacific, in May 1936 the US President issued an order for Howland, Baker and Jarvis Islands to become US territory. As justification, he referred to the Guano Act of 1856, under which US companies could acquire unclaimed islands for their country merely by digging for guano on them. Companies had done this much on the three islands in question.[2]

In December 1936 the crew of the British warship *HMS Leith* raised the Union Jack on Canton Island in the name of King Edward VIII; when he abdicated, they did it again for George VI.[3] Then on 18 March 1937 His Majesty's government issued a proclamation that extended the boundaries of the Gilbert and Ellice Islands to include eight of the Phoenix Islands: Burnie, Canton,

Enderbury, Gardner, Hull, McKean, Phoenix and Sydney, which were most of the islands in the group that the US had not already claimed.

The British annexed the uninhabited Gardner, Hull and Sydney Islands specifically for the purpose of resettling people there from the overcrowded southern Gilberts. Of course the resettlement scheme also ensured that it was Gilbertese who occupied the islands, supporting British claims of sovereignty over them. (At the time, Sydney and Hull Islands were actually again inhabited by 'British' people—namely, Tokelauans working for Burns Philp in copra cutting as they had done earlier.)[4]

The British were also aware that Canton Island in particular had potential as an air base. Shortly after issuing the proclamation, they established a radio communications station there with two radio operators seconded from Fiji, F H Rostier and Geoffrey Vavasour Langdale, with one Fijian assistant.

There followed further visits to the Phoenix Islands by the *HMS Leith*. The New Zealand government also became involved, as it saw the Pacific islands as important to its own defence. Two cruisers of the New Zealand Division of the Royal Navy, sister ships *HMS Achilles* and *HMS Leander*, appraised both this group and several islands in the Gilbert Group as possible air bases. On an *Achilles* survey tour over July and August 1937, the Aerodrome Services Branch of the New Zealand Public Works Department sent an engineer, Eric Smart, to assess the possibilities of the various islands as bases for land planes and flying boats.[5]

The combined results of these visits were reported as follows.
- **Hull and Sydney Islands** had good lagoons for seaplane operations but no access into the lagoons nor anchorage for ships.
- **Canton Island** was better as a base for both land- and seaplanes, but coconut palms should be planted as only 11 were growing on the island.
- **Christmas Island (Map 3)** had good anchorage, access to the lagoon and ample areas for both land and sea runways. Smart considered that the island offered better facilities than any other British island in the Central Pacific.
- **Fanning Island** was also good for both land- and seaplanes.

- **Gardner Island** was considered as a possible site for two runways, one on the northwest and the other on the southwest side of the atoll.

The surveys ruled out use of the other islands in the Phoenix Group on the grounds that they were too small or difficult for landing supplies. However, many in the Gilbert Group were considered good or at least possible locations for either land- or seaplanes.[6]

Near the end of 1938 a further New Zealand expedition went to the Phoenix Islands to look into Smart's recommendations in greater detail. This time the party was comprised of more senior personnel. It included a survey team under surveyor J A Henderson; the aerodrome engineer of the Public Works Department, E A Gibson (who after the war became Director of Civil Aviation);

Figure 1. Surveying gang, Christmas Island. June 1941

and the Chiefs of Naval and Air Staff as well as the Staff Officer, Intelligence. The party marked areas for seaplanes with buoys on Christmas Island lagoons, while on Fanning, Hull and Gardner Islands it marked out both seaplane and airfield sites.[7]

US–British Tensions

The purpose of the 1938 New Zealand expedition was to investigate a trans-Pacific air route linking Australia, New Zealand and North America. Over 1938 and 1939 the British and New Zealand governments held discussions about a general scheme for trans-Pacific air routes. They hoped that it would be feasible to establish a route using only 'British' islands. To this end, one suggested route was New Zealand–Fiji–Nukunonu (one of the atolls in the Tokelau Group)–Hull Island–Christmas Island. However, it was found that such a route was impractical.[8] The intention behind such a route was to avoid Canton Island, which had become a bone of contention between the British and US governments. Refusing to recognise the 1937 British claim, in March 1938 the US President signed an administrative order placing Canton and Enderbury Islands under the jurisdiction of the US Department of the Interior. Both sides in the conflict stationed small numbers of occupation forces on Canton. For a time, a three-man British force stood guard over the Union Jack there while a seven-man US team watched over the Stars and Stripes.

The matter was finally resolved in April 1939 when the two governments signed an agreement for joint administration of Canton and Enderbury for 50 years. They agreed that, without prejudice to their respective claims, they would set up joint control and allow the islands to be available for use as airports for international civil aviation, although only by British and US airlines.[9] Yet in this same year the Americans were making aerial photographic surveys of Gardner and Hull Islands, which sparked an official protest from the British who had already settled Gilbertese on both islands. On 29 April the aviation tender *USS Pelican*, accompanied by *USS Swan* of the US fleet air base in Honolulu, began survey work using small float planes. The April agreement likewise did not prevent the US government from announcing further claims to 25 islands in the Gilbert, Ellice, Line and Phoenix Groups, later in 1939.[10]

More Detailed Survey and Development Work

In June 1940 the US government advised the British that it proposed spending US$1.5 million on dredging work and runways on Canton Island and asked whether they had any objections. The British did not: the lagoon at Canton was cluttered with a mass of coral reefs, over an area 4.8 kilometres by 460 metres, and they could not meet the cost of clearing it themselves.[11]

Then, following the earlier British–New Zealand discussions, in September 1940 the Aerodrome Services Branch of the New Zealand Public Works Department sent out a team of surveyors on a secret project code-named 'Operation Grandpass'. Its purpose was to prepare plans for a seaplane runway at Laucala Bay in Suva and for land- and seaplane runways on Christmas and Fanning Islands. The team of six men comprised chief surveyor N J Till, three surveyors, a chainman and a radio operator/depth sounder technician, E J Paton. They took a launch fitted with an echo sounder for the seaplane runway surveys. Arriving in Suva on 13 September 1940, the team had determined alighting areas and approaches and completed the Laucala Bay project by 20 December. After other survey work around Fiji, they departed for Christmas Island on the *Aorangi* on 31 March 1941.

At that time, Christmas Island was the only major point on the trans-Pacific air route on which the New Zealand government still lacked detailed information. The team's task was to conduct detailed surveys of the sites that the 1938 expedition had selected: aerodromes at 'Le Bourget' and 'Croydon' and a seadrome at St Stanislas Bay. They were also to investigate the possibility of seaplane-alighting areas on four other lagoons: Wilkes, Deepwater, Motutabu and Ellis .

For transport over the vast desert areas of the large atoll (its total land area being 460 square kilometres), the team had brought a three-tonne truck, but this proved too heavy for the soft sand terrain. Luckily, in a shed they discovered the remains of three old Ford trucks, a 1926 Model T and two 1929 Model A vehicles, all much lighter and more suitable for the island. They managed to get one Model A operating, thus dealing with their transport problems—until Kima Pedro, the labour overseer on the island, ran it into a coconut tree and cracked the clutch housing irreparably. With more work and cannibalising of the broken vehicle for spare parts, they ended up with two working vehicles (**Figure 2**).

The survey work was extensive, requiring six months of hard work in trying conditions. Under the equatorial sun, the temperature and humidity were high, and the white coral sand reflected a blinding glare. Finally, on 11 October 1941 the team left for Fanning Island on the *Tagua*, a two-masted auxiliary schooner registered in New Zealand. However, due to an alert that a German raider was in the area, they were recalled to Christmas Island.

Back on Christmas Island the team were awaiting developments from the German raider warning when suddenly a destroyer arrived off the lagoon entrance. They were much relieved to learn that it was not German but the *USS Ellet*. The Americans were not yet at war but had similar ideas to the New Zealanders about surveying the island and building airstrips. The US contingent consisted of 30 enlisted men, meteorologists, surveyors and army engineers. Very well-equipped, they arrived with a mass of new outboard motors, four-wheel drive vehicles and sand motorbikes—rather outshining the New Zealanders and their 1926 Model T Ford. But credit is due to the New Zealand team who had completed their task with very limited resources.

Over the next few days the New Zealand and US groups collaborated closely. The New Zealanders handed over the results of their six months' work to the Americans, who were most grateful as it reduced their work substantially. The detailed work included specific details for two land aerodromes, two seadromes and a complete, detailed coastal survey of the whole island. Good relations between the US and 'British' groups (see the flag in **Figure 3**) were further cemented after a motor skiff from the *Ellet* tried to enter the harbour and capsized in the breakers. Four Gilbertese men working for the New Zealand team rescued the Americans, quickly and seemingly effortlessly. To the Gilbertese who are

Figure 2. New Zealand survey team between London and Paris, Christmas Island, 1941

competent and much at ease in the surf it was nothing, but to the Americans it meant a great deal.[12]

After the New Zealand team departed from Christmas Island on 27 October 1941, the Americans continued with the airfield project. On 18 November, the *Haleakala*, a chartered Hawaiian inter-island steamer, arrived with six officers and 150 enlisted men of the 804th Army Engineer Aviation Battalion and 70 civilian workers from Hawaiian Constructors, to begin airfield construction. However, US policy meant that ultimately Christmas Island would be home to the second military airfield of the Central Pacific.[13]

The First Military Airfields

In October 1941 the US Secretary of War decided that the initial air ferry route across the Pacific should be Hawai'i–Canton–Fiji–Townsville. As a result

Figure 3. British flag flies at Christmas Island, 1941

of this decision, the Americans gave priority to building air facilities on Canton ahead of those on Christmas Island.[14]

The navy supply ship *USS Antares* then left Honolulu for Canton with a team to build the airport, with a derrick and two pineapple barges loaded with construction materials in tow. It took more than two weeks to get to Canton. After breaking loose several times, both barges were eventually lost: one became so waterlogged that the party had to sink it by blowing it up with dynamite and the other went missing at sea. However, the party salvaged some of the lumber that the barges had been carrying, and eventually made it to Canton on 14 November. Six days later, a civilian construction team arrived on the *SS Mariposa*.[15]

Another dredge, the *Holland*, arrived on Canton on 7 December, the day that the Japanese attacked Pearl Harbor. After a few days of waiting, during which time the Americans on Canton expected to be attacked themselves, they decided to evacuate all civilians from the island. The tug *Mamo* towed the *Holland*, carrying 200 civilian workers and a few Gilbertese and Tuvaluan civil servants, to the US naval base on Pagopago; it would have made an easy target had Japanese attack planes arrived during the voyage. From Pagopago the civilians were kept uncomfortably in quarantine on the barge for several days, and then went to their home countries.[16]

The Pearl Harbor attack placed a new urgency on completing the base on Canton. On 17 December the commanding officer received a message that 'General Short expects you to present him with a Xmas present… a runway… 5000 feet long and 200 feet wide…'[17] Completed with two days to spare, the airstrip then received its first planes, three B-17 bombers, on 5 January. Landing there on their way to Townsville, these bombers became the first planes to complete the South Pacific ferry route which had been announced open on 28 December: Hawai'i–Canton–Nadi–Tontouta–Townsville.[18]

But although the air facilities were constructed, they were almost entirely unprotected. The Canton Island garrison consisted of just 78 army engineers, who had only light weapons—carbines, rifles and a few machine guns. There were no large guns, no radar, no searchlights. Work on gun emplacements was soon underway and preliminary defences were complete by the end of January 1942. Then on 13 February a task force of 1124 Army officers and men, under the command of Colonel Herbert D Gibson, arrived at Canton Island after a 14-day direct sea voyage from San Francisco. Their transport ship was the 10,700-tonne *SS President Taylor*, owned by the US President Line and under charter to the Army.

At Canton Island, the ship drifted half a mile off the lagoon entrance as it was far too large to enter the channel, and unloading via barges commenced. An advance party of anti-aircraft artillery units was amongst the first troops ashore, to set up gun positions to protect the remainder of the unloading operation. While most of the troops and equipment were still aboard the ship, their escort, a destroyer that was patrolling nearby, detected the presence of a submarine and ordered the *President Taylor* to move in closer to the island for protection. There was a ten-foot swell running, whose surge was causing the ship to swing towards then away from the reef. Unfortunately the ship was taken a little too close and the surge brought her down onto the reef where her hull was pierced and held fast. This accident happened close to the time of high tide and when the tide receded the ship became stuck even harder. The situation was worsened that night when a westerly gale blew up and drove the ship higher onto the reef. The remainder of the troops were disembarked without incident the next day but the ship's engine room was flooded and much of the cargo damaged by seawater.[19]

There was a wait of two weeks for tug boats to arrive from Honolulu. By that time the *President Taylor* had been further damaged by the surf and irrecoverably stuck on the reef. The tugs attempted to move her but they were unsuccessful and shore parties were sent out daily to salvage everything useful and bring it ashore. This salvage work continued for three months at which point the ship was abandoned. In addition to the loss of the ship itself, the Army estimated that 80 per cent of the equipment and supplies carried on the ship were lost or ruined as a result of the grounding.[20]

Meanwhile, on Christmas Island after the Pearl Harbor attack, there was near panic and the island was placed under martial law. All men, both army and civilian, were ordered to work on constructing the airfield seven days a week. The first plane, a B-17 Flying Fortress from Honolulu, landed on the runway on 22 January 1942.[21]

Rickenbacker Misses Canton Island

Captain Eddie Rickenbacker, who had been the US ace fighter pilot of World War One, went missing in October 1942 while attempting to fly from Hawai'i to Canton Island.

Captain Edward Vernon Rickenbacker had lived an adventurous life. As a young man he raced automobiles, and in 1914 he held the World Land-speed Record. Then, serving in World War One, he became a war hero, bringing down more German aircraft than any other American pilot: 22 planes and 4 balloons. During the 1930s he was a leader in the American air-transport industry, becoming president of Eastern Airlines. When the US was drawn into World War Two, he undertook special assignments related to military aviation. He was 52 years old when the Boeing B-17 bomber on which he was travelling became lost in the Central Pacific.[22]

Rickenbacker and his aide, Colonel Adamson, had been engaged on a secret mission which involved a flight of 2700 kilometres from Honolulu to Canton Island. As Canton is less than 16 kilometres across, to locate it after a flight of this distance over featureless, open ocean, required highly precise navigation. The plane, with a crew of six plus Rickenbacker and Adamson, took off at 1:29 am on 21 October. After several hours of uneventful flying, at the point when they should have been near to their island destination, there was nothing to be seen but ocean. Radio bearings were requested from Canton Island but Canton Radio was unable to oblige as it was not equipped with direction-finding gear. Even a volley of anti-aircraft fire, which it was hoped might pinpoint the island, was not seen by those aboard the B-17. And after searching until the plane had used all of its fuel, an emergency landing was made in the sea. The eight men — Rickenbacker, Adamson, pilot, second pilot, engineer, second engineer, navigator, and radio operator—all transferred to the plane's three life rafts. Their aircraft went down rapidly and they were not able to remove any food or water before it sank. This was a pitiful beginning to what was to be a long drift-voyage covering at least 600 nautical miles (1110 kilometres).[23]

Four days later at Palmyra Island in the Line Group, the *USS Hilo* (Patrol Torpedo Boat Tender) with four patrol boats (PT boats) departed for Funafuti in the Ellice Islands where they were to be stationed. Their route was to take them via Canton Island and so they were requested to keep a lookout for survivors from the missing plane. Landfall at Funafuti was made on the morning of 2 November, without having sighted the rafts.

The survivors drifted on, catching a few noddy birds and fish, and were lucky to encounter rain squalls which provided a little drinking water. All were in bad shape physically after a few days of exposure but they managed to keep their spirits up. The condition of second engineer Alexander Kaczmarczyk deteriorated, however, and on the 12th day at sea he died. On days 18 and 19 pontoon planes were sighted which, unbeknown to those on the rafts, were on patrol out of Funafuti. But the small rafts were not spotted from the air and

Captain William Cherry, commander of the lost B-17, decided that the three rafts should separate and spread out so as to present a better chance of being found. Cherry cut loose his smaller raft from the other two and drifted away alone, leaving three men in each of the remaining rafts. Some time later the second pilot, Lt James Whittaker, cut away the raft with himself, the navigator and the radio operator, leaving Rickenbacker, Adamson and Bartek, the engineer, to drift independently. Just before sunrise on their 21st day adrift, Whittaker and his two companions spotted land, broke out their paddles and used their remaining energies to keep the raft moving towards it. They hit the surf and shot in over the reef at 2 pm but, because of the fear that they might have landed on a Japanese-held island, concealed themselves and their raft in the undergrowth. They had actually landed on the east side of Nukufetau, the atoll just north of Funafuti. Whittaker was the fittest of the three and managed to get some coconuts for them to drink.

It was on the 21st day also that Captain Cherry's raft was spotted and he was rescued. A naval Vought Kingfisher floatplane was on a routine patrol from Funafuti when the radioman sighted the yellow life raft, 40 kilometres from base. One of the recently arrived patrol boats, Ml, was sent out and brought Cherry to the sick bay on the *Hilo*. Extensive air and PT boat searches then commenced for the other two rafts; but it was not until late the following day that Rickenbacker's raft was located. It was further away than they had anticipated, as it had drifted past Funafuti and was now 60 kilometres from the island.

It was almost dark when the seaplane pilot, Lt Eadie, spotted the raft. Fearing that he would not be able to guide surface craft to the position, he risked landing his small aircraft in the open ocean. The manoeuvre was successful and the raft and plane were brought together. Adamson was found to be in poor condition and, because of the ocean swell, it was only with great difficulty that they managed to transfer him to the cockpit of the Kingfisher. There was then no more room inside, so Rickenbacker and Bartek were lashed on to the wings of the plane and their raft tied to one of its floats. The plane was unable to take off in this state and so began a long, over-water taxi back to Funafuti. After about an hour, PT26 reached them and took off Rickenbacker and Bartek. It was decided to bring Adamson back in the seaplane rather than to risk attempting to transfer him to the PT boat.[24]

Meanwhile a plane had been sent to Nukufetau to drop a note to the New Zealand coast-watchers, asking them to search the atoll for the last missing raft and for any survivors. No radio communication was used because of the need to maintain secrecy. The New Zealand coast-watcher, radio operator Colin Davis, immediately arranged for Ellice Islanders to search the atoll in canoes, and it was 19-year-old Toma who found Whittaker. He assured him that there was nothing to fear as the island was under Allied control. It was by now the 22nd day since the B-17 had been lost. Whittaker, Second Lt John DeAngelis, the navigator, and Sgt James Reynolds, the radio operator, were brought in canoes across Nukufetau lagoon to the coast-watchers' quarters in the village.[25]

The *Hilo* departed Funafuti immediately. It reached Nukufetau the same afternoon but, because of poor visibility in the lagoon, the ship did not attempt to enter. A whaleboat with the ship's doctor and executive officer on board was sent ashore. Reynolds' condition was the most serious of the three men, and coast-watcher Davis stayed all night with the doctor to help care for him. The following day all the survivors were taken to Funafuti. Whittaker and DeAngelis went immediately to a temporary Funafuti Field Hospital which had been hastily constructed soon after the first sighting of Cherry's raft. Reynolds was kept aboard *Hilo* for several days while the doctor administered plasma and glucose, before transferring him ashore. After a further few days of recuperation, the seven survivors were all moved to the area base hospital in Pagopago, American Samoa.

It was the two oldest men, Rickenbacker and Whittaker, who survived the ordeal best. Lt Gordon, the *Hilo*'s executive officer, recalled that:

> One interesting sidelight on Captain Rickenbacker's condition was that when taken aboard he said that he had never seen a P.T. boat before, and, therefore, he would like to inspect it, in spite of the fact that he had been on this raft 21 days, and the captain of the P.T. boat took him all over his ship, showing him the various features.[26]

While recovering in Funafuti Hospital, Rickenbacker was interviewed by Richard Seither, a line sergeant and war correspondent with the Marine Corps at Funafuti. The interview took place on 15 November; the rescue was a top news story at the time and perhaps Seither could not resist breaking the censorship rules. He had his story smuggled out to Hawai'i, where it appeared in the *Honolulu Advertiser* on the 23rd, under his own name and with the title 'Rickenbacker Well Knows About "Nearness to Death"'.[27] He did not reveal the name of the island nor the location where the rescue and interview had taken place, other than to state '… somewhere in the South Pacific'. At the time the existence of the base at Funafuti was kept very secret and later newspaper articles referred to 'an advanced naval base'. As a result of his publication of the story, Seither was reprimanded and demoted to the rank of private first class.[28]

Rickenbacker wrote an account of the drift voyage and his rescue which appeared in editions of *Life* in 1943.[29] As a result of the raft ordeal, the publicity and Rickenbacker's influence, many improvements were rapidly made to the safety equipment carried on planes. Life-rafts were made larger and carried emergency food supplies. Each one had a map made of rubberised material so that it could be used as a sail, sun-shield and rain-catcher. The Air Force demonstrated these improvements to Rickenbacker and sought his opinion before making them standard.[30]

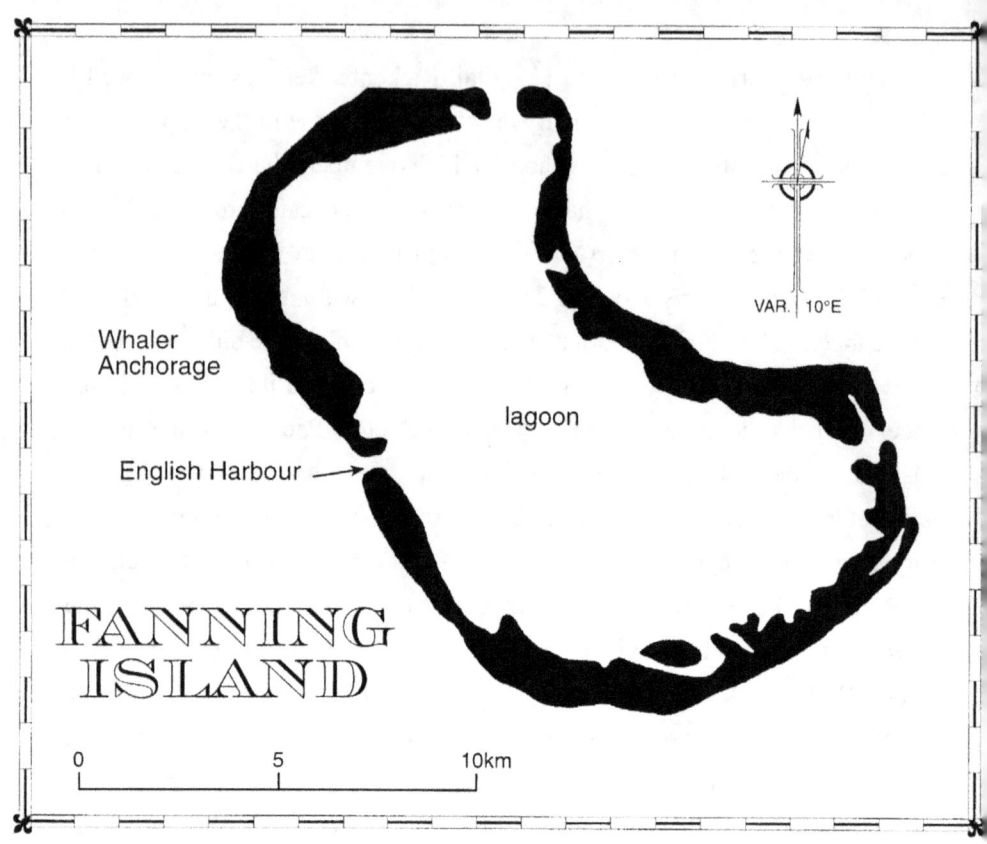

Map 4. Fanning Island (Tabuaeran), northern Line Islands

3
Fanning Island Garrison

The first military activity in the Gilbert Islands in World War Two was also New Zealand's first instance of active participation. On 30 August 1939, four days before Britain, France, Australia and New Zealand officially declared war on Germany, troops from the New Zealand Army left from Auckland on the warship *HMS Leander* to guard the submarine cable station, owned by the British company Cable and Wireless, on Fanning Island (**Map 4**). They arrived there on 5 September.[1]

Planning for the Protection of Fanning

Fanning Island (Tabuaeran) had been the site of a communications relay station since the first trans-Pacific cable opened in 1902. Vital to telecommunications, it linked Australia and New Zealand with the northern hemisphere. It also linked Fiji with Canada via a cable from Fanning to Vancouver that was the longest in the world (5547 kilometres).

The strategic value of the Fanning Island station had not gone unnoticed by the Germans in World War One. Within a month of the declaration of that war, the German raider *Nurnberg* appeared off Whalers Anchorage on the island, flying the French flag. But far from being friendly French, the Germans soon came ashore with fixed bayonets and drawn revolvers. Sailors with axes smashed all the communications equipment and cut the cables.

Although no one was harmed in that incident, there was a strong feeling that the British government should have provided naval protection to this important station. The same mistake was not to be made in World War Two. In 1929 the Committee of Imperial Defence on Local Forces in the Pacific first recommended the provision of protection when necessary. Then in August 1930 the New Zealand government agreed that it would send two platoons when His Majesty's government requested it to do so. Following a review of this commitment in 1937, the New Zealand government agreed it would increase that force to a company of 150 men.

In 1939 a further effort was made to coordinate the defence of the South Pacific region when the New Zealand Prime Minister, Michael Savage, initiated a meeting of representatives of the Australian, British and New Zealand governments. At this meeting, held in Wellington on 14 April, it was confirmed that New Zealand would send troops to Fiji and Fanning Island as soon as war in the Pacific was inevitable. The New Zealand Cabinet reconfirmed the decision in May. By mid-1939 planning was underway to send a preliminary force to Fanning Island, which would be reinforced later.[2]

The operation was surrounded by much secrecy. The troops involved—Number One Platoon, A Company—secretly began training in Wellington in June 1939. The two officers and 30 men of other ranks that comprised this small unit were themselves unaware of the operation details until 2 September when, en route for Fanning Island, they were informed of their destination and of their task of protecting the cable station there. The next day while still at sea they learned that their country had declared war on Germany.[3]

Maintaining the attempt at secrecy, the *Leander* tried to reach Fanning with great haste and unnoticed. Unfortunately she could not carry enough fuel to steam at full speed directly to Fanning; the direct route would have required travelling at an economical speed of 12 knots, which would take an estimated 21 days. Instead the ship travelled at speeds of up to 25 knots, quickly and quietly refuelled at Suva and made it to Fanning in less than six days.

However, their transit through Suva attracted more attention than had been planned. As the ship arrived there before the war had actually started, many people did not realise the seriousness of disclosing information about its movements. The Asiatic Petroleum Company, which supplied fuel for the *Leander*, sent a message to the manager of the Melbourne Hotel in Suva telling him to 'get more beer in as the *Leander* is coming again'. In addition, the women working in the government offices and at the Burns Philp store knew when the

Figure 4. Unloading supplies for the New Zealand Army garrison on Fanning Island from *HMS Leander*, 5 September, 1939

ship was coming and how long she would be in port, as did the women on the Suva telephone switchboard.[4]

When the ship approached Fanning, she sent the small float plane, which she carried on deck to reconnoitre and to ensure that the island was clear of enemy ships before she made her presence known.[5] The *Leander* did not attempt to enter the lagoon, dumping the 163 tonnes of stores for the soldiers on the ocean beach and then hastening away south.[6]

The First Tour of Duty

On arrival (**Figure 4**), the two officers on Fanning Island were provided with single quarters at the cable station while the enlisted men made camp with tents and constructed a few wooden huts with materials that they brought from New Zealand. They soon discovered that the Gilbert Islands thatched-roof huts were much more comfortable than tents in the tropical heat, and local labour was employed to construct them. When the soldiers added their own concrete floors to these huts, they gained very comfortable and clean accommodation.[7]

The Cable and Wireless station had good provisions: it had the only large-scale electricity supply in the Gilbert Islands at the time, a good water supply and spacious concrete buildings. All facilities were run by Chinese workers who provided most of the engineering expertise, while the managers were all Australians and New Zealanders.

Soon the soldiers settled down to a routine of little work and ample spare time. They were able to enjoy some of the amenities of the Cable and Wireless staff club, which included a day and night tennis court, billiards and later even movies and a swimming pool. Cable and Wireless also hosted occasional parties. Fishing in the lagoon and ocean was a popular pastime, using boats belonging to the cable station.

Fresh food was in short supply, as shipping to the island was irregular and they had no refrigeration. One soldier has described their diet as 'World War One food':[8] they ate a lot of biscuits and bully-beef. However, they supplemented this with fresh coconuts, the fish that they caught, and infrequent local limes and pawpaw. On rare occasions, they were also able to obtain a coconut crab from the islanders. A later detachment experimented with growing vegetables by hydroponics, but managed to produce only a little food.

The garrison had arrived armed with just rifles and machine guns. Machine gun posts were set up to cover the entrance to English Harbour, the only ship entrance into the lagoon on Fanning.

When a large ship arrived unannounced off the coast of the island on 29 September 1939, the alarm was raised, and women and children were evacuated from the settlement. However, it turned out that the vessel was a Swedish tanker, which was apparently only using the island to obtain a navigational 'fix', and then it disappeared.[9]

The other excitement in the early months of the New Zealanders' stay on Fanning was caused by their commanding officer. In the *Official History of New Zealand in the Second World War*, Gillespie describes him as 'not temperamentally suited to command an isolated garrison in a trying climate'. In truth, the commanding officer turned to alcohol, made a nuisance of himself and became dangerous. Sergeant Major Campbell Prentice placed the commanding officer under arrest for his own safety and everyone else's,[10] and the *Aorangi* of the Union Steam Ship Company was diverted to take him off the island in November. A replacement, Captain G P O'Leary, arrived on the *Atholdike* in the same month.

After their six-month prescribed tour of duty was over, the first group was relieved by a platoon under the command of Captain W A Moore on 7 March 1940. They returned to New Zealand on the British warship *HMS Hector*, which was an old tramp merchantman with a four-inch (102-millimetre) gun mounted on the stern. En route, they called at Apia and Nukualofa, as well as Suva where they collected an advance of salary and had a week's leave, before arriving in Auckland on 29 March.[11]

A Strengthened Garrison

The second relief arrived on 3 October 1940 in the New Zealand ship *Matai* under charter to the army. On 7 March 1941 the garrison strength was increased to 105 men, when an additional 42 infantry and 30 artillery personnel, along with a six-inch (150-millimetre) naval gun, arrived on the *Aorangi*.[12] The ship had been escorted by the New Zealand *HMS Monowai* and on the same voyage had dropped off the airfield surveyors on Christmas Island (Chapter 2). The increased supply of weaponry now included rifles, eight machine guns, one three-inch (76-millimetre) mortar, 250 grenades and the quick-firing six-inch gun with 150 rounds of ammunition.

The New Zealanders had asked for two six-inch guns from the British government, which turned them down on the grounds that the demand for such guns was too high for it to meet all requests. So instead the single gun that the reinforcements brought came from Australia, where it had been mounted at Sydney Heads, protecting the harbour entrance. On Fanning, the garrison then resorted to constructing a number of 'palm tree gun positions', or imitation six-inch guns made from coconut logs. Set up along the ocean coast between

Whaler Anchorage and English Harbour, these 'guns' would be observed by arriving ships and, it was hoped, frighten off any potential attackers. A 22-metre high watch tower, erected prior to the soldiers' arrival, stood near the only real six-inch gun.[13]

Four army signalmen were added to the garrison in August as part of the coast-watching service. On 15 September they established radio communications with Washington Island (Teraina) and Christmas Island, and with Suva. A few days later Suva advised that a German raider was believed to be in the area and the island again went on alert, but nothing was seen.[14]

By October the Aerodrome Services team had completed their work on Christmas Island and turned their attention to Fanning. They arrived off the island on 12 October in the *Tagua*, one of the small auxiliary sailing vessels chartered by the Public Works Department for such work.[15] They arrived during another of the German raider scares and no one came from the island to greet the ship. Indeed, the new arrivals could see no signs of life on the island at all, although the coconut cannons guarding the coast were visible.[16]

Eventually a canoe with four Gilbertese, two men and two women, came alongside. They spoke with the captain and with one of the Gilbertese survey assistants, asking a few questions about the *Tagua* and her crew, and then returned to shore. Soon after, the beach came to life with soldiers, civilians and Gilbertese, all waving. The canoe party had assured those on shore that the vessel was not a raider. The surveyors and soldiers held a small party that night where they drank New Zealand beer but, before any survey work could be planned, the *Tagua* was recalled to Christmas Island because of the raider warning.[17] The last relief, consisting of 41 soldiers, came to Fanning on 24 November 1941, when 38 men were also uplifted for the return home. Two weeks later the Japanese attacked Hawai'i and the garrison increased its vigilance, expecting a Japanese attack which never came.[18]

A Historic US Arrival

On 25 April 1942 the Americans took over the defence of Fanning after the New Zealand government invited them to assume responsibility for it along with French Polynesia and Western Samoa. It was a historic occasion, representing the first time in the war that US forces took over from forces of the British Empire. A contingent of 141 Army officers and enlisted men arrived on the destroyer tender *USS Rigel*, accompanied by the *USS Gridley* which by prior agreement transported the relieved New Zealand garrison home. They arrived in Auckland on 17 May.[19] After an uneventful two years of garrison duties, the Americans left Fanning on 9 July 1944. By this time, the war had moved far away and protection of the island was no longer necessary.[20]

4

Coast-Watching

Coast-watching in the Gilbert and Ellice Islands began in September 1939 with the declaration of war on Germany.[1] It was seen as necessary in the light of events in World War One, when German raiders had attacked shipping and put the Fanning Island cable station out of service (Chapter 3). The fear of a repeat attack was well founded, as raiders again operated in the Pacific during World War Two. Between April 1940 and December 1942 the Germans had 10 ships operating worldwide that were fitted out as cruisers but masqueraded as harmless merchant vessels, flying the Japanese flag before Japan entered the war. With the goal of disrupting and destroying merchant shipping, these raiders sank several phosphate ships near Ocean Island and Nauru (Chapter 5), in addition to others in Australian and New Zealand waters.[2]

The First Two Years

From September 1939 until the coast-watching system was upgraded in August and September of 1941, islanders reported any ship, aeroplane or other object that they sighted from their coasts to their island magistrate, who was the government representative on each island. Island magistrates in turn reported to their district officers at the first opportunity. If considered important, reports were then forwarded to the colony headquarters on Ocean Island by radio.

Although this system operated throughout all islands within the Gilbert and Ellice Islands Colony, it could only be really effective on those islands that had radio communications. The coast-watching stations in the Gilbert Group were:

- Ocean Island, headquarters, reporting to the Australian Naval Board;
- Butaritari radio station, northern Gilberts, reporting to Ocean Island;

- Tarawa radio station, northern Gilberts, reporting to Ocean Island;
- Beru radio station, southern Gilberts, reporting to Ocean Island.[3]

There was no government radio station at Tarawa. The only station there was owned and operated by the Burns Philp trading company, at Betio. This station, 'VSZ', Tarawa Radio, provided communication to shipping and to the colonial government headquarters at Ocean Island, as well as to Burns Philp trading stations around the Pacific islands. At Beru Island in the southern Gilberts, the London Missionary Society (LMS) operated a radio station from its mission station at Rongorongo. This station had been established in 1926 by the head of the mission, Rev. Eastman, who had trained a number of Gilbert and Ellice Islanders as radio operators. Elsewhere, in the Phoenix Islands there were radio stations on the islands of Canton, Gardner, Hull and Sydney and in the Line Group there was a government-operated station on Christmas Island, and good telecommunications with Fanning Island due to the submarine cable relay station there. Washington Island was in radio communications with Fanning Island by means of a private radio system operated by the Burns Philp copra plantations on each island.[4]

The inhabitants of the Phoenix Islands were settlers who were taking part in the government-sponsored scheme to relieve overpopulation in the southern Gilberts (Chapter 2). Altogether some 700 colonists went to the Phoenix Islands between 1938 and 1940. On Gardner Island the total population was only 66 so no formal watch system was set up there; however, any unusual sightings of ships or planes were to be reported. On the more populated Sydney and Hull Islands, all able-bodied men took turns in patrolling the length of coast associated with the settlements. In addition, Hull Island had the services of an Australian radio operator, Arnold Cookson, who had been a telegraphist in the Royal Australian Navy in World War One and who had joined the Gilbert and Ellice colonial service on Ocean Island.[5]

Coast-watching at the four Gilbert Island stations operated on a more formal basis with lookouts maintained in several directions from each island and the radio stations operating to regular schedules. At the headquarters on Ocean Island, the radio station was in continuous operation.

Under this system, it appears that no significant sightings were made. However, it established the concept of coast-watching and the procedures associated with it.

A Change in Focus

By mid-1941, although the German threat remained, the emphasis of coast-watching had shifted towards looking for aircraft and ships of a Japanese invasion force. Many people believed that a war in the Pacific was inevitable after the Axis powers of Japan, German and Italy signed a tripartite pact for mutual military assistance. In this context, in May 1940 President Roosevelt had shifted the US fleet from southern California to a position of readiness in Pearl Harbor, Hawai'i.

The Gilbert and Ellice Islands now held a key position between the Japanese Marshall Islands and British Fiji, which increased the importance of early reporting from the colony. In an effort to improve the effectiveness of coast-watching, the Australian, British and New Zealand governments agreed, at a meeting in Wellington in March 1941, that the New Zealand government would provide radio equipment and personnel to upgrade the network. The British Western Pacific High Commission (WPHC), headquartered in Suva, would provide shipping to transport men and stores to the islands from Fiji.

The system planned would comprise a control station in Suva and 14 smaller stations scattered strategically throughout the Gilbert and Ellice Islands, all operated by New Zealanders. Nine of these new stations would be in the Gilbert Islands. In addition, the existing colony radio stations on Ocean Island, on Tarawa and in the Line and Phoenix Islands would continue to carry out coast-watching duties. They would become part of a large South Pacific network controlled by the New Zealand Naval Board in Wellington.

The colonial government took control of the Burns Philp radio station at Betio using local radio operators. One operator was John Milne who had previously been radio operator on the government ship *Nimanoa*. As all messages were to be transmitted in cypher, the government stations were supplied with code books for the 'Playfair' code, the same code as the New Zealand coast-watchers used. The LMS mission radio station at Beru Island was taken over by the New Zealand coast-watcher, Alan Taylor.

Altogether the New Zealand Navy would have responsibility for 58 coast-watching stations in the tropical Pacific, covering Fiji, the Cook Islands, Tokelau, Tonga and Western Samoa as well as the vast territory of the Gilbert and Ellice Islands Colony. The New Zealanders would undertake the greater part of communications work, while the islanders would continue to be responsible for watching for ships and aircraft. Some local men would in addition receive wireless training and many islands would benefit from radio communications for the first time.[6]

Training and Recruitment

With the collaboration of the Director of Education, Captain F G L Holland, the Bairiki Wireless Training School was set up early in 1941, based at King George V (KGV) School, on Tarawa. Its objective was to train, at one time, 25 local wireless operators to assist the New Zealand staff of the coast-watching radio stations. Planned to take about 10 months, the course was based on a standard portable short-wave transmitting and receiving set, the 'Teleradio', made by Amalgamated Wireless Australia Limited.[7]

The school was under the charge of Reginald Morgan, an Australian who had been operating Tarawa Radio for Burns Philp. When the colonial government took over Tarawa Radio he assumed his new post. Trainees included some of the pupils who already attended the KGV School and had an aptitude for wireless telegraphy work. Other recruits were young men with a background in wireless transmitting and receiving, through their work as assistants to wireless operators of peace-time radio stations for the government, Beru Mission Station, and stations of local firms or on local vessels. The trainees were Gilbertese, Ellice Islanders and of mixed race (German-Marshallese and British-Gilbertese).

A more well-established training centre was the Suva School for Wireless Operators, run by Edwin Higgings who had previously operated a radio station on Tarawa for Burns Philp and was married to Carla Reymond of the Butaritari Reymond family (Chapter 1). It also provided a few Gilbertese and Ellice Island radio operators for the Gilbert and Ellice Islands service. Trained here were Frank Christopher, the grandson of a European trader and with Banaban ancestry; Tito Homasi, an Ellice Islander from Nanumea; and Korina Takeimoa, an Gilbertese from Marakei and ex-KGV student. When they completed their training in 1942, these three operators all went to coast-watching stations in the Phoenix Group, by which time the main Gilbert and Ellice Islands service had been in operation for more than six months.[8]

Meanwhile in New Zealand another group of young men was undergoing special training for coast-watching duties. They were all New Zealand Post and Telegraph Department employees who had completed basic training as telegraphists. Now they received additional technical instruction in basic maintenance of radio equipment. The New Zealand Meteorological Department headquarters in Kelburn, Wellington, also trained them in weather reporting procedures, as one of their tasks would be to set up the first meteorological stations on the islands. Finally, with all messages to be transmitted in cypher, further training was given in New Zealand, and later also in Fiji when the Royal New Zealand Air Force (RNZAF) gave instruction in using the 'play fair' code.

All of the New Zealanders had volunteered for 'special duties outside New Zealand'; half of them were below the legal age of consent (21 years), so their parents had to give their approval. While the fear of being captured by the Germans (or even the Japanese) may have deterred some from volunteering, a positive incentive was the remuneration. In their peace-time work, most of the operators were earning around £115 per year, which was taxable, while some earned only £80 or £95. As volunteers they were offered £300 tax free, a considerable increase. There was no real explanation provided for the increase other than that it was an incentive to work overseas. Perhaps the implication was that the salary now included some sort of 'danger money'.[9]

There was strict secrecy about the whole operation so that the Japanese would not learn of the move nor of the exact locations of the radio stations when they began transmitting. However, the men and their families rightly believed that they would be sent somewhere in the Pacific to keep a lookout for German raiders. They were informed that they might be stationed anywhere from the Auckland Islands in southern latitudes to islands on the Equator, and from the western Pacific to easternmost Pitcairn Island. Neither the Gilbert and Ellice Islands nor even the Western Pacific High Commission were specifically mentioned.

It had been decided in New Zealand that because of the youth and inexperience of the New Zealand operators, they should each be accompanied by two unarmed soldier companions if they were stationed on very isolated outer islands anywhere in the Pacific. The majority of the soldiers selected were mature—at least one was a veteran of World War One—and all were volunteers from troops of the 2nd New Zealand Expeditionary Forces already stationed in Fiji. However, the resident commissioner of the Gilbert and Ellice Islands, R H Garvey, was concerned that the soldiers would not have enough work to occupy their time, which would create problems with the local people. Despite his request to reconsider the stationing of the soldiers, the New Zealand Chiefs of Staff held to their decision and the soldiers remained part of the plan.[10]

On some islands, the soldiers were not required. For example, there was no need for them on Tarawa, given that the government had its own radio station and the wireless training school there. Likewise, the island of Abaiang could communicate by sailing canoe with nearby Tarawa, the headquarters of the district officer of the northern Gilberts, and the district officer for the southern Gilberts and European missionaries resided on Beru, so no soldiers were posted to these stations.

A sore point for the soldiers was their level of pay. Despite their maturity, they received £126 per annum, which was taxable. It was a far cry from the tax-free £300 paid to the young radio operators, whom the soldiers nicknamed the

'Millionaire Signalmen'. It might also be noted that the local radio operators were paid only £18 a year.

Establishing the Radio Stations

On 13 July 1941 the New Zealand team sailed from Auckland on the *MV Matua*, reaching Suva on 16 July.[11] Waiting for them was the ship commissioned to take them north to the remote atolls, the *HMFS Viti* under the command of Lt Commander Mullins RNR. Built in Hong Kong in July 1940 as *RCS Viti*, the official yacht of the Western Pacific High Commissioner, she was redesignated as a colonial vessel of war on reaching Fiji, in view of the approaching war. As such she was involved in operations throughout all territories of the western Pacific during the war years.

The *Viti* departed from Suva on 19 July with the New Zealand coast-watchers and their soldier companions, bound first for the Ellice Islands then for the Gilberts, Ocean Island and the Phoenix Group.[12] It was on board the *Viti* that the radio operators and their soldier companions met each other for the first time. They also found out which islands they were going to, with their destination determined on religious grounds: Catholics were sent to the predominantly Catholic northern Gilberts, while Protestants went to the southern Gilbert and Ellice Islands, strongholds of the Protestant LMS.

Off the coast of Niulakita, the first island in the Ellice Group, the sea was too rough to land people and equipment safely, so the *Viti* steamed north to other islands, delaying the installation of the Niulakita station until the return voyage. By the time she left the Ellice Islands on 12 August, the five stations of Funafuti, Nukufetau, Vaitupu, Nui and Nanumea were on the air.

Tamana was the first island the *Viti* reached in the Gilbert Group, and the installation of its Teleradio set was completed on 14 August (**Figure 5**). The ship then departed for Beru, site of the parent station for the southern Gilberts. Here a working party was left behind to install the required station which was larger and more complex than the stations using the simpler Teleradio equipment.

Figure 5. Coast-watchers' stores are unloaded at Tamana Island, 13 August 1941

After calling at Kuria, the *Viti* arrived at Maiana to discover that the coast-watching lookout posts were some 10 kilometres from the selected site for the radio station. Such a distance made supervision of the lookouts difficult; eventually coast-watchers dealt with the problem by requisitioning a bicycle to shorten their travelling time.

On Tarawa, the cargo and personnel for the islands of Nonouti and Abemama were transhipped to the *RCS Nimanoa*, under command of Captain Harness. The *Nimanoa* had been the first government-owned ship in the colony, ending the government's reliance on ships owned by religious missions and trading companies. When it reached Abemama on 21 August, the New Zealanders were very impressed by the great strength of the Gilbertese men who single-handedly lifted full 200-litre drums of fuel over the rails of the ship and passed them to men in the whaleboats below.

On Nonouti, they met the retired Scottish trader A M McArthur, known locally as Makata, who became a personal friend of the radio operator and two soldiers stationed on the island. McArthur lived with his Gilbertese wife, Nei Kaeka, in a modest, European-style weatherboard house about one and a half kilometres south of Matang village. As his book-lined walls confirmed, McArthur was an avid reader. Now aged about 60 years, he had spent the greater part of his life in the Gilbert Group, working for various trading companies such as Burns Philp, before finally retiring to Nonouti, his wife's home island. He became the coast-watcher's adviser on all matters concerning customs and life on Nonouti. From there, the *Nimanoa* collected the installation team from Beru and then returned to Tarawa to meet the *Viti* after it had delivered the remainder of the personnel and equipment.[13]

Before leaving Tarawa, the *Viti* had collected about 10 trainee operators from the Bairiki school. Even though they had not completed the 10-month course, they were considered ready for duty. Then she sailed for Ocean Island, location of the colony headquarters and parent station for the whole Gilbert Group. In 1940 two New Zealand telegraphists, Ronald Third and Philip Thorburn, had been seconded to operate the parent station on Ocean Island where the officer in charge was Rupe Bastin, an Australian. Two of the KGV trainees, Peleti and Solomona, disembarked there to assist the operators.[14]

At Ocean Island the crew of the *Viti* had been hoping to take on fuel oil from the *Nortum* and the coast-watchers to purchase butter and other supplies, but no goods had yet arrived. The *Viti* returned to Tarawa on 27 August, staying on there while several New Zealanders received medical treatment for septic sores caused by coral cuts and one was treated for dengue fever.

Then on 30 August the *Viti* sailed for the northern Gilberts, to the last islands that were to have stations in the Gilbert Group. On Butaritari the station was installed on Bikati Islet at the extreme northern end of the lagoon, far away from the main island and villages. Next the *Viti* called at Makin, the northernmost island in the Gilberts. After calling in again at Ocean Island only to find that the butter had still not arrived, once more she made her way back to Tarawa. On 9 September she arrived at Ocean Island for the third time, took on stores and headed for Beru to pick up settlers for the Phoenix Islands. One of the KGV trainees, Falavii Sosene of Vaitupu in the Ellice Group, disembarked at Beru as the senior local operator.

Other Personnel

Some islands already had radio stations and/or operators who had not been part of the main recruitment process for the coast-watching scheme. Such was the case in several islands of the Phoenix Group, where the *Viti* called with the settlers from Beru. First, a radio station on Gardner Island was already in operation under the control of Reuben Uatioa who later became a prominent politician and Leader of Government Business of the colony. Next the ship travelled to Hull Island where there was also an existing radio station, operated by Arnold Cookson and Faasamata O'Brien, an Ellice Islander. On Canton Island, the British administrative officer, Fleming, operated the radio; he had been sent there to 'show the flag' in support of British claims for sovereignty. Another Ellice Islander from the Tarawa operator school, Metusela Neeia, disembarked to assist there.[15]

Coast-watchers on Beru also arrived by different processes of recruitment. The New Zealand operator was Allan Taylor, a volunteer from the Communications Centre headquarters at Tamavua in Suva. Two local operators were recruited to assist him. One was Irata Kaisala, who had an Ellice Islander father from the island of Niutao and a Gilbertese mother from Arorae Island. He had spent several years in charge of the short-wave radio set maintained by the LMS mission on Beru. Now he volunteered to work at the new coast-watching station until a second New Zealand operator could be sent there. The other local operator had also worked at the LMS station. He was 'Tekarara' (Stephen Brechtefeld), from the part-German family of Abemama (Chapter 1).[16]

By February 1942 Beru was taking full responsibilities as the auxiliary parent station, after a Japanese bombing attack on the Ocean Island parent station had downgraded its status. Thus assistance for Taylor was sought from among the New Zealand operators in the Communications Centre headquarters. Several volunteered, a brave move as there was a strong risk of being captured by the Japanese who by then had the whole Gilbert Group under surveillance. The British had lost Singapore in the same month, leaving all the South Pacific vulnerable to Japanese attack and occupation. The selected volunteer was Tom C Murray, who travelled to Beru on the Fiji ship *Degei* when it took supplies to the coast-watchers in March 1942 (and there is more to this story—see Chapter 8). Murray and Taylor were later captured on Beru by the Japanese and executed on Tarawa (Chapter 11).

On Tarawa itself, there were two other local operators. John Milne, of British, Gilbertese and Marshallese ancestry, was from Maiana Island. He was 25 years old and had been an operator since October 1940. Working with him was Willie Schutz, another German-Marshallese who had trained at the Tarawa KGV School.[17] In mid-1942 two more New Zealand operators were transferred from Suva to the Phoenix Islands. J M (Mike) Lee and Allan (Oscar) Wilde flew to their new station, Canton Island, landing at a newly constructed US airfield in the north. After the bombing of Pearl Harbor, all civilians had been evacuated from Canton, leaving only Fleming and his wife on the southern portion of the island. The New Zealanders were later joined by local operators. KGV-trained Metusela returned on the *Degei*, along with Tito Homasi. The *Degei* also brought equipment to install a new radio station on Sydney Island, as the previous radio set belonging to the resettlement scheme had been taken to Gardner Island. At this opportunity, too, Reuben was replaced by Frank Christopher. From that time, the Phoenix stations sent their reports to Canton Radio.[18]

Appendix B gives a complete summary of the New Zealanders and islanders involved in coast-watching operations in the Gilbert Islands.

5

German Raiders

Fear that German raiders might attack led to the stationing of troops on Fanning Island and the introduction of coast-watching in September 1939 (see Chapters 3 and 4 respectively). The fear became a reality more than one year before the Japanese made the surprise attack on Pearl Harbor which brought the full sense of the impending war to most islands. In December 1940 German gun boats, disguised as Japanese merchant ships, attacked defenceless shipping near Nauru, 300 kilometres northwest of Ocean Island, and began the war in the Pacific islands. When they then turned against Nauru itself, they became the only raiders in the war to attack a land target.

The attack was the first hostile action of World War Two in the Pacific, and the result was an outstanding success for the Germans. In their conventional role of destroying defenceless merchant shipping, the raiders sank five phosphate ships in three days. Among these ships were the *Triona*, *Triadic* and *Triaster*, three of the four ships specially designed for the Ocean Island and Nauru operations of the British Phosphate Commission (BPC). Moreover, in their unique land offensive, the Germans destroyed Nauru's phosphate plant and oil tanks.

Attack on Merchant Shipping

The first raider to enter the Pacific, the *Orion*, mined the approaches to Auckland Harbour in New Zealand then sailed north. In the Japanese-held Marshall Islands, the *Orion* took on fuel and supplies and teamed up with another raider, the *Komet*, and the supply ship *Kulmerland*.[1]

Then, on 6 December 1940, the BPC vessel *Triona* was heading for Nauru when it was intercepted by the *Orion* north of Solomon Islands. The Germans transferred the *Triona* crew, passengers (mostly BPC employees and their families) and some food supplies to the *Orion*, then sank the *Triona*.[2]

People on Nauru remained unaware of the attack. Early in the engagement, when a shell killed four of the *Triona*'s crew members, it also destroyed its radio equipment, so it had sent no distress message. On the afternoon of 7 December, an unidentified ship passed very close to the shore of Nauru. It aroused some interest among people ashore, but Nauru Radio did not alert the phosphate ships in the area.

That night, four phosphate ships were drifting off Nauru, waiting for the westerly weather to improve so that they could land passengers and begin loading phosphate. This kind of accumulation of ships was to be expected in westerly weather. As on Ocean Island, the Nauru landing is on the western side of the island where there is some shelter from the prevailing easterly trade winds and accompanying sea swells. When westerly storms come up between November and March, ships are unable to approach and must wait for the wind to drop or change direction. The BPC was later criticised for sending unprotected vessels to Nauru, to drift around like sitting ducks, when it was aware of the implications of the westerly conditions and the presence of the raiders.

The first of the four ships to be sunk off Nauru that night was the *Vinni*, a Norwegian vessel under charter to the BPC. Then at 5:00 am on 8 December, the BPC ship *Triadic* came under gunfire from the *Komet* and a shell burst in the saloon, setting it on fire and killing one of the crew. After the signal to abandon ship was given, women and children were put into the first lifeboat, and the crew (mostly Filipino and Chinese) went in the second boat. A distress message was also sent out by Morse code, which was received at the radio station on nearby Ocean Island and perhaps elsewhere as well. The Germans quickly sent out another message cancelling the distress call and misleading the radio operator on Ocean Island, Maheu Naniseni.[3]

Hoping that the Germans would allow them to land on Nauru, the people in the lifeboats headed towards the island. However, their hopes of escape were soon disappointed when two ships blocked their route. Bearing the names *Tokyo Maru* and *Manyo Maru*, these ships were in reality the *Kulmerland* and *Komet*.

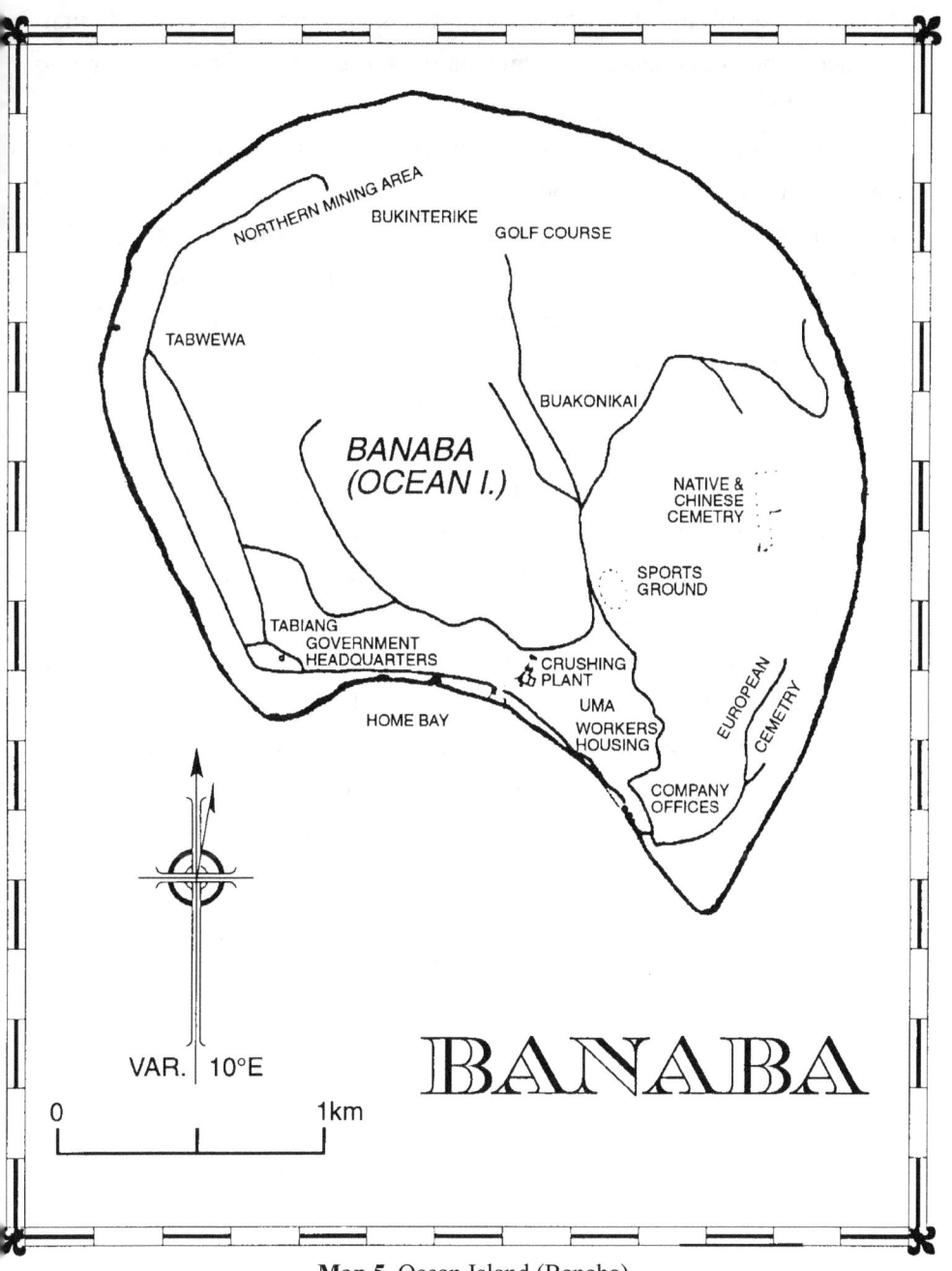

Map 5. Ocean Island (Banaba)

The third raider *Orion* showed no colours and had no markings visible to indicate her name or nationality. For this reason, those in the lifeboats referred to her as the 'black ship'.

Survivors from the lifeboats were taken aboard the *Manyo Maru*, which now displayed a Nazi flag from her rail. One of *Triadic*'s officers berated the German commander, 'Why the hell did you fire without warning?' The German's response showed the irony of their situation: 'You were an armed ship, why do you carry passengers on a ship with a gun on it?' He was referring to the mounted gun on the deck which was there, as on some other BPC ships, to be used in self-defence. Far from providing any defence against the German gunboats, these guns had brought the ships under needless attack.[4]

A little later, the third BPC ship *Triaster* came under attack from the *Orion*. Along with the other phosphate ships, the *Triaster* had been drifting off Nauru with its navigation lights on when those aboard heard gunfire and saw a ship on fire. With its lights hurriedly extinguished, the *Triaster* ran from the island at maximum speed, trying to escape under cover of darkness. But as dawn broke those aboard saw that another ship was astern of them and at 7:00 am it opened fire. Stopping the ship, the *Triaster* captain ordered everyone to the lifeboats. However, they were soon intercepted by a launch full of armed German sailors who ordered them to the enemy ship. The Germans placed bombs in the hold and engine room of the *Triaster*, and sank her at 8:00 am.[5]

The last to be attacked and sunk was the New Zealand ship *Komata*. Under shellfire, its chief mate was killed outright and the second mate mortally wounded.

Thus as a result of the attacks, five ships were destroyed around Nauru, and seven lives were lost. The prisoners were kept aboard the *Komet* for two weeks, after which time the civilians were put ashore in Papua New Guinea and the merchant navy officers were transferred to German prisons.

The loss of the ships was a severe blow to the BPC but one for which it had to accept some responsibility. It might have reduced the extent of the loss had it not allowed its ships to wait near the island in bad weather. Other mistakes were that the ships had shown navigation lights, and used radio communications too freely in passing on weather reports and other messages. Carrying passengers on ships fitted with guns was also an error.

Nonetheless, as serious as this loss was to the phosphate industry of Ocean Island and Nauru, worse was yet to come.

Land Attack on Nauru

Early in the morning of 27 December, the *Komet* returned to Nauru, this time clearly flying the Nazi flag. By means of a signalling lamp her commander indicated that he was going to open fire on the phosphate loading equipment. The crowd of Nauruan spectators who had gathered around to look at the ship were told to move away from the area. Europeans dispersed to places of safety, while the Chinese phosphate workers and the 50 Gilbertese and Ellice Islander workers headed inland to the phosphate fields or rode around towards the other side of the island on their bicycles.

Originally, the Germans had planned to send a demolition party ashore on Nauru, for the dual purposes of destroying the phosphate equipment and landing the civilians captured from the destroyed ships. Prevented from doing so by rough weather, they had to be content with inflicting damage with their ship's guns.

Under heavy fire, the cantilever teetered but was not brought down. One set of the huge mooring buoys was sunk. However, because the buoys had been made with several separate watertight compartments, another set survived and the shell holes were later patched successfully. Incendiary shells hit the island's fuel storage tanks, resulting in a huge oil spillage and fire. The great heat of the blaze softened the steel of the 12,240-tonne phosphate storage bin which fed the cantilever; the bin then crumpled, spilling its contents. The oil blaze burnt for several days.[6]

Aftermath

The Australian Prime Minister stated that the world would view the attack with contempt because the Germans had attacked defenceless people on Nauru.

The Germans must have been aware that, under the terms of the League of Nations mandate which gave the administration of the island to Australia, the island was not fortified. Moreover, he said, the Germans had attacked using the neutral colours of a Japanese name and flag.[7]

On both Nauru and the other phosphate island, Ocean Island, general opinion was that raiders would return as soon as shipping began again. BPC officials had to decide whether, given the wrecked plant on Nauru and lack of available ships, they could produce and ship phosphate at all, even if there were no further German attacks. A further worry was that Japan would formally enter the war and commence hostilities. It might be diplomatically useful to try to maintain phosphate supplies to Japan, but the result would be a drop in phosphate supplies for Australia and New Zealand.

There was also an attempt to improve security at the radio station on Ocean Island. The WPHC sent a radio officer to investigate operations. From examining the station's log book, he found that operators had been too careless in disclosing information on the positions of ships. In a communication with the raider, the European superintendent of the station had been fooled by a message that should have aroused his suspicions. He had then told Nauru to cancel the distress message. On the investigating officer's recommendation, the superintendent was replaced by Rupert Stanley Bastin, who took up the position of chief wireless officer on 15 August 1941. Another recommendation was to install new equipment to the value of £5000, because the station had only one receiver and therefore could not keep continuous watch on both the ship-calling and distress frequencies.[8]

A further question was whether to fortify the islands. Although the League of Nations mandate expressly forbade building military bases or fortifications on Nauru, it was felt the German attack had absolved the Australian government from that obligation. Thus in February 1941 the Australian government sent a small infantry force with field artillery guns to establish anti-raid defences. The garrison was poorly equipped but it boosted morale for the Australian workers on the island and may have helped to deter potential raider attacks.

Figure 6. First parade in uniform of the Ocean Island Defence Force, on the cricket ground. July 1940

On Ocean Island (**Map 5**), the Defence Force Ordinance of 1917 provided that a defence force could be called out for compulsory service. After this provision had been invoked in July 1940, a small force was formed, consisting of 37 Europeans (mostly Australians), supported by a detachment of native armed constabulary comprising eight Ellice Islanders and seven Gilbertese (**Figure 6**). From the outset there was dissatisfaction among the Australian members of the force, who felt that they should not have been subject to compulsory service abroad and that they had no moral obligation to defend Ocean Island which was part of a British Crown colony. There was also disagreement as to how much, if any, resistance they should give to a superior force. There was constant bickering among different sections of the force and, on more than one occasion, men threatened to lay down arms. The discontent continued until March 1942 when the force was disbanded.[9]

In fairness to the force, it must be recorded that its members turned out each morning at 3:45 in readiness for an attack and it is believed that, had the order to open fire been given, the majority would have given a good account of themselves. On one occasion the sergeant of the Uma Section said to the resident commissioner, 'We know you think we are a lot of bastards, but if you order us to attack the Japs we'll give them bloody hell too.'[10]

After the German raider attacks and in anticipation of a coming war with Japan, moves were made to evacuate all Australian and New Zealand women and children from both Ocean Island and Nauru. The Australian merchant ships *Vito* and *Kenilworth* were used for this purpose on Ocean Island, and the *Skegerak* on Nauru, with the armed merchant cruiser *Westralia* providing protection. No German raiders were encountered and the evacuation was completed without incident on 17 July 1941.[11]

Part II

THE RISING SUN

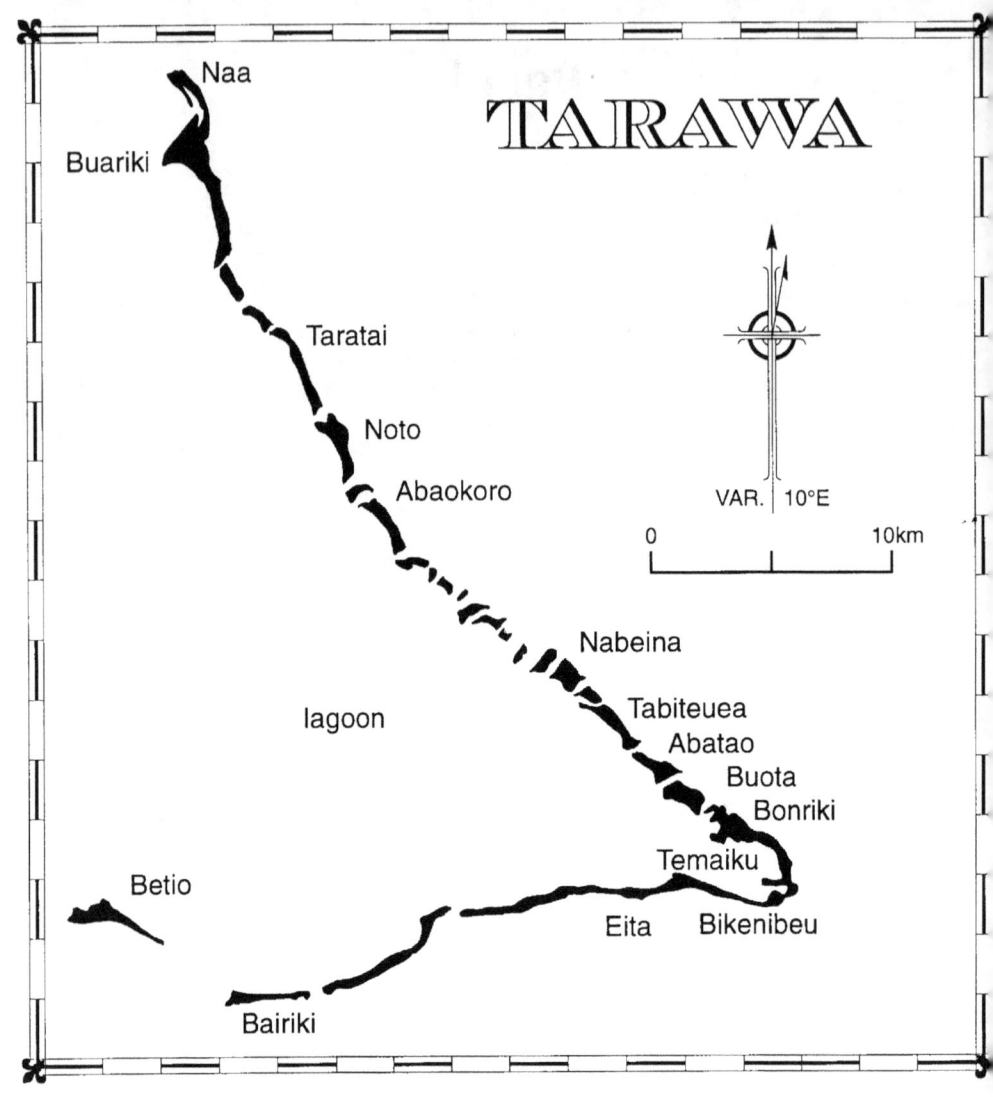

Map 6. Tarawa Atoll

6
After Pearl Harbor—Ocean Island and Tarawa

With its surprise attack against the US naval base at Pearl Harbor in Hawai'i, Japan made a dramatic start to its war in the Pacific. Although anticipating aggression from the Japanese, the Allies were expecting them to strike in the Philippines, Singapore or Malaya. The Americans in particular felt that the Japanese would not dare to target Pearl Harbor and risk the wrath of the US Navy. But they were wrong. Starting before 8:00 am on 7 December 1941, Japanese torpedo bombers destroyed 188 US planes and sank or seriously damaged 18 warships, with a total loss of 2400 US lives. The expected Japanese attacks against the Philippines, Singapore, Malaya and Hong Kong happened almost simultaneously. Other Pacific island targets were Guam, Midway, Wake and the Gilbert Islands.

Air Raids on Ocean Island

Hearing the news of the Pearl Harbor raid on their radios, most European residents on Ocean Island were wondering how it would affect their lives. They did not have to wait long before they found out. Six hours after the attack on Pearl Harbor, Japan took its first aggressive action against the Gilbert and Ellice Islands Colony by bombing its headquarters on Ocean Island. A large, four-engine seaplane arrived over the island from the northeast and dropped several bombs which were obviously aimed at the Residency. None of the bombs found its target and there was no damage to buildings, nor were there any casualties.[1]

At 4:00 pm the defence force was called out for active service, and an order was issued enforcing a blackout of the island from dusk until dawn. As there were no air raid shelters on Ocean Island, the population was advised to find shelter in worked-out phosphate mining areas as soon as they heard planes approaching. The coral pinnacles that remained after the phosphate had been extracted formed very good protection. The BPC suspended all phosphate mining work, and all Chinese and Pacific islanders were evacuated to locations away in the bush.

The next day, 9 December local time (Ocean Island being across the dateline from Hawai'i), three Japanese seaplanes arrived and again bombed the island. This time they hit the Residency and completely demolished its upper storey. No other buildings were damaged and there were again no casualties. With the planes out of range of their machine guns, the defence force did not open fire as such action would have given their positions away to no advantage.[2]

The Ocean Island radio station broadcast the news that it was under attack and this report was received at Tarawa Radio and by the ship *Nimanoa*, which was heading for Tarawa. The *Nimanoa* was bringing sisters of the Catholic Church from the outer islands to Tarawa, ready for evacuation to Australia along with other missionaries. Lloyd Sinclair, the chief engineer on the ship, left a written record of the events of that time:

> At lunch Monday I had an awful premonition and it was all I could do to keep steady and some time later we trapped O.I. [Ocean Island] signals to say their place was being raided by aircraft by this time we were nearing the South Eastern side of Betio, and every officer aboard was quite calm, somehow now things were happening so close I steadied up. The sisters were not informed but Harness [the captain] told the Bishop and the only thing that prevented us from turning around was that some of the people would be left on Tarawa and the other islands, anyway we came on fully expecting to see the Jap warships in Tarawa lagoon. Feelings were many and various and the Sisters were kept in ignorance of the O.I. raid.
>
> On arrival in sight of the lagoon there was nothing to be seen bar the *Helena* (B.P. Co. schooner). We anchored and the Capt. went ashore to ask Dr Stinson [Steenson], who in the absence of the D.O. Bevington [Eric Bevington, the district officer], was officer in charge, what we were to do. Tarawa station had heard the O.I. signals but the boys not

knowing what they meant had not reported them. Capt. wrote off to me and said as there were too many Sisters aboard to put to sea with that they were to be sent ashore and we worked until about 10.00 pm (in the rain) and took water and oil etc and were ready to make a dash for it at about 8.15 pm. I went ashore and informed Capt. that we were almost ready. The buoy had been lighted in readiness with a hood or guard so that the light did not shine out to sea but only towards the anchorage.[3]

But the *Nimanoa* had not begun its dash south to safety when the Japanese arrived.

Naval Capture of Tarawa

The Japanese Navy sent five ships from Jaluit, their headquarters in the Marshall Islands, to capture the northern Gilberts. Chapter 7 covers how three of these ships went to capture the coast-watchers on Butaritari and nearby Makin, and to begin constructing a seaplane base on Butaritari. The remaining two destroyers, *Asanagi* and *Yunagi*, arrived at Tarawa (**Map 6**) at midnight on 9 December. A landing force of approximately 200 marines went ashore over the ocean reef at Takoronga, the eastern end of Betio islet. They formed a line across the island and marched westwards, sweeping all the people before them.

At this time, most of the Europeans in the Gilbert Islands (with the exception of the Catholic nuns) had already been evacuated to safer locations in Fiji, Australia or New Zealand. Only a handful remained on Tarawa. Doctor Steenson, head of the Medical Department, was acting administrative officer. He instructed the radio operator to send out the signal that the Japanese were landing and to destroy any copies of messages in the radio station. He then took the code books and concealed them where the Japanese wouldn't find them.

At the Betio radio station, the Japanese caught the operator on duty, Willie Schutz, as he was sending out the enemy-has-landed message (LLLL) to Ocean Island. Bob Narruhn, another operator, tells the story:

They caught Willie sending a distress call, it was a series of L's—you know, "Landing". They roughed him up a bit and jabbed at him with

Figure 7. RCS Nimanoa, in Tarawa lagoon. August 1941

a bayonet. On Betio there was a great big barque anchor which stands about six feet, it was one of those sailing boat anchors with big flukes. They tied him up to that and then they started machine-gunning the *Nimanoa* [**Figure 7**].[4]

Sinclair tells how he was also captured and tied to the anchor with Schutz:

The tide was dead low and outside the reef on our side of the island the sea was as calm as a mill pond. I'd just come off the beach when I met John [Milne], the wireless boy and Joe Randolph and they told me that the Capt. wanted me at the Hospital Dispensary so I immediately started at the double. I'd just past Pat's [Pat English, the government sub-accountant] office (the P.O. treasury, etc) when I heard them coming at the double towards me and then I saw their bayonets fixed, so I slowed to a walk, two or three passed me and apparently didn't see me, talk about grunts or perhaps Japanese curses—they sounded like a lot of a gruntsome fellow challenged me and I halted and a couple of his mates made signs that I should raise my hands and then they descended on me (after I had raised my hands and herded me over in front of the wireless shack where they had Willie Schutz and a native bailed up. They pinched my torch and felt my pockets and I told them I had nothing, they weren't at all rough they put my hands behind my back and tied me with a rope and by the feel of things they were very excited indeed and fumbled like hell, (I'm glad it happened to me because I was scared inside of the way I might conduct myself in such a case and I know I'm O.K.). When eventually the soldier tied my hands I was coupled to Willie Schutz at the end of the rope and herded around for a bit and then they led me towards the boat harbour and intended to tie us to the concrete mooring post, we used for the lighters which could only come in at high tide, and signalled for us to sit down. So I immediately sat down on the mooring post but they then signalled that I should arise so I arose and then they repeated that we should sit so I sat down on the post again. (Incidentally it was still raining and there was about three inches of water all around and I did not feel inclined to sit down on the ground unless forced) so after a few seconds (luckily) they pushed us along towards a large anchor (that we used for mooring the entrance buoy in the passage) out in front of Pat's office and made us sit there and tied us to it. While they were doing this there was a continual barrage of questioning. Where the wireless station, the post office, how many white men on the island, how many guns, any war ships, English or American, where the doctor and every other thing they could think of and as where you come from and when I pointed in the general direction of the lagoon they sent some men along the jetty with machine guns. It was still dark and by the light of torches the commanding officer continued to question me and flashed his sword around in front of my face and pointed to the Japanese flag trying to impress me but I was very dumb at the same time he was doing his best to tell me that as long as I kept quiet nothing would happen to me. (He seemed to have so many parrot phrases and beyond that he was stumped). I gathered from the honour of being interrogated by the O.I.C. and the questions he was asking that I was the first of our blokes to be captured (another honour). When his men came to make reports on the situation they did not salute but bowed on one knee before him. This chappie in charge or in command was very officious and touchy. I played dumb for about 10–15 minutes asking him to repeat his demands and kidding that I would not understand his English then as he approached very closely and flashed his sword around in my face I suddenly pretended to understand his very [sic] and pointed in the general direction of the Hospital. (Just before the Japs took me I had received a message from the Capt that we would all meet at the Hospital and meet the Japs there). During the absence of the O.I.C. I managed to sign to the N.C.O. in charge of the group of guards around Willie and I (all with fixed bayonets within about 6" of our bodies and a machine gun and a revolver carried by the N.C.O.) that I wanted my hands untied saying that I would not try to run off. (Not with all that armoury around us, certainly not). At first he just looked at the lashings, but I looked at his eyes as he flashed the torch to take a look at the lashings and I was sure that he understood English. You will remember the wristwatch straps I used to make well the ropes were causing mine to bite into my wrists, at last he freed my left hand. I said thank you very much and told him not to worry I wasn't going to bolt and he appeared to understand and nodded to one of his men.

By jove they were touchy when they first landed. Guess I was the first prisoner. So I was marched off and led them to the Hospital where it had been arranged by Dr S that we should all meet, he was the O.I.C. in the absence of Bevington and it had also been arranged that there should be no resistance of any kind and it was just as well because of the younger were just spoiling to shoot someone or stick a bayonet in someone. Willie and a native were marched along with me and when we got to Dr S house I told him (the N.C.O.) that is the Drs. house. Doctor me don't know and shrugged my shoulders like a froggy (but I knew that Dr S and the Capt and Bas [Basil Cleary, the Pharmacist].

were further on at the Dispensary. Then the native fellow said Dr. down there. When we were fairly close to the Dispensary (it was still dark and they were still as touchy as hell) I said for the benefit of the Doctor etc "It has turned out nice again" there was an audible sigh and they all came off the verandah and surrendered. All their pockets were gone over, smokes removed, they did not smash anything at the Hospital and then we were all herded back towards the P.O. but they did not tie the Doctor or anyone else up until further on it the day, especially after the mate came ashore.

Harness, captain of the *Nimanoa*, had sent the ship's radio operator Bubu to the ship with instructions to the first officer, Stead, who was on duty, that he should destroy the code books. A policeman woke the senior radio operator, John Milne, to tell him that the Japanese had landed. Milne had been the radio operator on the *Nimanoa* and was familiar with its radio equipment. He made his way out to the ship and, with Bubu, also began sending out the LLLL message. When the Japanese began firing on the *Nimanoa*, all the crew and Milne jumped overboard and swam ashore.[5]

The Japanese rounded up all Europeans on Betio. In the early hours of the morning, Japanese marines woke the Catholic sisters who the *Nimanoa* had brought to Tarawa for evacuation to Australia. Walked to the post office at bayonet point, they were confined there with part-European women. The wives and children of European workers on Tarawa had been evacuated to Suva on the LMS ship *John Williams* on 3 December. The bishop, priests, brothers and other European men were put under guard under the veranda of the Burns Philp store.[6]

As part of a government scheme to evacuate missionaries and government officials and their wives to Australia, the Sacred Heart Mission schooner *Santa Teretia* had been collecting nuns from the outer islands when the Japanese arrived on Betio. With 19 sisters already assembled on Betio, the *Santa Teretia* was bringing more from Abemama and Maiana when she received the news that Tarawa had been attacked. The two sisters and Father Ramuz on Maiana remained there and the ship turned south to return the Abemama nuns to their island and then head for the safety of Fiji. Thus Bishop Terrienne, two priests and 22 nuns remained on Tarawa.[7]

On Betio the Burns Philp manager, George W Jenner, along with the accountant, T L Clark, and storeman, Leslie Copeland, stood by the store waiting for the Japanese to arrive. They had already hidden all the Burns Philp cash in the ceiling of the manager's house. On capturing the three men, the Japanese took their personal possessions such as keys, torches and tobacco, then marched them along the beach to the Burns Philp office where they arrived in time to see the government wireless mast falling.[8]

Hands tied behind them, the Burns Philp staff were told to sit down with the other European men on the veranda. The Japanese then made it known that all islanders were required to carry goods from the Burns Philp and government stores to the wharf for loading onto the Japanese warships. Sinclair's account continues:

> But first of all they took the Marshall-German bloke outside and had him interpret to the natives that they were going to work but that they would be paid for their work. They rounded up all the natives and had them sitting around the P.O. fence. I suppose they also told them that Japan was their new master, etc. etc. as they had already told us, anyway there was a cheer and next thing the Govt. store was looted and everything laid out in front of the P.O. All natives took part, police, N.M.Ps., and personal servants, they had no choice and they all fully expected that they were going to be taken away and so did we ourselves. When the Govt. store had been turned inside out and they had put aside what they wanted and then gave the natives a free hand telling them to help themselves and they did.
>
> Next came the looting of B.P. store and they employed the natives as a chain gang and soon had the entire stock out in front of the P.O. Stores were piled into two lots, those they finally took with them consisting of marine gear and steel goods and those they afterwards flung to the natives as presents and the promised payment for their work, such as cloth, perfume and all fancy goods…
>
> The natives had a grand time and lots of them got away with cases of meat, kerosene, bolts of cloth, etc. etc, and they went wild and pillaged

all the houses. The Japs made a nice mess of Bev's house all that new furniture was smashed. The flag staff was blown down, lighters at B.P.'s were holed, boats were burned and every single canoe on the island was holed. The natives are simply running wild and I am very pleased that you and the other women were not here when it all happened and after.

Having had responsibility for fuel, Pat English, the government sub-accountant, had begun destroying stocks by breaking open drums with an axe and had almost completed the task before the Japanese seized him. The Japanese killed two inmates of the lunatic asylum (Korambati Aretima of Arorae and Toma Tonana of Marakei) who were unable to understand their orders, but there were no other casualties.[9]

One of the destroyers proceeded along the south coast of the atoll to Bairiki and landed a party there, which destroyed boats, canoes and wireless equipment at the school. Reg Morgan, head of the wireless school, had hidden a short-wave receiver and transmitter. Undiscovered by the invading force, it was recovered after the Japanese left, and used to keep in touch with the outside world.

By slipping the mooring cable before abandoning ship, the mate of the *Nimanoa*, Harold Stead, prevented his ship from falling into Japanese hands. It drifted up onto the reef and, when they could not refloat it, the Japanese instead had to blow it up with explosives. A different fate met the Burns Philp ship *Helena A*, which was also in port at Betio with Captain Doughty aboard. After destroying all ship papers and rowing himself ashore in the ship's boat, he was taken into charge by the Japanese. They then used the *Helena A* to transport stores from the wharf to the other Japanese destroyer that had entered the lagoon.[10] Sinclair continues:

> Just about daylight they handed in some crew biscuits or should I say threw them on the floor and they tasted good, several times later they handed us more biscuits and at about 1 pm, tinned fruit, meat and some milk as well. By this time Jenner who had vantage point at a window said "the Nimanoa is drifting ashore" and do you know the Japs didn't

notice anything amiss. Bravo old Stead who cut the anchor chain and let the ship drift ashore. (Harness had slept with Steenson and that is how he came to be at the Hospital when the Japs first came ashore. I slept in the house I was occupying and Stead and Wal slept aboard the ship)...

The Nimanoa, after the Japs were aware that she was ashore had a demolition charge in the engine room and was blown up and then burned far into the night and all my belongings went with her. Now she is just a twisted mass of iron and charred wood marking the reef where she went up just to the west of the jetty end.

Later in the afternoon, a Japanese officer attempted to read a proclamation to the effect that the Japanese had taken over the Gilbert Islands. However, due to his very poor knowledge of English, he could not complete the task. As reported by Sinclair, he said:

'Japanese Navy occupied Her (meaning Hawai'i), Hong Kong. Singapore and all the Gilbert Islands today. You obey me you see, supposing you no obey me, all white man this island I keel.' (But he did not deliver the speech like that there were a lot of pauses and hums and ahs while he apparently was trying to memorise the whole speech).

The Japanese then erected a pole in front of the post office on which the proclamation was displayed. It said:

Declaration
The Empire of Japan declared war on America, Britain and Dutch Indies to break down these hostilities on Dec 8th and Japanese Naval Forces have occupied Gilbert Islands today in the morning. It is our duty to secure the military supremacy in our hands but we have never enmity for the Gilbert peoples. Accordingly the peoples to do the peaceful conduct will be protected sufficiently, but if you will do hostile acts or do not submit my order, you will be punished with heavy penalties.

December 10th 1941
Commander of Japanese Squadron[11]

At 5:30 pm the Japanese left Betio after warning the Europeans that they were prisoners of Japan and that no one was allowed to leave the island. Sinclair explains that the Japanese had Captain Doughty pilot them in and out of the lagoon to demonstrate that the passage was not mined:

> They then took Capt. Doughty out to the Helena and put him aboard with a guard and he had to show the destroyer by preceding it into the lagoon that the passage was not mined. (After the raid Capt. Doughty had to pilot the destroyer out of the lagoon just before dark and J. Narruhn went along because he was the Engineer). When the destroyer was safely anchored in the lagoon Doughty and Joe Narruhn rejoined us on the floor of the P.O. All this time there was another destroyer on our side of Betio, i.e. the weather side, and the two destroyers remained one in the lagoon and the other on station outside.

The war ships left Tarawa at dusk, towing the *Helena A* and taking her Gilbertese and Ellice Islander crew of 10 sailors to Butaritari.

The Japanese Navy next returned to Tarawa on Christmas Day, this time in a cruiser. The visit is described by Sinclair:

> Some days have passed and the next visit was on Christmas day. A cruiser hove off the passage and sent two launches and boats ashore but they only came for more of the stores from B.P.'s. The naval officers were very nice apparently and after asking Pat to open his safe and lay all the money out on the floor they asked him what the money was used for as his reply was so as to pay Govt. servants, dressers, police, etc. so that they could buy food and after consulting with a higher ranking officer they left it all. By the way Tim has come back home for the present and he is company at least.
>
> The marines who came ashore off the cruiser were much more mature than the marines from the destroyers and the naval men seemed much smarter and tougher to look at. The first lot that landed on 10/12/41 all wore sand shoes or felt slippers or nothing much better, they appeared to be all types. The type of pillaging was fishing lines, razors, razor blades even the old ones were taken from our bathrooms.

After the visit by the Navy cruiser, the Japanese Navy made periodic inspections of Tarawa, arriving by air from its seaplane base at Butaritari and landing on Tarawa lagoon. Sinclair's record describes one such visit:

> The Japs visited us on another occasion arriving in a large flying boat, much like the Air N.Z. machines that plied between NZ and Aust and Fiji in those days. They landed on the lagoon and we assembled on the inner end of the jetty as usual to greet them (although they as usual walked right past us and again as usual we stood there until they were ready to depart).

During this period the Japanese showed little interest in Tarawa. Initially their main focus in the Gilbert Islands was on establishing a seaplane base at Butaritari.

7

Butaritari Captured

When news of the Pearl Harbor attack reached Butaritari on 8 December 1941, the district officer for the northern Gilberts, Charles (Chas) Fulford Williams, placed the only Japanese nationals in the colony under house arrest. These prisoners were Kanzaki, the manager of the Nanyo Boyeki Kabushiki Kaisha trading station on Butaritari, and Suzuki, his assistant.[1] On 10 December the roles of captive and captor were reversed, when a convoy of Japanese warships entered Butaritari lagoon.

Arrival and Capture

At midnight on 9 December 1941 the destroyers *Okinoshima* and *Tenyo Maru*, with a land combat unit of the 51st Naval Garrison, reached Butaritari. At dawn, troops landed at three points on the island: the government pier in the lagoon, the ocean reef opposite On Chong and Company's station and the beach to the west of Ukiangang village (**Map 7**). Arriving shortly after with construction materials for a seaplane base, the *Nagata Maru* of the 8th Gunboat Division began unloading before dawn.[2] Now taken captive himself, Williams was locked in one of the buildings at the head of On Chong's wharf.

Before Williams' arrest he sent a radio message to the New Zealand coastwatchers on Bikati islet, 23 kilometres away at the northern end of Butaritari lagoon, advising them of the Japanese landing. Government radio operator Beriki tried to warn Ocean Island of the situation but could not make contact. Instead, the Bikati operator, John M Jones (**Figures 8 and 9**), accepted the message and successfully transmitted it to Ocean Island; Beriki then destroyed his radio equipment.[3]

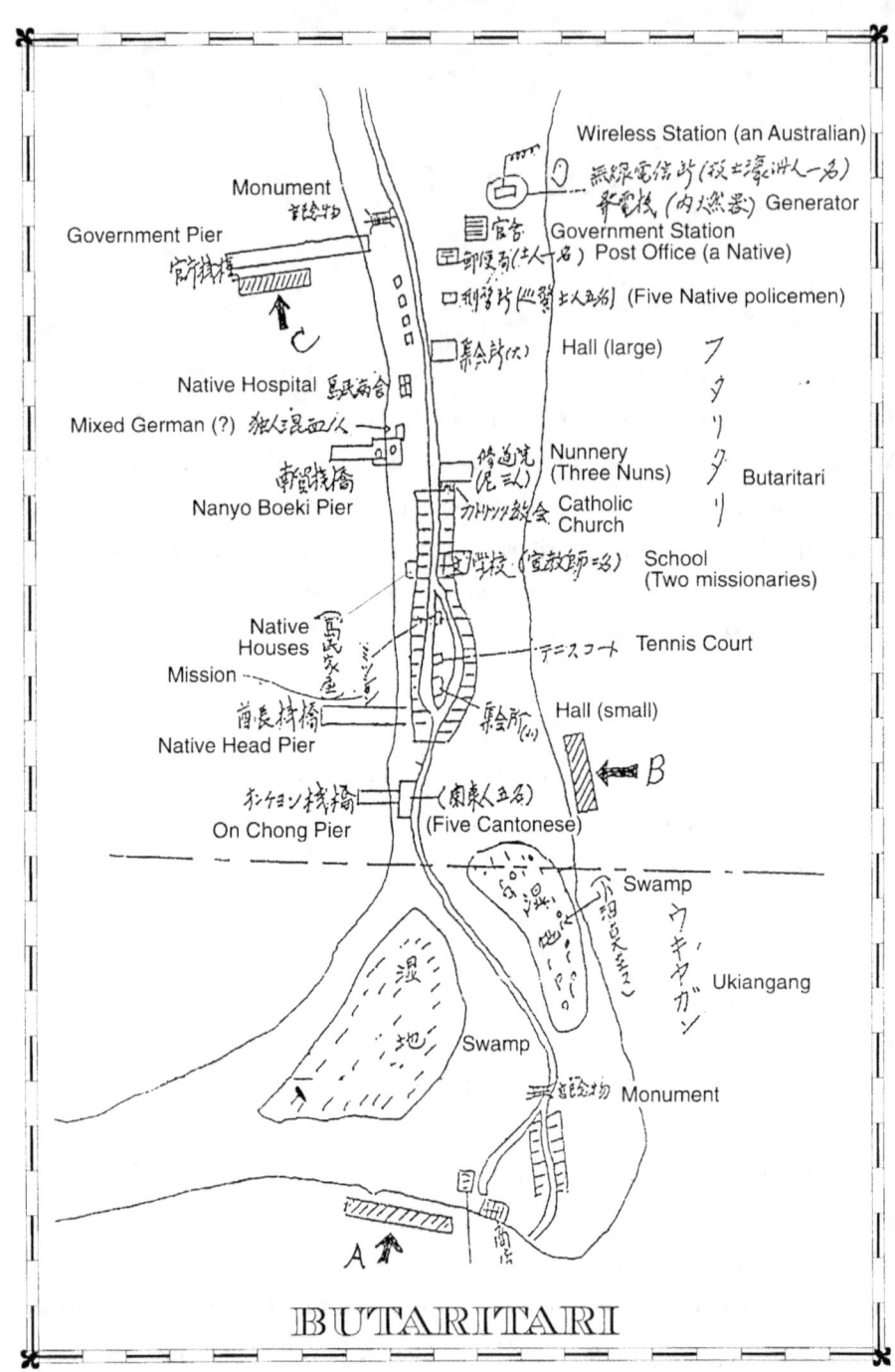

Map 7. Japanese intelligence map of the main settlement on Butaritari

Three coast-watchers had been stationed on Bikati since the end of August. Jones was accompanied by two soldiers, brothers Michael and John (Jack) Menzies, who supervised groups of local men taking turns in keeping a lookout for ships and aircraft. At his own expense, Williams had fitted out the men in uniform *be* (loincloth, lavalava) and had them build a bunkhouse near the radio shack, which was then occupied by six men on seven-day shifts. A 24-hour watch was also maintained from lookout towers, made of coral rock, in three positions on Bikati. From Bikati they saw and reported on the many Japanese ships that sailed past on their way to the southern end of the atoll and to Tarawa.[4]

On 11 December a small float biplane circled over the island, apparently trying to locate the coast-watchers. It flew directly over their station and then south. Not long afterwards, their lookouts reported that a launch towing two whale boats was approaching Bikati from outside the ocean reef. Realising that their capture was imminent, they sent out the 'LLLL' message, burned their code books and destroyed all radio equipment. At this time Iabeta Tarakai (**Figure 9**), a local Bikati man, assisted the coast-watchers considerably, helping the Menzies brothers to bury half of the coast-watchers' stores, covering them with tarpaulins and sand, then releasing the gasoline from the fuel drums and helping to destroy equipment and code books.[5]

The Japanese arrived from the ocean side of the islet, the launch towing two whale boats full of marines who wore camouflage uniforms, displayed the navy's anchor insignia, and carried rifles and light machine guns. After rushing the radio station with fixed bayonets, they found that the building was deserted and the New Zealanders were waiting for them on the beach. The Japanese then forced the coast-watchers to sit on the sand alongside the radio shack for several hours while they loaded everything moveable on to their boats. During this time they gathered all the islanders, about 40 people in total, and made them watch the proceedings.

The dozen or so Japanese marines who surrounded the three coast-watchers frequently used graphic signs to indicate that the New Zealanders would be beheaded. However, the next action was to ship them down the lagoon to question them aboard a cruiser, before at last they were taken to the village and locked up near Williams in another On Chong shed.[6]

Also arrested on Butaritari were the male representatives of the seven Chinese families who lived in the On Chong compound. The On Chong manager, Jong Kum Kee, had a house on stilts over the lagoon. When the Japanese took over his house, they threw all his belongings outside into the mud and water, which his family had to collect before finding somewhere else to live. The seven arrested Chinese men disappeared for seven days before they were released unharmed.[7] (Appendix C provides more details of the Chinese experience of the conflict in the Gilbert Islands during World War Two.)

Before the Japanese arrived at nearby Makin, operator Maxwell McQuinn gave a wristwatch of sentimental value to Father Jonchere, of the Catholic mission, for safekeeping. At about midnight, a party of approximately 40 marines visited McQuinn (**Figure 8**) and soldiers Basil Were and Lewis Muller. The Japanese took possession of everything there, including the wireless set. Unharmed, these coast-watchers were taken to join the other prisoners on Butaritari early the next morning.[8]

The Fate of the Prisoners

While the Japanese were capturing Hong Kong and strengthening their Pacific perimeter, the seven European prisoners on Butaritari were kept locked up at On Chong's wharf. On Christmas day, the other Europeans on Tarawa learned of their fate, when the crew of the *Helena A* were repatriated to Tarawa while the Japanese kept their ship at Butaritari.[9]

On 27 December the Butaritari prisoners were placed on board a Japanese cruiser. Along the way, on the main road to the wharf, the Japanese lined up the Butaritari islanders to witness the belittling of their former administrator, Williams, as he was made to pull a copra cart carrying all their personal belongings. Father Guichard was also forced to watch, and members of the Japanese garrison mixed among the crowd, jeering. No one was allowed to offer Williams any assistance. It is believed that his good relationship with Kanzaki before the war may actually have ameliorated the treatment that Williams received at the hands of the Japanese.[10]

The seven Europeans were taken to Jaluit, the Japanese military headquarters and capital of the Marshall Islands, then transferred to another ship where they met up with Sydney Wallace (**Figure 8**), the coast-watching radio operator on Abaiang who had been captured there. Wallace's assistant, Telavi Faati of Nanumea, later made a statement concerning the capture on Abaiang:

> On 30.8.41, I went to Abaiang. I was assistant to Mr S R Wallace. He was the only European coast-watcher there. On 24.12.41 the Japanese arrived at Abaiang at 12 noon. They asked Mr Wallace for his code books but he told them they had already been burnt. They asked to see the ashes, so they went to the kitchen to see the ashes... They took Mr Wallace. The code books were still hidden in the trees. After they left I got the code books and burned them.[11]

An interesting aside to Wallace's capture is that, like McQuinn on Makin, he was concerned about the Japanese confiscating his personal effects. Before the Japanese arrived at Abaiang, he hid his fountain pen and a ring. Seven years later, these were recovered and returned to him in New Zealand—as the wristwatch was to McQuinn.

The prisoners were moved further north to Kwajalein and then to Yokosuka Naval Base and a house in Yokohama. Arriving there on 7 January 1942, they were the first prisoners of war to reach Japan. As a result, their arrival was widely publicised and they were initially treated very well. Accommodated in a house belonging to Standard Oil of New Jersey, at 250 The Bluff, Yokohama, they were provided with servants and fed well for a week during which time many photographs were taken to show how well Japan was treating its prisoners of war.[12]

Thereafter, conditions worsened. At Japan's first prisoner of war camp, Zentsuji on Shikoku Island, where they went on 15 January 1942, their treatment deteriorated as the war went increasingly badly for Japan. They managed to survive poor living conditions and lack of food largely by stealing food while working as stevedores in a railway yard. In September 1945 all were released and made their way back to New Zealand. Fortunately, none of their families had seen an article in the *Statesman* (3 July 1945) which described, wrongly, how 154 prisoners at Zentsuji had been bayoneted to death on 26 April.[13] However, although that story was untrue, in about July the prisoners had been made to dig a long trench outside their barracks. According to US troops who occupied Japan, that trench was intended for the prisoners' own bodies: they were to have been killed when the Allies began landing on Japanese soil. The tragedy was averted by the Japanese surrender.[14]

Life Alongside a Japanese Garrison

On Butaritari, a detachment of the 51ˢᵗ Naval Garrison remained after the main group returned to the Marshall Islands. Its duty was to guard the Butaritari seaplane base, which several large flying boats of the Yokohama Naval Air Group would use to patrol a wide area to the south. The Japanese garrison was small, fitted in with island life and had good relations with the islanders. Thus, as the following selection of accounts shows, its presence did not affect the local community greatly:

> The Japanese bought eggs, pawpaw, drinking coconuts, breadfruit, with cigarettes. They lived like Gilbertese, even ate babai. They had names for all our foods, babai was 'imo', coconuts 'asi'.
> (Robuti of Ukiangang)[15]

> We were warned that any offence against a Japanese would be punished by death but we had many Japanese friends. I used to go and sell eggs to them, they paid in cigarettes. I would auction them to the highest bidder, there was no force. One brand of cigarettes was pink 'Cherry Blossom', another was green…
> (Oscar Reymond)[16]

> The Japanese were strictly forbidden to touch our women, on fear of death. I think Kanzaki helped in protecting our women.
> (Iaonibure Unaia)[17]

Figure 8. Japanese photograph of the three captured New Zealand radio operators from the northern Gilberts. Rear centre: John M. Jones (Butaritari), left front: Sydney Wallace (Marakei), right front: Max McQuinn (Makin)

As Iaonibure Unaia's comment above suggests, Kanzaki is credited with obtaining favourable treatment generally for the islanders, Europeans and Chinese, as well as for Williams early in the occupation. Married to local woman Lina Muller, he had lived on Butaritari for a number of years. Another Japanese friend of the Butaritari people was Masubusi who had also married a local woman, Lina Brechtefeld, and had been Kanzaki's predecessor as Butaritari NBK manager. Although he had not been on Butaritari for some years, Masubusi returned with the Japanese military as a guide and interpreter.[18]

Although the Japanese undertook little construction on Butaritari, they did build a radio communications station with electrical power. In addition, they enlarged and modified the King's Wharf to make it a suitable base for refuelling flying boats. Following up on plans for a small railway network using narrow gauge tracks, the Japanese also brought materials and equipment, including four or five railway cars, to Butaritari but never completed the project.

Because Japanese activity was centred around the King's Wharf, people who moved out to more remote parts of the atoll generally managed to avoid involvement with them. Those who moved out of the Butaritari village area included Chinese such as the Leong family and the family of Jong Kum Kee, who became manager of the W R Carpenter store after it took over the On Chong business. Receiving a certain amount of respect owing to their nationalities, French priest Father Guichard and German Brother Engelhardt also lived generally unmolested.

Figure 9. Coast-watcher John M. Jones and Iabeta Tarakai meet again at Bikati, Butaritari, 51 years after the coast-watchers were captured there

8

Launch Escape

When they departed Tarawa on 10 December 1941, the landing party of Japanese marines warned that no one was to leave the area without their permission (see Chapter 6). Despite the warning, most of the small group of Europeans on the atoll decided that they would try to escape. With hindsight, this decision was clearly wise as later the Japanese killed all Europeans who opted to remain on Tarawa (Chapter 11), apart from members of the Catholic mission.

Fluctuating Plans for Escape

Contacting the High Commissioner in Suva by wireless telegraphy, the Europeans asked for permission to escape in a repaired boat and estimated that they would be ready to depart in about three weeks.[1] On 19 December 1941, they received a telegram granting them permission and suggesting that a ship might pick them up further south, from Funafuti in the Ellice Group, if they could get that far. But doubts and indecision grew among the main party, under the leadership of Captain Harness of the *Nimanoa*. Japanese reconnaissance flights from Butaritari were becoming more frequent, increasing fear of detection, and a spell of rough weather raised questions about the best time to leave. The resulting delay to their departure aroused impatience in some who were eager to get away.

Early in the new year, the size of the group trying to escape grew substantially, following the arrival of two separate groups of castaways in quick succession.

First, on 17 January, a lifeboat washed ashore on Tarawa after a 39-day voyage from a point 800 nautical miles south of Hawai'i, amounting to more than 2000 nautical miles away. It belonged to the Norwegian merchant vessel

Donerail, which had been on a voyage from Suva to Vancouver carrying a cargo of Fiji sugar, until it had been stopped by an attack two days after the Japanese had bombed Pearl Harbor and other Pacific targets. This was around the same time as they were bombing Ocean Island and capturing the first coast-watchers on Butaritari. After firing a torpedo at it and missing, a Japanese submarine (the I-10) had sunk the *Donerail* with gunfire.[2]

The attack began at 9 pm and was a terrifying experience. Of the 40 people on board the *Donerail*, 15 had been killed outright in the attack. One lifeboat was swung out on its davits, and received a direct hit, killing all eight passengers—two women, five men and an 18-month-old baby. Although the other lifeboat managed to escape with 25 crew on board, it was damaged by the gunfire and leaked badly. For the first 24 hours of the voyage the boat was awash and was only kept afloat by its buoyancy tanks. Those on board had to beat off sharks with oars, including one that actually swam inside the low-lying boat. Available food consisted of about 14 kilograms of wet biscuits and 40 tins of milk.

Gradually, the castaways plugged all the holes with clothing and bailed out the boat. However, during the long drift voyage to Tarawa a further 16 people died of wounds, starvation and exposure, and the master, Captain Niels Pii, was washed overboard and drowned. The eight survivors landed on Tarawa in a poor condition, physically and mentally. As far as is known, the Japanese were unaware that there were survivors of the original sinking, or that the lifeboat eventually came ashore on Tarawa.

The logistics of escape from the Gilbert Islands became even more complicated when two days later another lifeboat washed ashore on Nikunau, 270 nautical miles southeast of Tarawa. It came from the *USS Prusa*, which had been sailing between Honolulu and Panama when without warning she was torpedoed south of Hawai'i, and sank in nine minutes. It was 10 days after the *Donerail* had met a similar fate, and perhaps from the same submarine. Again, there is nothing to indicate that the Japanese knew or cared that there were survivors or that they later arrived in the Gilbert Islands.

Two of *Prusa*'s lifeboats had managed to escape with a total of 25 seamen. One lifeboat containing 13 men was rescued in December and the occupants taken to Honolulu. The second boat drifted, one man died and after a 31-day voyage, with 11 men surviving, the boat overturned in the high surf which was breaking heavily over the reef on the eastern side of Nikunau. With all crew exhausted by their ordeal, they were fortunate to escape with only minor cuts. The captain later paid tribute to the people of Nikunau: 'They didn't have much in the way of food apart from coconuts and fish, but what they had we were welcome to. They fed us for several days and also supplied us with some clothing.'[3]

Thus the number of people trying to escape now rose to around 30. The Director of Education, Captain Holland, suggested that an approach should be made to the Japanese senior naval officer at Jaluit in the Marshall Islands, requesting safe conduct for a vessel from Fiji to evacuate all Europeans. Although the High Commission in Suva advised him that this suggestion was both impractical and unwise, the request was made in a letter handed to the Japanese Commandant of Butaritari when he arrived by flying boat on Tarawa on 23 January. At about the same time the Americans were making a hit-and-run carrier raid against the Marshall Islands and Butaritari, their first in the Pacific War. Perhaps for this reason, the Europeans received no reply to their request; the Commandant would hardly have been in the mood to grant safe conduct.

The First Escape

Initiating the first escape from Tarawa was Captain Harold Stead, Chief Officer of the *Nimanoa*, who had been frustrated with what he considered to be undue procrastination by the main group. At 56 years of age, and as a commander in the Royal Naval Reserve and a master mariner, he probably felt that he was as competent as anyone to lead a small boat to safety. His one handicap was a gammy leg from wounds received in World War One.

Knowing that the brothers Fritz and Henry Reiher had repaired a Burns Philp sailing boat for their own use in the lagoon, Stead approached them and offered £10 for the boat. The Reihers told Stead to take it without payment of any kind and wished him good luck. Stead departed Tarawa on 9 February in the company of Yee On Bonto, a 17-year-old Chinese Gilbertese sailor from the *Nimanoa*; George Jenner, the Burns Philp manager who was keen to escape from Tarawa with the company's money before it fell into enemy hands; and M Chambers, a survivor and the sole Australian crew member of the *Donerail*. On 20 February, after island-hopping to Maiana and Abemama, they arrived at Nonouti—quite a feat of seamanship and navigation in an open sailboat without any engine. They planned to sail all the way to Fiji if necessary, but they remained on Nonouti when they learned that a ship would come from Fiji to pick them up.[4]

Escape of the Main Group

Meanwhile, the High Commissioner in Suva asked the US military to help rescue the main group of Europeans escaping from Tarawa. However, the US told him that it could not undertake a special operation for this purpose and that he should instead find a small local ship, which he did. Through radio communications, the High Commission informed the Europeans on Tarawa that the Fiji government ship *Degei* could collect any escapees who could reach Nonouti in small boats. The *Prusa* survivors were then transferred from Nikunau to Beru with the assistance of James Coode, the district officer for the southern Gilbert Islands; the LMS church on Beru; and the people of Nikunau. The *Degei* would collect them along with Coode and the Reverent Eastman, Principal of the LMS Training School, from Beru.

Originally sent with supplies for the coast-watchers in the Ellice Islands and southern Gilberts, the captain of the *Degei,* Gordon Webster, now had new orders. His ship was to go only as far north as Nonouti, to keep radio silence and to move only at night. People on Tarawa, and sometimes on neighbouring Maiana, regularly saw or heard Japanese reconnaissance flights over the Gilberts, but such flights were noted once per week at most over the islands further south. It was therefore judged that a small boat would have a good chance of getting away to the south undetected and meeting up with the *Degei.*

Another launch owned by Burns Philp on Tarawa had not been irreparably damaged by the Japanese. Moreover, the Japanese had not discovered a new engine, suitable for this launch, in the Burns Philp store. A few days after the Japanese visit to Betio, the captain of the *Nimanoa*, E W Harness, and chief engineer, P. L. G. Sinclair, had found a new diesel engine, complete with shaft and propeller, in the store. Eventually repaired and ready, the launch departed Tarawa on 27 February. It had in tow two lifeboats: a wooden one from the *Nimanoa* and a larger steel boat which had brought the *Donerail* survivors ashore.

Aboard these three small boats were a total of 25 men. They were:
- Captain Doughty of *Helena A*;
- the remaining survivors from the *Nimanoa*, who were Captain Harness, three engineers—chief engineer P L G Sinclair, second engineer W L Hunt, and his assistant, Tom Pall, who was responsible for keeping the launch engine in operation—and the bosun, Tabokai, a Gilbertese;
- two government doctors—Dr K R Steenson, the senior medical officer, and Dr Isaac;
- the seven Norwegian crew of the *Donerail*;
- Captain Holland, the Director of Education;
- T L Clark, Burns Philp accountant;
- Mr English, government sub-accountant; and
- seven local radio operators, who were a mixed bunch of young men trained at the Bairiki school (Chapter 4)—Willie Schutz, Bob Narruhn and Paul Muller were of German-Marshallese descent, Ruotake Iantin was Gilbertese, and Kapoa, Maatusi and Taukiei were Ellice Islanders.

One man who could have travelled with the group but chose to remain was Basil Cleary. The officers of the *Nimanoa* urged him to escape with them but he refused. Basil Cleary, the government dispenser, was British, born in Suva, Fiji. He was the son of John and Sylvia Cleary and his mother was of the well-known Ragg family of Suva. He had trained as a pharmacist in Sydney and was working as a chemist in the Morris Hedstrom department store in Suva when recruited for the Gilbert Islands. It is believed that he had some training as a medical doctor in Sydney before switching to pharmacy and with both the European doctors planning to escape from Tarawa, this was a factor that compelled him to stay and help the Gilbertese people.[5] This compassionate act, which he chose to do when he was just 30 years old, cost him his life.

The first step of the voyage was the easiest. From Tarawa they motored directly south to Maiana, 32 nautical miles away, which became visible on the horizon virtually as soon as Tarawa was out of sight. At Maiana, Ruotake left the group to assist the New Zealand coast-watching radio operator there, A C Heenan.

The next leg of the journey, from Maiana to Kuria, was more difficult. The distance was greater, 50 nautical miles, and the island lay more to the east, which meant travelling into the prevailing weather. On this stretch, the group encountered the greatest danger in their endeavour, when the engine broke down and they drifted away from their destination. With only one engine among three boats, they would drift off into the vastness of the Central Pacific if it failed, and would likely die of thirst and exposure before reaching land. Luckily their engineers were able to get the boats underway again. However, even with the engine at full power, they were lucky if they made a speed of 2 knots with the two heavy boats in tow and heading into the wind and ocean swell.

It was necessary to ration the limited supply of food and water that they could carry with them. The poor Norwegians were so starved that they pounced on every morsel they could get, grabbing the chicken bones after the others had thrown them away and gnawing them hungrily. Drinking water was eked out by mixing a small portion of sea water in with the fresh; when everyone got diarrhoea, it was blamed on the poor drinking water.

Reaching Kuria on 1 March, the boats stayed there for a week to rest and prepare for the final leg of the journey to Nonouti. During their stay, they saw a Japanese reconnaissance plane—the only one they encountered on the whole journey. It flew low over the island and probably observed the launch which was anchored in a small passage in the reef. Luckily, though, the lifeboats were hidden among the trees, and the plane did not return.

The passage to Nonouti would be the longest and most difficult yet, 78 nautical miles to the southeast. In anticipation of the long beat windward, they decided to leave the smaller of the two lifeboats on Kuria to reduce drag and windage. Another radio operator, Maatusi, also remained behind to assist the New Zealand operator, H Hearn. The others recommenced their journey, which continued slowly but uneventfully. As they approached the entrance into the Nonouti lagoon on 9 March, their spirits rose for there they saw the *Degei*.[6] On board the *Degei* were the *Prusa* crew plus Coode and Eastman who the *Degei* had collected from Beru.

Passengers and Supplies
With neither the escapees' boats nor the *Degei* entering the lagoon, the passengers from Tarawa were transferred to the Fiji ship, and its supplies for the coast-watchers were unloaded. Disembarking from the launch at Nonouti were radio operators Kapoa and Taukiei. Kapoa was to remain on Nonouti to assist the New Zealand coast-watching operator, McKenna and Taukiei was to travel on by launch to Abemama to assist McCarthy there. The *Degei* departed the same day for Suva.

George Brechtefeld, from the German-Marshallese family of Abemama, had the problem of delivering the *Degei*'s supplies to the coast-watchers on the other islands. The *Degei* itself had been unable to fulfil this part of its original mission, because of its strict orders to go no further north than Nonouti. Fortunately for all concerned, Brechtefeld courageously volunteered to take the launch back to Abemama, and succeeded in towing the lifeboat there loaded with provisions. Then during April he achieved a still greater feat when he successfully travelled to Kuria and Maiana to deliver supplies to the coast-watchers. With only a compass to guide him, his seamanship and navigation skills would have been impressive even if he had not had the added complication of travelling mostly at night to avoid detection by Japanese flying boats. Given its nearness to Tarawa, Maiana was well within the area of regular Japanese reconnaissance and Brechtefeld's launch moved very slowly with the lifeboat in tow. For this service he did not expect nor receive payment. However, there is no doubt that his actions helped to convince the British of the loyalty of the part-German families in the Gilbert Islands.[7]

The *Degei* proceeded to Fiji. On the way it called at Niulakita, the southernmost island of the Ellice Group. Niulakita was owned by the Burns Philp South Seas Company, which operated a copra plantation and had a few cattle there. Burns Philp had abandoned the island for the duration of the Pacific War. Provisions on board the *Degei* were running low so an attempt was made to shoot one of the cattle, which were running wild, to obtain fresh meat. Although several shots were fired and at least one cow was hit, none of the animals was brought down and they all disappeared into the dense bush. Later, Burns Philp made an official complaint about the incident.[8]

Two days before the ship arrived in Suva Harbour, a thank you letter was presented to Captain Webster and the officers and crew of the *Degei* (**Figure 10**). The letter thanked them for their courage in undertaking the rescue mission and was signed by 29 of the 38 escapees on board.[9]

In official reports, engineer Lloyd Sinclair is praised for the excellent work he did in rebuilding and maintaining the launch engine. Sinclair himself recognised the contribution of the Gilbertese people in his written account of the escape:

> First and foremost I would like to state it was made possible by the loyalty of the local people and the assistance I personally received from them. In no way did they betray us from the drizzly early morning of the Invasion until the evening of our departure… [10]

About the Men who Escaped

Who were the men who escaped, some of whom appear elsewhere in this book? Some rose to prominence during or after the war, in Fiji or the Gilbert or Ellice Islands. Some were decorated for bravery or valuable service. The following is some further information of what little we know of their stories.

M.V. DEGEI,

nearing SUVA, Fiji.

March 16th 1942

WE, the undersigned Residents of the Gilbert Islands leaving under stress of circumstances and Survivors from vessels torpedoed by the enemy, desire to express to Captain G.J. WEBSTER, Master of the M.V. DEGEI, our warm appreciation of his skill, courage, and thoughtfulness for others in taking his vessel to the Gilbert and Ellice Islands without convoy, when those islands were in partial occupation by the enemy, for purposes incidental to the defence of the Empire, and at the same time bringing away fellow-citizens and others, who through enemy action were left in difficult circumstances.

We should like to thank not only Captain Webster, but also his Officers, Messrs G. RADDOCK, D. DONOVAN, R. CROSS, H. CROSS, and the other members of the ship's company for all that has been done for our safety and comfort on the hazardous voyage now happily ending. At the same time we express to them all our good wishes for their future voyages and trust we may meet them again in the happier days of Victory and Peace.

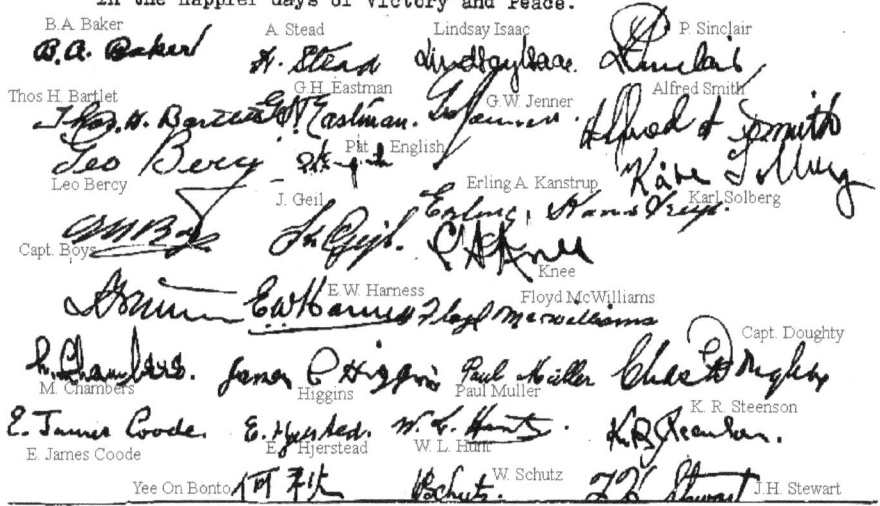

Figure 10. Thank you letter presented to Captain Webster of *Degei*. The printed names near signatures have been added by the author

Captain T C Doughty was captain of the *Helena A* and had been the master of other Burns Philp ships over a number of years. In 1937 he had been in charge of the Burns Philp ship *Makoa* when it was driven by a storm on to a reef in the Phoenix Islands and wrecked.

Captain Gordon Jack Webster was captain of the Gilbert and Ellice Islands Colony (GEIC) ship *Kiakia*, heading for Tarawa on the day the Japanese first visited Betio. He turned the *Kiakia* around and headed for the safety of Fiji, then later volunteered to return to the Gilbert Islands with the *Degei*. In September 1943, as Lieutenant G J Webster of the Royal New Zealand Naval Reserve (RNZNR), he travelled to Hawai'i as one of the local experts on the Gilbert Islands. He advised the US military in the planning of their amphibious attack against the Japanese on Betio and piloted US warships into Tarawa lagoon.

Captain E W Harness was captain of the GEIC ship *Nimanoa*. He also went to Hawai'i in 1943 as an adviser to the US military planners. In the 1950s he was Harbour Master in Suva, Fiji.

Captain Harold Stead was first officer of the *Nimanoa* from October 1941. A New Zealander, he was master mariner and lieutenant commander, RNZNR. He had seen action and was wounded in World War One.

P L G Sinclair, chief engineer of the *Nimanoa*, was of Scottish descent, born in Ba, Fiji. During the war he joined the Fiji Navy and later the merchant navy, serving on several ships as chief engineer. In the 1950s he returned to the Gilbert Islands as a senior engineer, head of the Public Works Department in the Gilbert and Ellice Islands. He later worked in Suva, Fiji and eventually retired in Auckland, New Zealand.

W L Hunt, second engineer on the *Nimanoa*, was similarly of British ancestry but born in Fiji. After escaping from Tarawa to Fiji, he made his way to Australia and attempted to enlist in the Royal Australian Navy, but was advised to continue to serve in the merchant navy where there was a need for him. He was eventually accepted into the US Navy (or the USCG) and served with the Americans in the Pacific War.

Tom Pall was third engineer on the *Nimanoa*. He was born on Betio, Tarawa, of an English father and Gilbertese mother. Before joining the *Nimanoa* he had served on the government ship *Kiakia* and, after escaping to Fiji, he again joined the *Kiakia* which operated within Fiji waters for the remainder of the war. When the war ended he returned to Tarawa.

Tabokai was Gilbertese, the bosun on the *Nimanoa*. After arriving in Fiji on the *Degei*, he apparently resided in Suva for the rest of his life, working as a fisherman, supplying the Suva fish market.

F G L (Frank) Holland, Director of Education for the GEIC government, was awarded the OBE for maintaining secret wireless communications from Tarawa when the island was under Japanese control. He had lived on Tarawa for 20 years before the Japanese arrived and accompanied the US Marine invasion force to Tarawa in November 1943, as an adviser. He had advised the Americans not to land during neap tides but was ignored, at a cost of many casualties to the Americans. After Tarawa was captured from the Japanese he remained there as one of His Majesty's government representatives, helping to re-establish the British civil government.

Dr K R Steenson was the GEIC senior medical officer and in 1941 also the acting administrative officer for the Northern Gilbert Islands District. He returned to work in the Gilbert Islands in 1944 and is remembered as a decent man and a compassionate doctor.

Dr Walter Lindsay Isaac was the doctor in the Medical Department of the GEIC. While working in Tarawa he had examined the bones, found on Gardner Island, which were thought to be those of the aviator, Amelia Earhart. (Due to the degree of weathering of the bones he decided that they had been lying on Gardner Island much longer than Earhart had been missing.) He was Jewish and changed his name from Isaac to Verrier in March 1942, soon after arriving in Fiji from Tarawa. He worked as a doctor in Fiji for the rest of his life, mostly in private practice. He was a member of the Legislative Council of Fiji and the Alliance political party, which helped Fiji gain independence from Great Britain. He lived the remainder of his life in Fiji.

Paul Muller, Bob Narruhn and Willie Schutz, the three trainee radio operators from Tarawa, continued with further telecommunications training in Suva. They all joined the Fiji Navy and served during the war years. After the war Willie Schutz went back to the Gilbert Islands and had a career in the GEIC Marine Department. He rose to the senior position of Captain Superintendent of the department. Paul Muller also returned to the Gilbert Islands and Bob Narruhn emigrated to the United States of America.

Kapoa, Maatusi, Ruotake and Taukiei were the GEIC radio operators who worked with the New Zealand coast-watchers stationed in the Japanese-controlled Gilbert Islands. These men continued working right up until the Japanese closed their stations and arrested the New Zealanders. They were all awarded for their services to coast-watching. They all worked for the Posts and Telecommunications Department of the GEIC after the war. Ruotake also trained in New Zealand and qualified as a telecommunications technician. In 1975 Maatusi moved to Tuvalu and was employed by the Tuvalu Telecommunications Department.

Rev G H Eastman was the principal of the London Missionary Society training school on Beru, southern Gilbert Islands. He made two visits back to the Gilbert and Ellice Islands in 1943, while the war was still in progress, travelling on the mission ship *John Williams*. In 1944 he published a report on how the mission stations were faring under war-time conditions: *Frontline Islands – the Gilbert and Ellice Islands in Wartime*.

James Coode was the district officer of the southern Gilbert Islands District in 1941. He was responsible for making arrangements to evacuate the Prusa survivors and escaped with them on the Degei. He worked in the Fiji administration in Suva for a few months and was then stationed at Funafuti in the Ellice Islands, after the US Marines had occupied the island in October 1942.

Footnote: Cannibalism

A footnote to this story of courage and achievement under trying circumstances is one of grisly foul play. Shortly after the arrival of the escapees, rumours began in Suva about cannibalism on the *Donerail*'s lifeboat.[11] It was said that when the lifeboat had arrived at Tarawa there had been a strong smell of blood in the boat and in the men's clothes. In addition, the survivors were able to eat solid food without ill effect, which was inconsistent with the claim that they had been starving for weeks with very little food. There have been many cases when survivors of a ship wreck or plane crash have been forced to consider eating flesh from the bodies of their dead comrades as the only means of staying alive. But in this case the allegations were more serious: not only of cannibalism but that one of the survivors had been murdered in order that his body could become food for the others.

One month after the *Donerail*'s lifeboat arrived at Tarawa, the ship's third officer, Anton Petersen, had told Captain Holland that he wished to be lodged apart from the other survivors because he was afraid they were planning to kill him. He 'unburdened his mind' on 20 February, in a written statement to Holland, in which he alleged that men on the lifeboat had first eaten the body of a messman named 'Aas' who had died of wounds inflicted in the sinking of the *Donerail*. He stated that another man who died of wounds had also been eaten and that a junior engineer named Handeland had been murdered by a blow to the head so that his flesh could be eaten. Handeland had been wounded in the sinking of the *Donerail* but, according to Petersen, was recovering from his wounds at the time of his murder.

Some of the flesh had been eaten immediately after the men died; the remainder was sun-dried and eaten later. According to Petersen, there had been some of this dried meat on the boat as it approached Tarawa and it was thrown overboard just before the boat landed on the beach—hence the strong smell that stayed with the boat and the men's clothes.

Holland wrote to the Secretary of the WPHC, H Vaskess, enclosing a copy of Petersen's signed statement but the letter did not reach Vaskess until Holland himself delivered it after the *Degei* reached Suva on 18 March. A further month passed before Vaskess wrote to the US Consul in Fiji, Wainwright Abbott, advising him of the allegations. The letter informed the Consul that the Fiji courts had no jurisdiction in the matter as it involved foreigners in a foreign boat in international waters. Vaskess believed that the *Donerail* was registered in the United States of America.

In fact, the ship was the Danish *Nordhval* built in Copenhagen in 1924. It had been requisitioned by the United States Maritime Commission in June 1941 and was sailing in the service of the Union Steamship Company of New Zealand, under Panamanian registration and the name *Donerail*. Abbott advised the Secretary of State in Washington of the matter but the Americans also had no jurisdiction as the *Donerail* had been registered under the Panamanian flag. The end result was that no further action was taken in the matter.[12]

In May 1943 Murray Chambers, the Australian crewman of the *Donerail*, was interviewed on Radio 2FC Sydney. In the interview he stated that during the lifeboat voyage they survived by eating raw flying fish and drinking rainwater caught by the sail. This is consistent with the story he had told Captain Holland at Tarawa. He made no mention of cannibalism.[13]

9
Carlson's Raid and the Bombing of Keuea

In June 1942 the Americans were the victors in the Battle of Midway, a fight at sea between aircraft carriers. With the Japanese fleet crippled by the sinking of four of its carriers, this victory was a turning point in the war. By August, US forces were ready to make their first major counterattack against land-based Japanese forces. Marine corps were to land on Guadalcanal and Tulagi in Solomon Islands, the limits of Japan's perimeter in the southwest Pacific. The US plan for the western Pacific also turned the Central Pacific into a significant, turbulent battleground.[1]

Creating a Diversion

To divert Japanese resources away from Solomon Islands, Admiral Nimitz, Commander in Chief of the US Navy, Pacific Areas, planned a raid in the Central Pacific. A second purpose of the raid was to destroy Japanese installations, gather intelligence, test the raiding tactics of the US Marines and boost home-front morale.

With the Americans well aware of the enemy's weakness in the Gilberts, their selected target was the Japanese seaplane base on Butaritari (**Map 8**), the only Japanese base in the island group at the time. Nimitz believed that the small garrison on the island consisted of only 43 men (actually there were 73 men of the 62nd Naval Garrison Unit), led by a sergeant major. He considered that a small force of marines could do damage out of all proportion to their numbers.[2]

Much impressed with the British commandos, President Roosevelt had been instrumental in establishing similar units (raiders) in the US. Selected for the Butaritari operation were 222 marines of the 2nd Raider Battalion, with

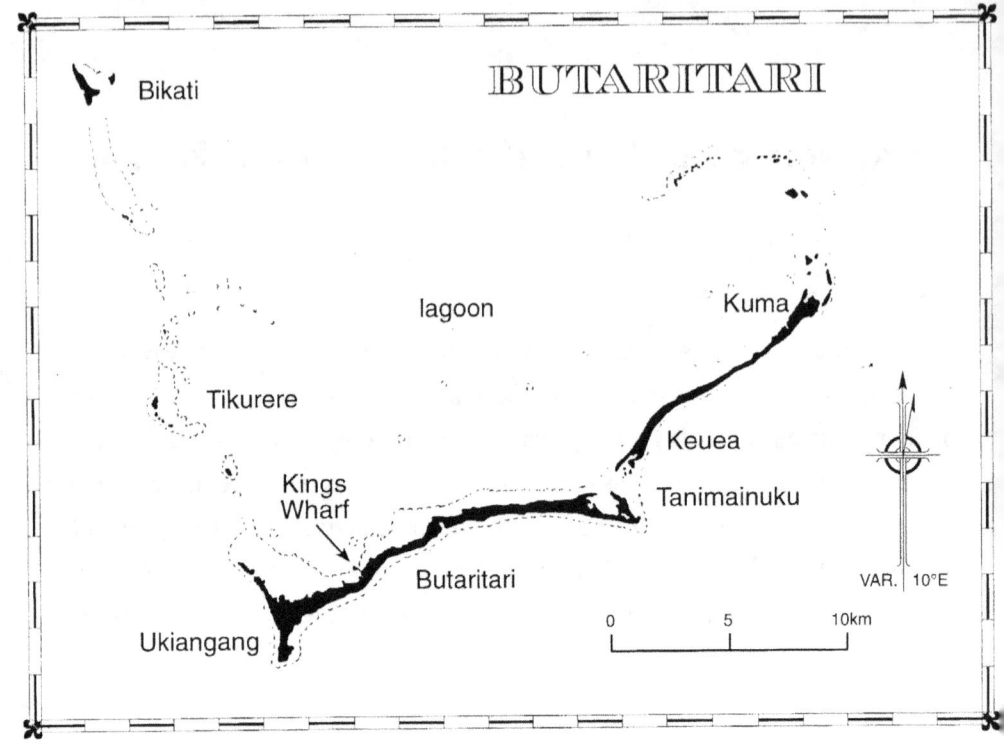

Map 8. Butaritari Atoll

Lieutenant Colonel Evans F Carlson in command and the President's son, Major James Roosevelt, as second in command.

On 8 August they left Honolulu for Butaritari aboard the submarines *Argonaut* and *Nautilus*. It was a long and uncomfortable voyage of 2000 nautical miles with no place to sit or stand, so for most of the eight days on board the marines were kept to their bunks. The air inside the submarines was constantly hot and stale.[3]

The two submarines made their rendezvous at a point south of Butaritari at 9:16 pm on 16 August. Because of the need to maintain radio silence, the operation orders were passed from the *Nautilus* to the *Argonaut* in a watertight barrel. Next day at 4:00 am, under cover of darkness, the raiders left the submarines in inflatable rubber boats. Coming in over the ocean reef not far from Butaritari village, the main settlement, they made their way to the lagoon shore and then began to advance towards the southwest. At 5:30 am, they established radio communications with the submarines.[4]

Local people soon joined the marines, and informed them that most Japanese installations lay about three kilometres further to the southwest. There, a radio communications station stood at the head of King's Wharf, the seaplane mooring area.[5] Of the several people who gave assistance to the marines, the most outstanding were Joseph Muller, who acted as a guide, and Beriki, who had been the Butaritari radio operator before the Japanese occupation. Other Gilbertese who had personal friends among the Japanese went to warn them of the US landing.

Then Japanese troops began arriving to resist the invaders. Apart from two motorcycles with sidecars and one truck, bicycles were their only transport and these were soon stopped. Reporting the landing to the Marshall Islands, the Japanese communications station requested reinforcements. Soon the marines noticed a small transport and patrol boat coming down the lagoon from the north and they requested bombardment support from the *Nautilus*. Beginning their attack at 7:00 am, the gunners on the submarine were unable to see their targets. Nonetheless, after firing 65 salvos from their six-inch guns, concentrating their fire in the 'lake' (lagoon) and harbour areas, they hit and sank both craft, killing 60 Japanese sailors.[6]

By 9:00 am the Japanese commander, Sergeant Major Kyusaburo Kanemitsu, admitted that he was defeated. His men were fighting bravely but were outnumbered. He sent out his last radio message: 'All men are dying serenely in Battle.'

Some relief for the Japanese seemed possible when reinforcements arrived by air. Ten planes of the 19th Air Group bombed and strafed the area, so that the submarines had to dive quickly to avoid being hit. However, any other effects on the US forces were limited. Two more planes, big 'Mavis' flying boats, landed in the lagoon between the King's and On Chong's wharves. Automatic fire from the marines hit and burned one plane on the water and caused the other to crash as it attempted to take off again.[7]

A number of Gilbertese heard the shooting and came to look on. As the following extracts indicate, they were impressed with the superior US weaponry when they witnessed its impact on the Japanese forces:

> We heard the shooting from the location of the Japanese garrison and went to have a look. We then saw how weak the Japanese were in comparison to the Americans. The Americans had quick-firing automatics and the Japanese only single shot rifles apart from their few machine guns. We saw Japanese shot through the head, the bullets had gone right through their helmets.
> (Robuti of Ukiangang Village)[8]

> We saw a Japanese soldier, Ishi, his name was, he had been shot through the jaw. We asked him what was wrong but he couldn't speak. We helped ourselves to the goods in the store as all the Japanese had been killed.
> (Winnie Powell)[9]

Landing in their rubber boat too far to the west, 11 marines under the command of Lieutenant Oscar Peatross found themselves at the enemy's rear. Taking advantage of the situation, they destroyed the radio station and put it off the air at approximately 9:00 am, just after the commander had sent his last message. They burned equipment and stores then headed back to their submarine.

A Difficult Withdrawal

At 5:00 pm Carlson began to withdraw the rest of his men to the embarkation point, and at 7:00 pm launched the rubber boats that were to return them to the submarines. But the lightweight inflatables could not get through the breaking surf. Boats capsized and were cast back up on the beach. Only seven boats and fewer than 100 men made it back to the submarines that night, arriving alongside between 8:00 and 10:30 pm.

As an alternative means of reaching the submarines, the Americans could have launched the boats in the calm waters of the lagoon and motored out of the south channel into the ocean. However, such an approach would have meant a boat ride of 15 nautical miles and they were already having problems with their outboard motors. If they were still travelling after sunrise, they would have been seriously exposed to Japanese aircraft attacks. The submarines signalled that they would stay in position until all the marines were rescued.

Next morning, the marines tried to leave the island again, and four more boats made it through the surf. A boat coming from the *Nautilus* with a volunteer crew attempted to get a line ashore to pull the remaining boats through the breakers, but was strafed by a Japanese plane and disappeared. At this stage 70 men were still left on Butaritari and a high concentration of Japanese aircraft prevented any further attempts to escape. At 9:19 am the *Nautilus* was forced to dive to avoid being hit by enemy bombs and, while she was submerged, her crew heard a bomb explode.

The submarine surfaced again after 6:00 pm. When it was dark on the island, four rubber boats were taken over to the lagoon and lashed to Gilbertese canoes; locals then helped to paddle them out of the south passage and halfway around the atoll to the waiting submarines, reaching them about 11:00 pm. Here again Joseph Muller and other local people risked their lives, both in an immediate sense and through possible Japanese reprisals in future, to help the Americans.

Carlson believed that all the living marines were now aboard, and counted one officer and 29 enlisted men as killed or missing. What he did not know was that nine of the missing marines were still alive on Butaritari. The submarines departed for Pearl Harbor just before midnight, unwittingly leaving the men behind.[10]

Keuea Under Fire

On the morning of 18 August, while the Americans were escaping from the area around Butaritari village, Japanese planes bombed and strafed Keuea village, 15 kilometres to the northeast. Given that it was some distance from the action, it is unclear why Keuea was selected as the target. Perhaps the Japanese decided to bomb a village, any village, as a reprisal against Gilbertese cooperation with the marines; or perhaps they believed, mistakenly, that the nine

Figure 11. Memorial at Keuea, Butaritari to the people who died when the village was bombed by Japanese planes on 18 August, 1942. Inscription reads: Remembrance, Keuea people mourn the deaths of their beloved ones who died 16.8.1942. Keuea is with you.

stranded marines were sheltering there. Actually the people of Keuea had no involvement at all with the marines until the afternoon after the bombing, when the stranded marines passed through the bombed-out village, away from the scene of the fighting.

Whatever the motivation, five planes bombed and strafed Keuea without warning. Forty-eight innocent people were killed (see **Figure 11** and Appendix D). Among them were 38 Keuea villagers, including 10 children aged 10 years or younger. Also killed was the LMS pastor Tarekaua Tokamatawa from Marakei. Other victims were visitors from Kuma village and the islands of Abaiang, Maiana and Makin. The attack also wounded 30 others.[11]

One of the survivors, Buariki Tekateke (**Figure 12**), lost both his parents plus two sisters and a brother in the raid. He takes up the story:

> I was 13 years old. We heard the planes approaching and could tell by their sound that they were Japanese and not American. There were five planes flying in formation. I saw the bombs falling and told an old man, Tebari, who said, 'You fool, bombs would fall straight down and explode, there have been no explosions.' But I saw them glittering in the sunlight, about 10 of them. He said they must be the targets the Japanese use for shooting practice.
>
> Then we heard the sound of the bombs and they began exploding all around, on the road and beside the road. Bright lights flashed and we heard the whistling sound of things flying. There was smoke everywhere. Inside the house, the wife of the old man had her insides blown out and her child had a hole through him. Another child stood up and then fell again with lots of blood. The old man was hit and thrown between a coconut tree and a drum. A pregnant woman, Nei Kantetaake, was thrown outside, not hit by the shrapnel. The thatch on the roof was thrown up from the blast and there was blood on it. Three people had been killed and the blood dripped down through the floor of the house on to the ground.
>
> I was hit but didn't realise it until I saw all the blood. My thigh bone was shattered and my knee and a piece of shrapnel stuck into my shin bone, it was only removed years later in the hospital in Tarawa. When the Japanese returned about two or three weeks later they took

Figure 12. Na Buariki of Keuea, survivor of the bombing attack on his village

us wounded to their hospital for treatment. They never apologised or admitted that they made a mistake in bombing us.[12]

Buariki's right leg has been useless ever since and he walks only with the aid of crutches. Also injured in the bombing was one of his younger brothers, Reita, who recalls:

> They bombed and machine-gunned, three planes then two planes, in two waves. We ran out on to the beach or the reef. Houses were blown up, some burnt. I ran, didn't feel my foot. Someone told me, 'Hey your foot is nearly falling off, it got hit by a bomb.' I looked at it and saw all the blood and the mud stuck on it. In the Japanese hospital I had to have several operations. There was no anaesthetic, they used to hold me down on the operating table, like a pig. The pain was so great that I would bite those holding me. No one died in the hospital, some died of wounds after the bombing, before the Japanese returned with their doctor. Now there is no joint in my ankle, it is all joined solid and it is partly without feeling so that sometimes I fall over.[13]

Throughout the war, Tom Reiher (son of Fritz Reiher on Tarawa) lived on Butaritari with his family in a house in the bush not far from Keuea village. He recalls the day of the bombing:

> … one village not far from where we were staying… they machine gunned all the village… small village, Keuea… The same night we had to travel, to move away from there in case the Japanese came back… it was really dark when we went through the village… my wife said, 'Hey, I stood on somebody's hair', a lady was lying on the road… a small village, they nearly killed everyone, maybe about 200 people there…[14]

Several Chinese families had moved to Tanimainuku village when the Japanese took over the main settlement. After the Keuea bombing, it was rumoured that the Japanese would return to bomb other villages between Keuea and Butaritari village so they moved further away, to Kuma.

The nine marines who were left behind on Butaritari were captured a few days later when Japanese forces returned to the island. For a time, the Japanese kept them in a pen made from coconut timber, then shipped them out to Kwajalein in the Marshall Islands. Apparently the Japanese were intending to send them to a prisoner of war camp in Japan. However, the commanding officer at Kwajalein, Vice Admiral Kose Abe, became impatient with delays to move them and ordered their execution. They were beheaded on 16 October and buried in a mass grave on Kwajalein. In post-war trials, Abe was found guilty of the atrocity and was hanged at Guam.[15]

Assessing the Raid

To the Americans it seemed that the raid had been very successful. First, it had given the marines experience in atoll warfare and submarine troop transport. In addition, although they had lost 30 men, they counted 86 dead Japanese, with still more killed in the boats and seaplanes that they had destroyed.

However the raid was too successful in its aim of diverting Japanese resources to the Central Pacific. It had cost the people of Keuea 48 lives. Within two weeks of the raid, Japanese forces occupied Ocean Island (Banaba) and Nauru, ultimately resulting in the death of 600 Nauruans and over 500 Banabans, Gilbertese and Ellice Islanders. Less than one month after the raid, Butaritari was not only reoccupied by Japanese but strengthened, and Abemama was also occupied. Moreover, prompted by the raid, the Japanese began the fortifications of Betio that were to later take over 1000 US lives. The increased Japanese interest in the Gilbert Islands and Ocean Island also led to the deaths of 28 Europeans—New Zealand coast-watchers and others living there. The following chapters cover these events.

10

Occupation of Ocean Island and Abemama

Although for some time the Japanese had planned to strengthen their position in the Gilberts and Nauru, it seems that Carlson's raid was the catalyst to implement the plan. Within two weeks of the Butaritari attack, the Japanese were occupying Ocean Island and Nauru. Their occupation of Abemama and Tarawa soon followed (see also Chapter 11).

The Spectre of Occupation

The Japanese made their first moves to occupy Ocean Island and Nauru in May 1942. The plan was a part of Operation MO, which aimed to capture Port Moresby in New Guinea, thereby giving the Japanese superiority over the Coral Sea and ensuring their domination of the southwest Pacific, all the way to the Australian coast. The Americans strenuously opposed these early Japanese attempts with a counterattack that became a fight between aircraft carriers. It was the Battle of the Coral Sea, which began on 4 May. As a result, the Japanese advance southwards was checked although they sank one US carrier, the *Lexington*, and captured Tulagi in Solomon Islands.[1]

On 18 May the Japanese sent out an occupation force from Truk to occupy Ocean Island and Nauru. At this stage, it was a face-saving gesture: the earlier part of their plan to capture Port Moresby had not succeeded. The US reserve force for the Battle of the Coral Sea, with carriers *Enterprise* and *Hornet*, remained in the area as a deterrent. They were ordered to steam within 500 nautical miles of the eastern Solomons, where Japanese search planes would be sure to spot them. As predicted, the Japanese recalled the would-be occupation force when they learnt of the presence of the US carriers.

The Free French destroyer *Le Triomphant* had already evacuated most Europeans from both Ocean Island and Nauru at the end of February 1942.[2] Although before the evacuation, enemy air reconnaissance had been frequent, no planes were sighted during the evacuation itself. The ship arrived safely in Malekula in the New Hebrides, then the evacuees were transferred to Australia. Along with the Europeans, a group of Chinese men were evacuated. However, no attempt was made to evacuate any of the Pacific island workers.

For some time after the evacuation, there was concern in Australia and New Zealand about the welfare of the islanders on Ocean Island. In May 1942 the New Zealand Naval Board advised Washington that if possible the inhabitants should be evacuated as it was estimated their food reserves would last only to the beginning of September and the island could not produce enough food for the 1500 imported workers plus the 923 indigenous inhabitants. The New Zealand government expressed its willingness to cooperate in every way possible but pointed out that evacuation from the island was the responsibility of the US Navy.

In June the Americans were saying that the US Navy would consider the matter after the conclusion of operations in the Midway area. Early in July the WPHC suggested that if the danger to shipping was too great to repatriate islanders to their home islands, arrangements could be made to take them south to Fiji instead. On 6 August the administrator of Ocean Island, Cyril George Fox Cartwright (a young Oxford graduate), predicted trouble if evacuation was deferred as the food situation was by then serious.[3]

Any further consideration of the matter was curtailed three weeks later when the Japanese occupied the island. The High Commissioner of the WPHC had stated, 'It is unlikely that Gilbertese would suffer any serious molestation if the islands were occupied by Japan.' Unfortunately events in the islands, especially on Ocean Island and Nauru, were to prove him very wrong.

On 7 July 1942 Japanese forces landed on Guadalcanal in Solomon Islands to construct a base from which to launch renewed attacks against New Guinea and Australia. Then on 24 August, soon after the Carlson raid, Admiral Yamamoto, Commander in Chief of the Combined Japanese Fleet, ordered the capture of Abemama, Ocean Island, Nauru and Tarawa. Nine land-based attack planes and one flying boat of the 24th Air Flotilla bombed Ocean Island and Nauru on 22 August.[4]

Arrival on Ocean Island

On Ocean Island some of the bombs hit buildings in the Catholic mission compound. Then just after midnight, the *Yugure*, a destroyer of the 27th Destroyer Division, shelled the island. Correctly believing that the shelling was the prelude to a landing, administrator Cartwright destroyed the cypher for official messages and burnt records. The *Yugure* landed her combat unit unopposed at 3:00 pm on 26 August.

Living on the island were Banabans, Gilbertese, Ellice Islanders and a small number of Chinese workers. There was also a group of six Europeans who had volunteered to stay (**Figure 13**). Five of them had permission to remain: Cartwright, radio operator Ronald Third, Father Pujebet and Brother Brummell of the Sacred Heart Mission, and BPC staff member Cole. Soon after the Japanese landed, they were arrested.

The sixth European, Arthur Mercer, remained because he had refused to be evacuated and had gone into hiding, but he was discovered by the Japanese.

Before his arrest, Third had time to send some radio messages and then destroy his equipment (but apparently did not send the 'LLLL' message signalling that 'the enemy has landed'). Peleti Lauti, one of Third's assistants, remembers these events:

> I was on Ocean Island when the Japanese first came, working as a radio operator... when they first arrived we were working in the bush... there were a lot of big non trees [*Norinda citrofolia*], we took our radio set there with a European operator, Mr Third... We still communicated with Tarawa, as Tarawa had not yet been occupied by the Japanese... Two of us, [myself and] another operator, Fred, we went to a place where there were pawpaw trees to get some to eat... met someone who told us the Japanese had arrived. We returned to the place of the wireless and found that it had been all smashed up... Third had sent his final

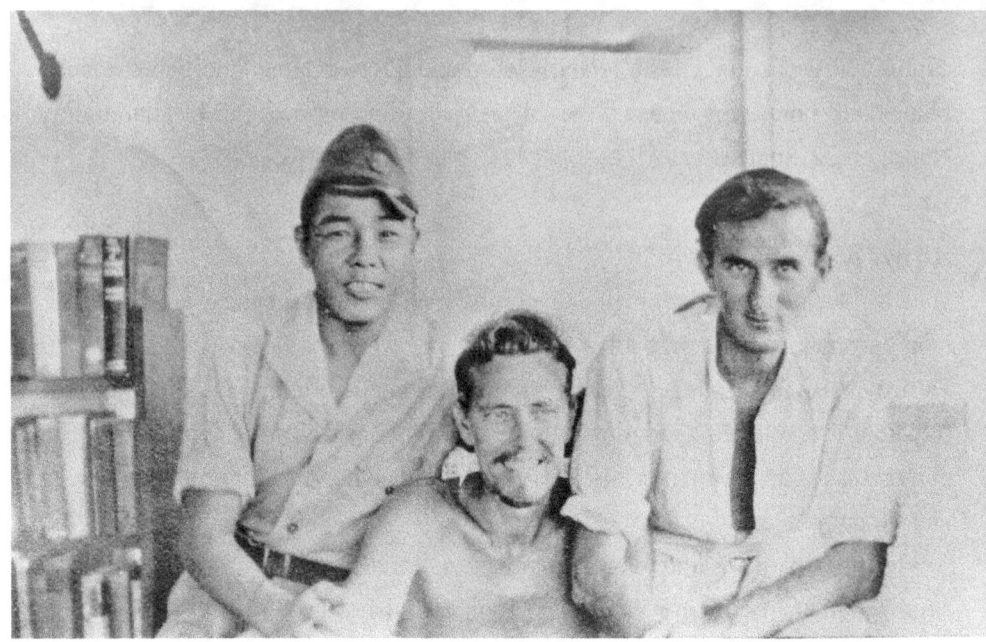

Figure 13. A happy moment on Ocean Island in 1942 before the period of famine and disease. Left to right: Okamoto, driver for the military commander of the island; Allan H. Mercer, Australian employee of the British Phosphate Commission; Ronald Third, New Zealand Post office radio operator.

message and then destroyed the equipment… the Japanese were shown the spot by islanders.[5]

At this time the Japanese were courteous and friendly towards the islanders. The Japanese showed them a map of the Pacific and informed them that Japanese forces would soon capture the Ellice Islands and then Fiji. On 1 September a detachment from the 63rd Naval Garrison Unit replaced the *Yugure* force as the garrison on Ocean Island, consisting of approximately 500 troops and 50 labourers. With the arrival of these troops, life for the islanders changed for the worse.

An Isolated Fortress

The Japanese had occupied Ocean Island in order to deny it to the Allies. The departing BPC staff had earlier sabotaged the phosphate mining plant and the Japanese made no serious attempt to recommence mining operations. Their sole focus in occupying the island was on fortifying and defending it.

Thus the occupying Japanese installed gun emplacements and traps to oppose any landing from the sea. Overlooking Uma bay, considered a logical landing site for an invasion, were six-inch guns, the largest in the garrison's weaponry. Uma village was completely destroyed, machine gun posts were everywhere and all trees and vegetation were removed to give the Japanese unobstructed vision around that section of the coast. Along with the two six-inch (150-millimetre) naval guns were a range finder and radar station. Out on the reef the Japanese placed many two-tonne phosphate train bogies as tank traps. With similar initiative to the New Zealanders on Fanning Island (Chapter 3), they also constructed a number of dummy coconut log guns alongside the Chinese compound.

Lacking a harbour and an airfield, the island became an isolated fortress, of little practical use. It was similarly of no military use to the Allies. So, rather than retake it, they left it to 'wither on the vine'.

Ever Worsening Conditions

Food and water supplies, in short supply even before the occupation, soon became a problem for both the Japanese and their captives. In spite of its rich phosphate deposits, the island produces few food crops because its rainfall is so low. Importing shipments of supplies became difficult as the Allies gained control of the sea and air in the area. The last Japanese supply ship to the island came in October 1943.

For a short time the Japanese managed to ship in small quantities of food by submarine, under cover of darkness. Yet eventually even this scheme became impossible as the Japanese supply lines became longer and more tenuous. Although the Japanese initiated a project to grow pumpkins in discarded fuel drums, using 'night soil' as manure, it was insufficient to meet the island's food needs. People were forced to eat the leaves of wild trees and plants, *ren*

(*Messerschmidia messerschmidia*), *ruku* (a creeper, *Convolvulus*) and other leaves.[6]

Nonetheless, in 1943 at least 130 islanders died on Ocean Island of malnutrition or related conditions. Captured Japanese records show that 48 of those deaths were attributed to beriberi and 31 to gastritis. Conspicuous by their absence are all records relating to deaths of Europeans.[7] The Japanese claimed later that all six Europeans died of illness but there is suspicion that at least some may have been murdered. Peleti Lauti remembers meeting Ronald Third on the road one day. Third was holding his stomach and Peleti asked him what was the matter. Third's reply was that he had been operated on by the Japanese doctor even though he was not ill. The doctor had been either practising his techniques or experimenting on him.[8]

Some Japanese took food from the islanders by force. However, for the islanders, stealing food was a capital offence. Three men—Toanikarawa Teaero, Tamoa and Robert Corrie—were publicly beheaded by Sergeant Major Otsaki for stealing food. Ituaso Laafai recalls the execution of two of them:

> Two Gilbertese were beheaded, they stole rice from the store. Everyone was forced to witness the executions, even the young children. It was translated to us, 'This is what will happen to anyone who steals food, do you understand?' We answered, 'Yes we understand.'[9]

Other memories of Ocean Island under Japanese rule are similarly disturbing:

> It would be better to be a soldier than a civilian prisoner. Soldiers have weapons and have a chance. We had no chance, we were slaves. We were the same as pigs—we had no human rights.
> (Tikaouti Bonabati)[10]

The Japanese built a fence out on the reef, where they expected an American landing. Two prisoners [Bangao and Tauantang] were sent out to test this fence. They were dressed up in military uniforms, like Americans, wore boots. They were told to climb over the fence but when they touched it they were electrocuted. They were buried in the graveyard, a single grave.

(Teveia Ntiua)[11]

The islanders were terrorised and starving. The Japanese pilfered uncontrollably. One Ellice Islander man, Lemuta, was bayoneted when he refused to unlock his cabin trunk to a Japanese looter. He died the following day. Two women were stripped naked and tied to a mango tree to be publicly humiliated, as punishment for showing a light during blackout. There were cases of rape. Moreover, it was said that a Japanese civilian, Taninta, was responsible for procuring young girls from the villages, and forcing them to go to Japanese officers who sexually abused them.

Removal from Ocean Island

To relieve the overpopulation of the island, the occupiers shipped islanders to other Japanese-held islands, despite the very real danger that the ships might be attacked. The ships used were the small *Nantaku Maru* which had been used to bring coconuts and *babai* to the island from Butaritari and the Marshall Islands; the *Ikuta Maru*, which was a larger armed merchantman; and the *Azuchi Maru*. Travelling mostly at night, these ships took nearly 2000 Banabans, Gilbertese and Ellice Islanders away: 750 went to Nauru in four trips over July and August 1943, 400 went to Tarawa, and many went to Kusaie in the Caroline Islands. It was intended that some of those taken to Nauru would go on to Ponape but instead they remained on Nauru until the end of the war.

In this way, all women and children and most men were removed from the island; there remained only about 150 young male islanders to work for the Japanese in fishing, toddy-cutting and pumpkin-growing (their fate is discussed in Chapter 15). Ituaso Laafai describes some of the harsh experiences involved in the removal of the islanders from Ocean Island:

> I was on the first ship to leave, it was a cargo ship and we were kept in the hold like cargo. We went first to Nauru where we got some food.

They threw the food down to us inside the hold as if we were pigs. Then they let us up on the deck. From there we saw four Chinese beheaded on the beach at Nauru, we were very close.[12]

The ship sailed to Kusaie where the evacuees from Ocean Island were put to work in agriculture, producing food for the Japanese military. They grew cassava, *kumala* (sweet potato) and melons, as well as looking after livestock. As Teveia Ntiua recalls, the perils continued as the island came under US attack:

> I looked after cows and pigs. The Americans bombed us. On Ocean Island the Japanese captured us and treated us as British prisoners, then on Kusaie, the Americans came and bombed us as if we were all Japanese. There was nowhere to hide, the American planes came in very low and fast. We lay down in the gardens amongst the cassava; another time I hid in a banana plantation. Some Gilbertese were killed in the bombing:
> ... There was little food, the Americans dropped leaflets 'Where is the Japanese Army? Where is the Navy? You will stay here and eat grass unless you surrender.'[13]

US forces did not land on Kusaie until 8 September 1945, one month after the war had ended. Nationals of the Gilbert and Ellice Islands Colony then had to live off the generosity of the Americans until 23 November, when the colony ship *MV Maureen* arrived with colonial officials looking for their nationals. They found 771 people; 657 were Gilbertese or Banaban, and the other 114 were Ellice Islanders. The *MV Maureen* and BPC vessel *Trienza* then took them to Tarawa, where some of the Gilbertese men joined the labour corps[14] (see Chapter 14).

Occupied Abemama

On 2 September 1942 several hundred troops landed on Abemama and the Japanese took up their first occupation of the island with land combat personnel from units stationed in the Marshall Islands.[15] They also had long-term plans to build an airfield there.

However, the occupation of Abemama was much less stressful than that of Ocean Island. The Japanese gave priority to building an airfield and establishing heavy defences on Tarawa. They left only 75 men to maintain lookout stations on Abemama, one of them in the extreme south of the island at Kabangaki. By the time the Americans captured Abemama in November the next year, there were only 24 Japanese there, as work on the airfield never began and the majority of the men were withdrawn to Tarawa.

On Abemama, the New Zealand coast-watchers hid themselves in the bush. During that time, radio operator Taukiei assisted and fed them, not giving them away despite being questioned and threatened by the Japanese.[16] After a few days, the New Zealanders heard that there would be reprisals against the islanders if they were not given up, so they surrendered.

Closure of Coast-Watching Stations

As well as occupying Abemama for the first time and strengthening their position on Tarawa, the Japanese took the opportunity to have a closer look at all the islands of the Gilberts. In so doing, they closed down the remainder of the New Zealand coast-watching stations. In particular, they paid close attention to Beru and Maiana, which they suspected of being radio communications centres (however, although Beru had been the parent station for the Gilberts since the closure of Ocean Island and Tarawa, the station on Maiana was only a small reporting station, identical to the other small stations).

The Maiana station sent its final message on 25 September, 'Japanese coming—regards to all'. Radio operator Ruotake Iantin recalls the events thereafter:

> I was in the radio station with Heenan [the Maiana radio operator], an LLLL message was sent to Beru. Heenan and I then took the radio equipment to the bush. Heenan and I destroyed all the code books by fire… I smashed the equipment with an axe… The Japanese were not able to find the New Zealanders and left… the New Zealanders came back to the government station on 28 September. They made arrange-

109

ments to leave by canoe to go to Kuria on 4 or 5 October. Before they got away the Japanese returned. Heenan and Owen [a private] surrendered but Speedy [the other private] went off into the bush again... The Japanese found Speedy who was bayoneted through the palm of his left hand, he was also wounded in the forehead by a bayonet.[17]

Leslie Copeland takes up the story, providing more information on Private Speedy's capture:

> ... Kanzaki took us aboard a ship called *Katori Maru*... we were told that two coast-watchers were at the government station and that one was hiding in the bush... walked on some coconut leaves which were covering the lid of a fox hole... the Japanese lifted the lid and found the man... The natives said the man found in the bush was Leslie [Speedy].[18]

On 26 September the Japanese arrived on Tamana. Sergeant Nateri of Baka village recalls that four Japanese came ashore about dawn, 'three with rifles, their leader with a fixed bayonet'.[19] The three New Zealand coast-watchers surrendered. Local witnesses recall the events as follows:

> The Japanese landed at Baka village in a launch from a ship. Kanzaki, the Jap man from Butaritari, accompanied them... They met the New Zealand operators... Kanzaki told some people to go into the house and collect the wireless set, foodstuffs and all other gear... The Japanese leader called all the people to the maneaba [communal meeting house] and addressed them. He said the Japanese had come to free the people from the governments of Great Britain and the United States which were very bad.
> (Tekemau of Barebuka village)[20]

> ... the hands of all three were tied behind them with telephone wire, then they were tied together... The interpreter asked the New Zealand soldiers to put on their uniforms because they were wearing only shorts... the operator only put on a white shirt and no hat.
> (Ueantabo)[21]

The parent station on Beru also went off on 26 September. The head of the LMS mission school on Rongorongo, Rev A Sadd, was arrested. For one week, the coast-watchers evaded capture before surrendering. Falavii Sosene, who was assisting the coast-watchers, remembers:

> Mr Taylor [radio operator in charge] said 'I have sent the first message but you can send the LLLL message when they land... I leave you in charge with Tekarara to help you'... I called BZO Suva but in vain, I heard him working a sub-station, so I called ZJU Funafuti and sent the LLLL plus remarks saying that four warships had arrived. After this we took the Teleradio transmitter and receiver to the bush and buried them... natives told Japanese that there were two European operators [Taylor and Tom Murray], one Gilbertese [Tekarara] and one Ellice [Falavii Sosene] operators... the enemy paid no notice of Tekarara and myself but were looking for Mr Taylor and Mr Murray...
>
> On Sunday 27 I reported to Mr Taylor and Mr Murray at Taboiaki village... they said to be ready that we will leave for Nikunau at 5:00 pm and gave me a suitcase to carry to Rongorongo. But when I got as far as Nuka village I met them again and Mr Murray said 'We are not going.'... On 3 October the Japanese returned and took them away to Tarawa.[22]

The government district clerk on Beru, Ikamawa, also told of the capture:

> 250 soldiers landed at 8:00 am on 29 September and spent the whole day looking for the Europeans. Kanzaki from Butaritari interpreted... the Catholic father and [Samoan] LMS pastor Iupeli were told to carry on as normal but to remember that they were now under Japanese control... The people informed the Japanese that wireless equipment was hidden in the kaubure's house... Before leaving they informed us that the coast-watchers were to be brought up to them next time they returned... Enemy returned on 7 October and the coast-watchers surrendered...[23]

Next to fall was Nonouti, on 27 September. Here the New Zealanders hid with one of their friends, Ben Kum Kee. The local radio operator, Kapoa, helped to remove and hide the radio equipment in the bush and then burnt the code books. Later, when the Japanese returned to the island on 4 October, the New Zealanders surrendered. At this time the Japanese also arrested their friend, the retired Scottish trader A M McArthur. A Gilbertese clerk and interpreter, Tiriata, witnessed the four Europeans at the government station:

> [The Japanese] were told that the Europeans were waiting for them on the government station. The Japanese found them inside the Native Government Office. They called them and lined them up and questioned them... While they were lined up one Japanese came forward and hit them hard on the head with his hand and they fell down. Three Japanese officers with stripes on their collar were watching. Then they were all taken on board and the ship left for Tarawa.[24]

On Kuria the coast-watchers—radio operator H Hearn and Privates R Jones and R Ellis—also went into hiding. Ellice Islander radio operator Maatusi Peniamina had been helping them since 1 March, when he arrived on the launch with the *Donerail* survivors and other Europeans who were escaping from Tarawa (Chapter 8). He recalls the arrival of the Japanese on the island:

> I worked with them [the New Zealanders] perhaps four or five months, weather reports and coast-watching observations. Coast-watching had been organised, there were lookouts at three places around the island. I didn't move around, I stayed near the station to receive reports from the lookouts. I slept with the code books, a bottle of kerosene and matches; when the Japanese came, if I wasn't caught I was ready to burn the records.
>
> One night a Japanese ship came, it was on its way to Abemama, Abemama had already been visited by the Japanese. Then another time, about one month later, another ship came, our radio had already been taken to the bush, we worked in the bush. All the other stations in Kiribati had been discovered by the Japanese, Kuria was the last.

I was communicating with Funafuti about 7:00 one morning when I heard someone nearby say that a ship had arrived at Kuria. I told Funafuti to stand by for 10 minutes then ran to the village where I met the European operator [Hearn], he gave me the last message to send. I sent this and said farewell to Funafuti. Three prisoners [islanders who had been convicted in the island court] and two other youths helped us to take the wireless equipment and hide it. On the way a Japanese plane flew over and we ducked for cover and took the wireless into a babai pit.

The Japanese landed on the island and we saw them. We slept in the babai pit and next morning awoke and saw the figure of a Japanese soldier, with a rifle, standing nearby, there was a babai pit full of water separating him from us. He left. We remained in hiding until we smelt smoke, the Japanese were burning the island...[25]

Because the island was small (with a total land area of about 12 square kilometres), the Japanese had decided to use fire to flush the coast-watchers out. They burned about half the centre part of the island, with the loss of thousands of coconut and other food-bearing trees, before the coast-watchers gave themselves up.[26]

Thus by September 1942 the mopping-up operations by the Japanese were complete, so ending New Zealand coast-watching in the Gilbert Islands. After the Japanese first visited the northern Gilberts in December 1941, there had been opportunities to evacuate the European coast-watchers from the central and southern islands. The matter had been considered at a meeting in Wellington on 28 December 1941, with both the New Zealand Prime Minister and the British High Commissioner for the Western Pacific present. It was unanimously agreed at the meeting that the coast-watchers would remain at their posts until, as the Prime Minister put it, 'a Japanese places his hand on their shoulder'.[27]

Thus the official position was that the coast-watchers' role was to observe and report and that their presence was even more important with renewed Japanese activity in the area. Perhaps, while knowing that all the coast-watchers would inevitably be captured, the Prime Minister and others in the New Zealand government honestly believed that the Japanese would treat their prisoners of war fairly. Later it became known that the Japanese had killed all the coast-watchers from the central and southern islands (Chapter 11). In retrospect, the New Zealand Minister of Defence still stood by the decision not to evacuate:

> There could… be no intention of withdrawing these men at that stage, when the very reason for which they had been sent to the islands had come into existence…[28]

11

Occupation of Tarawa and Fortification of Betio

After they had rounded up the New Zealand coast-watchers and closed all the Allied communication stations in the Gilbert Islands, the Japanese could turn their full attention to establishing their headquarters for the Gilbert Islands on Tarawa. On 15 September 1942 the Yokosuka 6th Special Naval Landing Force landed 1122 men on Betio.[1] The first Naval Commander was Matzu Shosa, with Lieutenant Yokata second in command. A further 500 went to Butaritari and 75 to Abemama. (These developments worried the Americans who feared that the Japanese might next move further south into the Ellice Islands. US Marines therefore occupied Funafuti atoll in the Ellice Islands on 2 October, to deny it to their enemy.)[2]

The Place to Hold Ground

Early in 1943 a fortifications specialist was brought in. The Japanese had lost their hold on Solomon Islands and were withdrawing from Guadalcanal, so decided to hold their ground from Tarawa. Under the command of Rear Admiral Tomanari Saichiro, a constructor and engineer, work commenced on Betio, an islet only 3 kilometres long by 500 metres at its widest. They built gun emplacements, bunkers and a barricade wall made of coconut logs wired together, along the lagoon beaches.

Eventually the result was a formidable fortress (**Map 9**). Betio bristled with guns all around its coast. There were 14 coastal defence guns with bomb-proof shelters for ammunition and gun crews, and another 90 guns of 20- to 40-millimetre calibre. Bomb-proof shelters and gun emplacements were protected by

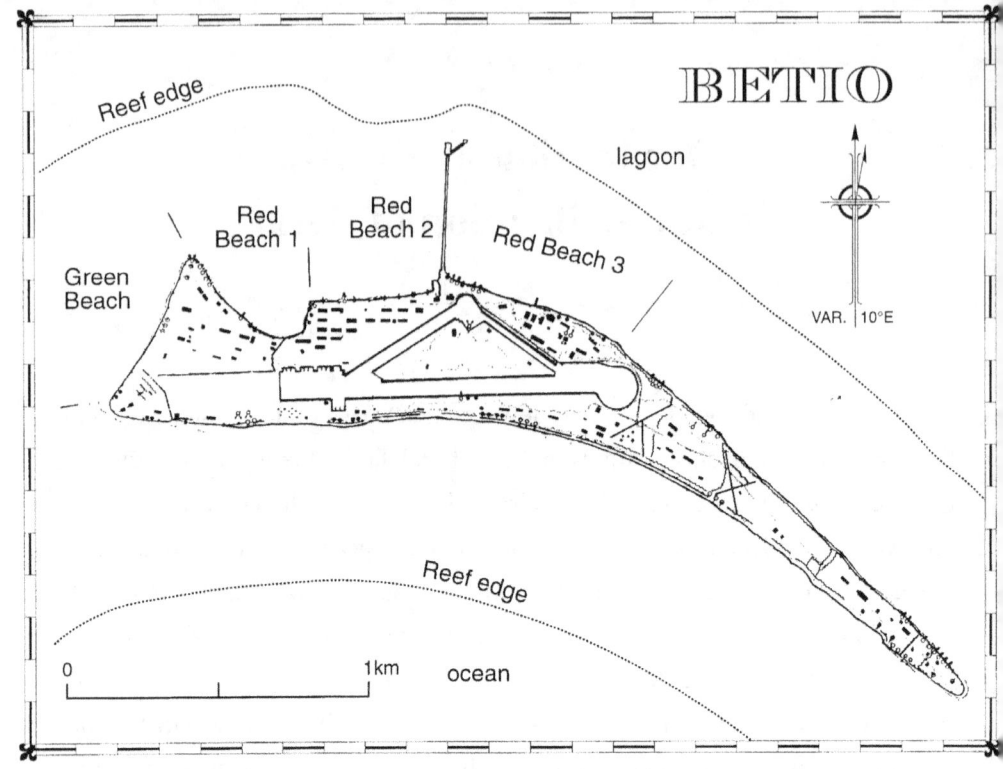

Map 9. Betio islet, Tarawa, showing Japanese airfield and fortification

concrete walls and layers of coconut logs and sand, and were interconnected by revetted trenches. At least 50 machine gun positions stood around the coast, along with anti-aircraft guns and searchlights. At each end of the islet were two of the largest guns on Betio, which fired eight-inch (zoom) shells (**Figure 14**).

Various publications have reported that the Japanese had captured these eight-inch guns in Singapore in February 1942 and taken them to Tarawa. Yet it was in January 1905 that the Japanese bought 12 such guns from the British manufacturer, Vickers Son and Maxim Limited.[3] At that time, Japan and Britain had a good relationship, reflected in the formal Anglo-Japanese Alliance. In a context where British yards were undertaking many shipbuilding and machinery contracts for large ships, Vickers built a number of warships and supplied arms and technical assistance to the Imperial Japanese Navy.[4] The battleships *Iwarri*, *Ibuki* and *Kurama* were launched in 1907, all fitted with eight-inch guns until they were disarmed over 1922 and 1923. It is likely that the guns from one

Figure 14. Two of the British 8-inch (203 mm) guns installed by the Japanese at Betio

of these ships were taken out of storage and sent to Betio after the naval mountings were modified for coastal defence installations. They definitely did not come from Singapore where the British did not have this type of gun.

With KGV School at Bairiki closed during the Japanese occupation, some of the senior boys worked for the Japanese as interpreters or guides, or in construction work. They were provided with a special 'student' armband and the Japanese generally treated them better than the average labourer. Pulekai Sogivalu, head boy of the school at the time, recalls:

> They were good people, the only thing, some of the officers were very rough to the Japanese [soldiers] but not to us... Gilbertese were taken as labourers, no pay only food... the food was always rice, rice in the morning, rice at noon, rice in the evening... no fish... We were divided into three teams, 60 of us, one party collecting stone from the ocean reef for construction work, some cleaning the land, digging holes etc.[5]

Another student, Fakatene Pili, was less favourable in his assessment of the Japanese treatment:

> The students were taken to Betio to work as slaves. There were no Sundays, we worked every day... lived day to day with no idea of the date or time passing... we worked to survive, were given one or two bowls of rice per day and water to drink. When supplies were cut off we ate coconuts.[6]

The Fate of the I-Matang

In October, during the construction activity, the Japanese executed the I-Matang (European) prisoners being held on Betio (**Figure 15**). Those executed were:

- the seven New Zealand coast-watching radio operators and their 10 soldier companions;
- Reginald Morgan, the Australian wireless instructor who had been attested into the Fiji military forces as a lieutenant;
- four civilians—government dispenser Basil Cleary, retired master mariner Isaac Handley, Reverend Sadd from the Beru mission station, and A M McArthur from Nonouti.

Apparently the Japanese had treated these prisoners badly, confining them in the compound of the Lunatic Asylum, tethered to coconut palms with their hands tied. It has been recorded that during a US air raid, Morgan escaped. The Japanese hunted him down on Betio and then killed all the Europeans in retaliation for the escape and the air raid.[7] In fact, the raid came not from the air but from the sea. The cruiser *USS Portland* was on a lone raid mission to investigate Tarawa, Maiana and Abemama islands. The ship approached from the southeast and Tarawa was sighted at 1:00 pm on 15 October. The two single-engine scout observation float planes (the Curtiss SOC 'Seagull'), which were carried aboard, were catapulted aloft. From the air, four Japanese ships were spotted at anchor in Tarawa lagoon (a light cruiser or mine layer, a destroyer and two transport ships). The *Portland* then steamed along the southern coast of

Figure 15. Memorial on Betio to the 22 Europeans massacred there by the Japanese

the atoll, firing at the Japanese ships. One of the Japanese ships returned their fire but the *Portland* was not hit. After firing 237 rounds from their main guns and observing heavy smoke coming from the transport ship, at 2:50 pm they ceased firing and changed course towards Maiana island. No ships or aircraft were spotted at Maiana or Abemama and just before dark the observation planes landed in the sea, were hoisted on board, and the *Portland* steamed away to the southeast.[8]

It seems likely that to the coast-watchers and other prisoners on Betio the raid came as an attempt to rescue them. They would have heard the shells flying over them towards the ships in the lagoon and apparently they heard, saw and waved to the small observation planes. Perhaps they cheered and made a lot of noise. This behaviour, in addition to Morgan's breakout, was more than the Japanese could tolerate and they executed all their prisoners.

Mikaere was an eye witness to two of the executions:

> One European ran away and the Japanese searched for him at the west end of Betio. One Japanese came to the Bishop's fence and showed them his sword, there was fresh blood on it, he said the European was dead... I saw the Europeans sitting down in line in front of the first house inside the lunatic enclosure. One Japanese stepped forward to the first European in line and cut off his head. Then I saw a second European have his head cut off, and I could not see the third one because I fainted.[9]

No one saw the remainder of the executions but two reliable witnesses, Frank Highland and Constable Takaua, saw the remains of the bodies after they had been burnt in an old *babai* pit. As Frank Highland (a part-European local who also features in Chapter 13) describes it:

> I went with Constable Takaua and saw the bodies... burnt in a babai pit. Takaua watched and I went in the pit and lifted up coconut branches and corrugated iron... There were no heads on the bodies. Then I kept watch while Takaua looked.[10]

At this time the Catholic missionaries became the only I-Matang left alive in the Gilbert Islands. Of course there remained many others of mixed European and Gilbertese or Marshallese descent, but the Japanese treated those of mixed race in the same way as they treated the full-blooded Gilbertese. (An exception was David Murdoch on Ocean Island; with only one-quarter Kiribati blood, he looked like a white man and was often beaten by the Japanese for that reason.)[11]

The Japanese spared the Catholic missionaries because most came from countries that were allies of Japan or neutral—France, Germany or Switzerland. Given that the Australian nuns on Abemama were treated no worse than the French sisters, another factor contributing to their special status may have been the close association between their church and Italy, the third Axis power. The Japanese Commander of Tarawa told Bishop Terrienne that leaving the Catholics alone made good propaganda.

Nonetheless, although the European members of the Catholic mission were not molested overtly by the Japanese, much of their property was stolen and they were frequently in fear of their lives. The Japanese regarded them with constant suspicion and refused to give them permission to travel between islands in the Gilbert Group.[12] The Marist brothers and fathers on Ocean Island and Nauru died as a result of Japanese ill treatment.

After the Gilbert Islands returned to British control in November 1943, the deaths of the 22 Europeans were investigated. In January 1944 Captain John R Grigg, a New Zealander on loan to the GEIC Labour Corps from the Fiji Military Forces, was assigned the task of locating the remains of the 22 Europeans killed by the Japanese. He reported on his work:

> When I received instructions to find the remains so that they might receive a decent burial, I asked Josefa to show me the spot. He also brought along a native medical dresser who knew the exact locality. Each separately walked to the only remaining landmark—a well with a circular stone top. From this point they paced some distance in a northerly direction and pointed to a certain spot. I contacted the officer in charge of the unit in that area and he told me that when he had first taken up his position there had been a deep hole but had noted nothing unusual about it. He reminded us that the whole place had been so bombed and shelled that everything had been changed beyond recognition. He had arranged for a bulldozer to fill in the excavation from which the Japs had probably obtained spoil for a fortification nearby and coconut tree trunks and heavy roots embedded in the coral sand would now make it extremely difficult to reexcavate. Even if the pit were laboriously cleared of all its debris it was problematical whether we should find what we were seeking. I reported accordingly to the Resident Commissioner.[13]

In October a court of inquiry convened on Betio established that, although their remains were never found, the Europeans had been killed by the Japanese on Betio, on or about 15 October 1942.[14] Sister Oliva of the Catholic mission stated that she thought the place of burial was covered by the airfield runway that the Japanese built later. In responding to a New Zealand inquiry, the resident commissioner explained that, during the US bombardment preceding the marine landing, a shell struck the spot where it was believed the bodies had been buried and that there was no possibility of identifying the remains now.[15] The three Japanese deemed responsible for the massacre, Commander Matzu Shosa, Lt Yokata and Shingo Masubusi (the NBK manager on Butaritari before Kanzaki), were never located.

Constructing the Airfield

To construct the airfield, the Japanese brought in the 111th Naval Construction Unit in December 1942. The Japanese had established such units for the particular purpose of building airfields in occupied territories. Because regular military officers had no experience in this type of work, these units were composed mostly of non-military men from the construction industry, and Korean labourers—an arrangement similar to that of the US Naval Construction Battalion (Sea Bees).[16]

The result was a bomber strip as the main runway, 1220 metres in length, running east to west along the centre of the island. It was first used while still incomplete, by land-based bombers from the Marshall Islands on 28 January 1943. By the end of May it was virtually finished and two shorter fighter strips were under construction, one running northeast to southwest, the other northwest to southeast.

Young Gilbertese men were recruited and forced to work on the construction. One of these men was Taberannang Teuaba of north Tarawa, who does not have pleasant memories of the experience:

> … we couldn't refuse because we were afraid of the Japanese. Our work was carrying rocks, digging holes, constructing the airfield. It was heavy work… we were beaten if not working hard enough. There was no pay and the food was only a handful of rice… we suffered… left our families, worked hard with little food. When the Americans attacked we were sent back to our villages.[17]

The Limits to the Japanese Defence

The Betio force was strengthened on 17 March 1943 with 1497 men of the Sasebo Naval Special Landing Force, who arrived on the destroyer *Asanagi*, Motor Torpedo Boat number 123 and transport vessel *Takunan Maru*. In April orders were issued for army ground forces to support the navy on Betio. In addition, the 1st South Seas Garrison, comprising one infantry battalion and one artillery company with a total strength of 1200 men, was despatched to Tarawa.[18]

In May 1943 the 1st South Seas Garrison sailed for Tarawa aboard the 5100-tonne auxiliary cruiser *Bangkok Maru*. However, it never reached its destination. On 20 May the US submarine *Pollack*, patrolling close to Jaluit in the Marshall Islands, discovered the *Bangkok Maru*. It planted four torpedoes into her stern, completely obliterating the rear of the ship. One-third of the passengers went down with the ship while the rest made it to Jaluit without weapons or equipment, where they spent the rest of the war. As a substitute for the unfortunate 1st Garrison, the Imperial Army intended to send the 4th South Seas Garrison, but instead diverted it to fill a greater need on Bougainville. Thus no Japanese army unit arrived in the Gilbert Islands, leaving their defence entirely in the hands of the navy.[19]

In July 1943 the navy sent Rear Admiral Keiji Shibasaki, a fighting officer, to take over from Admiral Saichiro, whose expertise was more in construction than defence. Admiral Shibasaki instituted stricter discipline and intensified training in preparation for the inevitable battle with the US Marines. He had at his command an estimated 4871 men: 2624 garrison troops, plus a large contingent of labourers, mostly Koreans, comprising 1247 from the 111th Construction Unit and 970 from the 4th Fleet Construction Department, and approximately 30 base personnel detached from the 955th Naval Air Group. In addition to 150 fixed gun positions scattered around the island, he commanded seven type 95 light tanks, each with a 37-millimetre cannon and two 7.7-millimetre machine guns.

Admiral Shibasaki boasted to his men that the Americans could not capture Betio with a million men in 100 years. Described as acre for acre the most formidable fortress in the world, Betio certainly became, acre for acre, the most expensive battleground in terms of human life.[20]

Part III

THE SETTING SUN

12

Bombing

For the Gilbert Islands, 1943 could be aptly described as the year of the bomb. Not only did the Japanese launch bombing attacks against American bases from the Gilberts, but the Japanese base on Tarawa came under attack also. On 26 January the first US photographic reconnaissance mission over Tarawa discovered the newly constructed Japanese airstrip on Betio.[1] (The first land-based Japanese plane to touch down on Betio arrived two days later.) Soon after US bombers from the 7th Army Air Force attacked Tarawa. This attack made the Japanese aware that a US air base existed on Funafuti in the Ellice Islands, where the bombers had come from. They retaliated with their own bombing missions from Tarawa, attacking US bases on Canton Island and Funafuti atolls.[2]

The Development of Forward Bases

Prior to 1943 the Americans conducted few land-based air operations in the Gilberts because of the vast distances involved. Although they completed a runway on Canton Island as early as December 1941, less than three weeks after the Japanese made their surprise attack on Pearl Harbor, its purpose was primarily as one of the stopovers in the South Pacific ferry route between Hawai'i and Australia (Chapter 2). A round trip from Canton Island to Tarawa carrying all the necessary fuel as well as a heavy load of bombs was impractical and dangerous, as the bombers of the period were not designed to operate over such great distances. They had trouble getting airborne and little time available to locate their targets. Thus the Americans decided that they needed forward bases that were closer to Tarawa.

Immediately after the US Marines occupied Funafuti in the Ellice Islands on 2 October 1942, the Navy Construction Battalion began building a bomber strip there. By January 1943 Funafuti was ready for the photo-reconnaissance bombers of the US Army Air Force. The distance to Tarawa from the Funafuti base was 1150 kilometres, considerably shorter than the 1700 kilometres from Canton Island, making it feasible to attack the Japanese from Funafuti with B-24 Liberator bombers. Conversely, of course, it placed the Funafuti base within range of the Japanese 'Nell' bombers (Mitsubishi type 96 attack bombers) based on Tarawa; indeed, bombers from Tarawa and Nauru bombed the island six times in 1943.

The first attack against Funafuti came on 28 March in which six Mitsubishi 'Nell' twin-engine attack bombers departed from Tarawa. They were detected by Funafuti radar and intercepted by two Grumman 'Wildcats' of US Marine Fighter Squadron 441. One bomber was shot down and a second one damaged. The rest withdrew to Tarawa without attacking the island.[3] The next attack from Tarawa was more successful for the Japanese. Nine bombers attacked Funafuti at night on 23 April with 100-kilogram bombs. Damage on Funafuti was high. Two Liberator bombers were destroyed on the runway; nine fighters and a small seaplane were damaged, as were vehicles and buildings. The Funafuti church was completely destroyed. Seven Americans died, 23 were wounded and one Funafuti man lost his life. The Japanese made more bombing attacks from Tarawa against the Ellice Islands. In total there were seven attacks against Funafuti and a few against Nanumea over an eight-month period from March 1943 until the US Marines captured Tarawa at the end of November.[4]

Prior to the completion of the Tarawa airbase, the closest Japanese base within striking range of Canton Island was the seaplane base at Butaritari, in the northern Gilberts. However, the long-range seaplanes could not carry a great bomb load over that distance and would have been incapable of inflicting any real damage to Canton Island. Such strikes would have been only 'nuisance' attacks and were not attempted. The first bombing attack against Canton Island came from Tarawa and commenced close to midnight on 19 March 1943 when three Japanese flying boats dropped several 300-pound bombs and anti-personnel explosives ('daisy cutters'). The attack came without warning even though Canton Island did have an early warning radar station and there was a hand-cranked alarm siren on the observation tower located close to the Pan Am hotel. Apparently the radar failed to detect the bombers and the soldier on watch at the observation tower saw nothing until it was too late. During this and subsequent bombing attacks, the Canton Island defenders used their searchlights and fired their 90-mm anti-aircraft guns. The Japanese planes were sighted but they were flying at high altitude and received no hits from the guns on the ground. There was no time for the Canton Island fighter aircraft to take off and it is doubtful whether these P39 (Air Cobra) fighters could have reached the altitude that the bombers were capable of attaining.[5]

The guards on duty near the wharf were in foxholes and survived some nearby bomb hits. Flying shrapnel ripped accommodation tents and a small wooden building where men were sleeping was demolished. No one received serious injuries, although a dog belonging to the Americans was found dead after the attack. After this first attack additional sirens were installed around the occupied areas.

US attacks on the Gilbert Islands steadily increased throughout 1943, culminating in November when planes from US aircraft carriers joined those from land bases to intensify the action. Their actions supported amphibious landings by US Marines on Tarawa, Butaritari and Abemama. During November, land-based navy and army Liberator bombers made 259 sorties against the Gilberts and Marshalls, while carrier planes flew 2284 sorties against the same targets.

The US photographic mission that detected the Betio airstrip also covered the Gilbert Islands to the south—Tamana, Beru and Abemama—where it did not detect the few Japanese coast-watchers on Abemama nor any other Japanese activity. Two days later, a single B-24 army bomber from Funafuti made a photographic survey of Nauru and Ocean Island, which revealed another Japanese airstrip on Nauru. Newly completed like its counterpart on Betio, the Nauru strip had received its first planes for landing only two days before the Americans flew over.[6]

On 11 September 1943 the Americans completed a runway on Baker Island in the Phoenix Group, giving them a new air base some 150 kilometres closer to the Gilberts.[7] Moreover, in the Ellice Islands they pushed north to occupy Nukufetau and the northernmost island of the group, Nanumea, only 840 kilometres from Tarawa. The advance was significant as when the Nanumea base became operational in November,[8] it gave the B-24 bombers the range they needed to attack Japanese bases in the Marshall Islands in addition to those in the Gilberts and Nauru. It became normal practice for bombers to stage through Canton Island and Funafuti before departing for their raids from Nanumea. Nonetheless, because of the long distances between home bases and targets, the bombers had to fill up with fuel and so were never able to carry large bomb loads as well. In addition, because navigation was a problem over vast open ocean with few landmarks as guides, pilots were often unable to locate their targets and so were forced to dump their bombs in the ocean before heading for base. Some had trouble finding their bases and crashed in the sea or crash-landed on the wrong island when they ran out of fuel.

Attacks Escalate

Japanese bombers again attacked Canton Island on 22 March 1943, inflicting just slight damage to the airfield.[9] The only bombs to hit the island landed in an undeveloped area between the wharf and the airfield and the Americans did not suffer any damage. This time the warning sirens sounded and there was time for the men to take shelter in their foxholes before the bombers arrived. Three nights then passed without further attack, until at 1:30 am on the 26th came what was to be the most damaging bombing attacked experienced at Canton Island during the war. This time the bombs landed on their intended target, the airfield. A new Catalina amphibian aircraft was hit on the airfield and caught fire. The Japanese planes kept circling over the island, having a good look while the fire from the burning Catalina was lighting up the whole air base.

The 7th Air Force, formed from the Hawaiian Air Force after the Pearl Harbor attack, was responsible for the defence of the Central Pacific. It was a force of limited strength, primarily engaged in training and reconnaissance work. It often had difficulty in furnishing more than a dozen bombers at any one time. On 23 April, 12 B-24s of the 7th Air Force bombed Tarawa, claiming direct hits on the fuel storage area and Japanese barracks on Betio.[10]

The last time that Canton Island was bombed was four months later on 18 July. Six bombs hit the island without causing any damage. Two nights after that, a solitary Japanese plane was seen flying over the island and the anti-aircraft gunners fired at it but the plane was not hit and no bombs fell.

The Americans continued to hit back in a small way. A single bomber attacked the Betio runway on 14 June. Then they sent four planes, then six. On 28 July they managed to muster 16 Liberators against Tarawa. On 18 September there were 24 planes, of which only 18 managed to locate their target and drop their bombs on the Betio installations. In doing so, one was shot down by Japanese Zeke fighters.[11]

The Japanese continued to attack Funafuti and then the Nanumea air base when they discovered it. On 8 September, 10 bombers from Tarawa and Nauru attacked Nanumea, inflicting minor damage.[12]

For both Americans and Japanese, the overall result of these bombing missions was not important in tactical terms. Although both sides lost life and valuable equipment, they repaired most damage to airfields within a few hours of an attack and the losses did not significantly affect the overall plan of the US advance northwards. Even the thousands of American attacks in November, which kept the Japanese bases out of action during the amphibious landings of the marines, did relatively little damage to the well-fortified Japanese base on Betio. However, what they did achieve was to eliminate the possibility of air attacks and allow ground forces to capture the island, which was of great significance.

On 7 November, just before the main air attacks began in support of the US Marine landing on Betio, the Americans sent a photographic reconnaissance plane to gather information on the Japanese seaplane base on Butaritari. From this base, Japanese flying boats had been conducting long-range surveillance over the Gilberts and Ocean Island since early 1942, except for three weeks in August 1942 when Carlson's raider attack put it out of action (Chapter 9). The photographic reconnaissance revealed that the Japanese had prepared new defences and were again conducting patrol operations with seaplanes.[13]

From 14 November the Americans conducted daily bombing and strafing attacks on Tarawa (**Figure 16**), in preparation for the marine landing.[14] Then on 20 November aircraft-carrier planes from *Belleau Woods*, *Princeton* and *Lexington*, the carrier groups involved in the invasion, undertook a total of 170 sorties.[15] The larger land-based bombers of the 7th Air Force made further attacks. The combined attacks destroyed the Betio runway, caused heavy casualties and knocked out some of the defence installations. The Japanese fought back with anti-aircraft fire, along with 15 to 20 Zero fighter planes which intercepted the bombers, shooting down one B-24 and damaging several others.

Impact on the Gilbertese

These bombing attacks did not create serious problems for most Gilbertese as most had been forced to move to other parts of the atoll after the Japanese took over the whole islet of Betio. The local people went to Abatao and other islets in north Tarawa; some went as far away as possible, to Buariki in the far north. Although there were thousands of Japanese troops and civilian workers on Betio, very few were stationed anywhere else on the island.

Before the US attacks began, the Japanese allowed the departure from Betio of the Gilbertese who had been slave labour on the construction projects there. However, a few decided to remain on the island, and seven of them—men aged 20 to 30 years—died in the US bombing. Others watched the bombing in safety from other parts of the island.[16]

Among the KGV School boys watching from Bairiki was head boy Pulekai Sogivalu, who later reports:

> We watched American planes dive together three at a time. They came in groups of 12 or 15 and bombed three at a time. The sound was delayed in reaching us; when the planes rose up again we heard the explosions. The bombing seemed to go on for a week.[17]

Figure 16. "Softening up" bombing of Betio in preparation for the American invasion, 11 November, 1943.

Tatou Kaburoro had previously worked in a Japanese kitchen on Betio. He was impressed by the effect of the bombing on the coconut palms:

> The coconut fronds were blown straight in the air, like a person with their hair standing on end, then after we heard the explosion.[18]

Apart from in the deaths in the disastrous bombing of Keuea village (Chapter 9), the local population of Butaritari was similarly distanced from the bombing attacks. In Butaritari village, the area that the Americans had made a lagoon beach landing and designated 'Yellow Beach' was vacated and most of the villagers moved northeast to live in the bush. In the southwest corner of the atoll, near Ukiangang village, the Americans planned two ocean beach landings, on 'Red Beaches One and Two'. For several days, bombing and shelling preceded the landings, with much concentrated around the Ukiangang area.[19]

133

Although most moved out of their homes, a few remained, sheltering in foxholes whenever the bombs fell. Some old men said that they would rather die on their own land than out in the bush. It was a common feeling among many Pacific islanders, but one that often changed once they experienced the war first hand. Most people found they were not killed but injured or frightened by staying at the centre of the action; they then became more willing to leave their land.

One foxhole in Ukiangang received a direct bomb hit, killing Teieta Hugill, his wife Nei Tita and four of their children.[20] An eight-inch shell, fired from a US warship, smashed its way through another foxhole at a low angle, sending fragments of broken coral stone flying and injuring the occupants. Luckily for them, the shell did not explode until after it left the foxhole and travelled some metres away. On another occasion a heavily pregnant woman got stuck in the entrance to a foxhole during the rush to get inside and had to shelter outside during the attack. A lot of praying went on inside the foxholes.

As Tebanini reports, the Japanese instructed the people on how to protect themselves during a raid:

> The Japanese taught us to put our thumbs in our ears to avoid broken eardrums, the first two fingers on each hand were pressed over our closed eyes and the third fingers were used to block our nostrils.[21]

In total, nine people died on Butaritari from the US attack, seven from bombs and two by shelling.

On Abemama, no Gilbertese were harmed in the pre-invasion bombing. Earlier however, on 29 May 1943, the Americans had conducted a bombing raid in which six women, a young girl and one man had been killed and several others injured.[22]

The US Army Air Force undertook regular bombing missions against Nauru throughout the war, aimed at neutralising the Japanese air base there. Approximately 30 Nauruans died as a result of these bombing raids; on a single day in August 1944, one such attack killed 19 Nauruans. Also killed in these raids against Nauru were 20 Gilbertese (see Chapter 5). Four Gilbertese are recorded as having been killed at Kosrae (Kusaie) by US bombing.

At the conclusion of the bombing, ground forces of the US Marines and Army launched their assault on the Japanese bases in the Gilberts.

13
Operation Galvanic

Several publications already cover Operation Galvanic and the Battle of Tarawa—all written by Americans and so, naturally enough, from an American perspective. They give detailed accounts of the battle, the tactical and strategic considerations, and the logistics of staging a major battle on an atoll in the middle of the Pacific (see the bibliography). Rather than revisiting these same topics in depth, this chapter simply gives an overview of the operation and focuses on the dimension of the story that emerges from non-American sources. It also describes the American build up in the Ellice Islands, in preparation for the Gilbert Islands offensive.

Planning for Attack

The Japanese strong points in the Pacific were Kwajalein in the Marshall Islands, Truk in the Carolines, and Saipan in the Marianas. Under Japanese control and development since 1914, each was the centre of a strong defence system easily supported from Japan. Although the Americans might have completely bypassed these islands and reached Japan via New Guinea and the Philippines, such an approach would have exposed a flank to attack from the islands. Instead, they decided to seize these islands, beginning with the Marshall Islands. Thus the purpose of the battles in the Gilberts was to secure American bases for the attacks further north.[1]

On 23 July 1943 the US Joint Chiefs of Staff decided to capture first the Gilberts (Tarawa and Abemama), then the Marshall Islands, in an invasion code-named Operation Galvanic.[2] Their original plan included Nauru as it would be unwise to leave an airfield in enemy hands, only 700 kilometres from Tarawa. In addition, they hoped to establish land-based bombers at Nauru's airstrip, in order to knock out the Truk naval base, although the distance was near the range limits of the US bombers. Unlike the other islands in the plan, however, Nauru is not an atoll. The Americans soon realised that with its 30-metre high cliffs and artillery defence hidden in caves, the island would be difficult to invade and not worth the cost of capture. Instead, they decided to bomb Nauru during the operation to neutralise its airfield, and to add Butaritari, in the northern Gilberts, to the invasion plan.

Operation Galvanic marked the beginning of an island-hopping campaign across the Central Pacific.

Prelude to Galvanic

In preparation for the Gilbert Islands invasion, there was expansion and development of the bases in the Ellice Islands. The American expansion in the Ellice Islands, which had begun with the push north from Funafuti to occupy two additional islands, Nanumea and Nukufetau, in August 1943, continued at a quickening pace until the commencement of the Battle of Tarawa on 20 November. The number of heavy bombers stationed in the Ellice Islands steadily increased, as did the bombing raids launched from Ellice Islands bases. The Americans who had previously been engaged in developing the bases and making a few reconnaissance and bombing raids, now increased their forces and began their counterattack in earnest. Eventually, all the land-based aircraft used in the Tarawa operation, both fighters and bombers, were based in the Ellice Islands. Funafuti lagoon became temporary home to dozens of ships and landing craft as the atoll was developed as a base to provide logistical support to the attacking amphibious task force.

Bombing raids from Funafuti against the Gilbert Islands bases had intensified from June 1943. On 18 June, ten Liberators attacked Tarawa from Funafuti[3] and on the 28th a further 18 of the bombers arrived at Funafuti; another 16 in July, and in September a further 13. Among the 18 Liberators that arrived on 28 June, the first plane to take off from Funafuti the next day crashed and exploded in the ocean about 400 metres north of the runway. It was 30 minutes after midnight and everyone on the island who was not watching the bombers take off was awoken by the loud explosion. When take-offs resumed after about an hour, to everyone's amazement the eighth plane crashed in exactly the same manner as the first and it too exploded. The aircraft were so heavy with fuel and bombs that they could hardly take off. There was no trace of the 10-man crew of the second plane; in spite of the first plane's full load of bombs which had exploded, six crew members survived. They were picked up by a PT boat and rescued by people along the shore. The remaining bombers of the group were then ordered to stay on the ground. Of the six that had successfully taken off; only two found the target at Tarawa. It was not therefore a very successful operation. After this inauspicious beginning, the inexperienced Liberator crews were given further training and practice before attempting another mission.

In July, 16 more Liberator bombers, of the 13th Army Air Force, joined the operations from Funafuti. On 28 July they attacked Tarawa where they dropped 126 bombs on Betio, the fortified islet where the Japanese had an airstrip.[4] None of the bombers was hit by Japanese anti-aircraft fire but two of the planes failed to make it back to Funafuti, either due to navigational errors or because they ran out of fuel. The round trip to Tarawa (2300 kilometres) left little spare fuel to cover delays caused by weather or poor navigation.

The above examples show that these early operations from Funafuti were characterised by a mixture of success and failure. Forces continued to build up and eventually by a sheer mass of numbers of men and machines, and with increased experience, the bombing raids had greater effect.

All shore-based aircraft to be deployed in Operation Galvanic came under the control of Rear Admiral J H Hoover, who had been posted as Commander of Land-based Aircraft, Central Pacific (COMAIRCENPAC). Hoover's Task Force 57 was comprised of the following units: 90 Liberator bombers of the VII Army Air Force, under General Hale, which formed the principal striking power; 56 Navy patrol bombers, directly under Hoover; 90 Marine fighters; 72 Marine scout bombers; and sundry Army and Navy transport planes. A total of approximately 350 aircraft was to be based in the Ellice Islands.[5] Task Force 57 was to attack bases at Tarawa, Nauru, Mili, Jaluit and other Marshall Islands, commencing on D-day minus three. On 12 November, 24 Liberator bombers, the last elements of the VII Army Air Force to be based at Funafuti, arrived. This brought the total of Army Air Force personnel on the island to 318 officers and 1680 men.

The VII Army Air Force developed mobile support facilities for use on small islands and the Air Service Support Squadron (ASSRON) was formed. By replacing the heavy equipment normally found at a large air base with motorised workshops and easily transportable machines, ASSRON became a mobile unit, tailored to the size of the island occupied. ASSRON 3 took over the servicing of the squadrons based at Funafuti, Nukufetau and Nanumea.[6] Admiral Hoover took station at Funafuti in his flagship, the large seaplane tender *Curtiss*, which dropped anchor in Funafuti lagoon. Communications between *Curtiss* and shore were maintained by telephone, teletype and FM radio, and the first joint Army, Navy and Marine Corps communications centre in the Pacific was established on shore at Funafuti.

The air squadrons that were to be based in the Ellice Islands then began moving up to Funafuti, Nukufetau and Nanumea. The heavy bombers, which were distributed throughout the three atoll bases in the Ellice Group, carried out daily 'softening-up' bombings of Tarawa and Butaritari and also attacked bases in the Nauru and the Marshall Islands to reduce their capability to interfere with the operation. Even from Nanumea, the northernmost American base, the missions to the Marshall Islands were not very successful because of the great distances involved. For example, in one group of eight Liberators sent to bomb Kwajalein during the operation, only one managed to reach the target, Roi-Namur, and drop bombs. But under fair weather conditions and with increased experience, the success rate improved. The immediate target was Tarawa; after this was captured, it would become much easier for American bombers to attack Kwajalein and other islands to the north.

Three months before D-day, Vice-Admiral Raymond A Spruance, Chief of Staff for Admiral Chester W Nimitz, Commander of the Pacific Fleet, had visited Funafuti and Nukufetau. His purpose was to inspect the two bases and to observe first-hand the reef and surf conditions on atolls similar to those in the Gilbert Islands.[7] Amphibious landings were planned on heavily fortified Tarawa, the seaplane base at Butaritari to the north, and at Abemama to the south, as the first objectives in Operation Galvanic.

At the time of the Funafuti visit, the Americans were still planning what would be the first ever landing on a coral atoll by US forces. Different types of vehicle were still being assessed for their suitability in this environment and developed accordingly. The manufacturer of the amphibious truck or DUKW (Duck) had supplied 21 of these to Funafuti for evaluation, and they were demonstrated to Admiral Spruance. But not enough DUKWs could be supplied in time for the Galvanic operation so the Landing Vehicle Tracked (LVT), or AMPHTRAC as it became known, was chosen as the assault craft.

During his visit to the Ellice Islands, Spruance confirmed that Funafuti, the nearest anchorage to the area of attack, would be used as the naval staging area. He ordered the dredging of the western lagoon passage, Te Ava Fuagea, to permit entrance into the lagoon of the large vessels required in the establishment of a mobile supply and repair base.[8] Fuagea Passage, later also known as the 'American Passage', is the deepest entrance into Funafuti lagoon, at over 30 metres deep throughout. It was, however, narrower than the other passages—down to 250 metres wide in one place—and had obstructions of coral, some of which the Americans removed. In addition to being a staging area, Funafuti lagoon would be used to hold in readiness such naval forces as might be required should the Japanese send great forces to defend the Gilbert Islands.

Operation Galvanic posed a logistics and support problem for the Navy. How was it to sustain over 200 warships, at sea for weeks, thousands of kilometres from their fleet base in Pearl Harbor, Hawai'i, and how was it to support the 20,000 men involved in the operation with everything required—food, medical services, munitions and fuel? The shore bases in the Ellice Islands could offer little of the facilities needed, but Funafuti's large lagoon would form a convenient supply and staging point. So the Navy created Service Squadron 4 (SERVRON 4), Funafuti's floating naval base, the first ever floating base in the history of naval warfare.[9] The main virtue of SERVRON was that it was a mobile naval base so it could move with the fleet. Some Japanese-held islands would be attacked but the invasion would leapfrog over others, leaving them to 'wither on the vine'. SERVRON came about as a result of this particular strategic need. Two service squadrons were formed, with the idea that as the fleet advanced across the Pacific, the first service squadron would supply it during an attack and then, upon capture of an area, the second squadron would immediately come in, while the first would re-form at the next captured area. This scheme was not used, however: after leaving Funafuti, SERVRON 4 was combined with the second squadron, SERVRON 10, and the single unit provided all required services. The mechanical services offered by SERVRON 4 included engine and boiler repairs, and divers were available for underwater work on hull and propeller damage. There were 300,000 barrels of diesel oil and 200,000 gallons of aviation gasoline available at Funafuti. One supply ship contained only refrigerated and frozen food, another only dry foods.

Before SERVRON 4 began assembling in Funafuti lagoon, the Navy dispatched Standard Landing Craft Unit 24 to establish a camp on Fualefeke, the northernmost islet of Funafuti atoll and uninhabited at the time. From a camp there, landing craft would service the floating base that would occupy the northwest region of the lagoon. The landing craft unit departed San Francisco on 10 October.

Two classes of landing craft were deployed: the single-engined Landing Craft Vehicle/Personnel (LCVP) which were 10 metres long and were used as ships' boats to service the ships of SERVRON; and the larger twin-engined Landing Craft Mechanical (LCM), which were 15 metres long and were capable of carrying larger vehicles, trucks, howitzers and other heavy machinery. For shipping purposes, the smaller LCVP fitted inside the LCM. About 50 landing craft were stationed at Fualefeke. The camp had been established on 7 November, two weeks before the start of the Battle of Tarawa. As the ships of SERVRON 4 began assembling at Funafuti, landing craft and their crews were assigned to them for the period that they stayed at the atoll.

Funafuti lagoon was valued as a submarine-proof harbour because of the surrounding reef, but mines were laid across the unused passages as a precaution against enemy shipping. A total of 201 mines were laid during November

1943 by the *USS Terror* which at the time was the largest, newest and the only purpose-designed minelayer that the Americans had. She was the only ship of her type built by the US Navy during World War Two and Funafuti was her first assignment in the Pacific.[10]

During the weeks leading up to the Battle of Tarawa, many surface vessels arrived at Funafuti. The hydrographic survey ship *USS Sumner* came first, to survey lagoons, draw charts, and install markers as aids to navigation. First, Nukufetau was investigated and found to be six nautical miles off the position ascribed to it on the available charts.[11] The Americans were using information 100 years old; their charts were based on the Wilkes survey of 1841.[12] In this regard, British information was no more accurate, except regarding Funafuti which had been the subject of an accurate and detailed survey by *HMS Penguin* in 1896. Taking soundings at Nukufetau for two weeks, the *Sumner* established without doubt that the lagoon passage was so shallow and cluttered with coral heads that it could not be used by the big ships of SERVRON 4. After carefully negotiating her way into Nukufetau lagoon, she actually had to blast some coral out of the way in order to get out safely again. Funafuti would therefore have to accommodate all the ships of Operation Galvanic.

The *Sumner*'s crew completed much clearance work at Funafuti. They blasted out coral heads from the anchorages and cleared some of the obstructions from Fuagea passage to facilitate its use by the more than 100 ships that would soon arrive. The coral on one lagoon reef was thought so beautiful that the leader of the demolition team instructed all his divers to enter the water and enjoy its fascination, before they destroyed it forever:

> In the northern end of the lagoon we found a coral castle right out of fairyland. My weirdest dreams had never pictured anything like its caves, tunnels, verandas, and grottoes, all decorated in extravagant colour schemes. In these rooms lived brilliant tropical fish, so tame they could almost be petted... Before we set off the explosives, I had every man of the diving party go down to see this wonderland. What a shame that military necessity compelled us to wreck it![13]

During November, a total of 131 vessels entered Funafuti lagoon. The Service Squadron consisted of 24 supply and repair vessels: tenders, tugs, minesweepers, 2000-ton-capacity barges, three huge concrete fuel barges (each 110 metres long), repair ships and a destroyer escort. The concrete fuel barges had the same silhouette as a ship. They generated their own electricity and had refrigerated storage as well as dry provisions, clothing and small stores. With a crew of 58 they had the general appearance of a ship, the difference being that there was no main engine, propeller or rudder and a tow was required when they needed to move. There were hospital ships, a floating dry dock, a degaussing vessel for demagnetising ships as protection against magnetic mines, and a floating crane. There were more ships than Funafuti had seen in the past 20 years combined, and larger ones than had ever been seen there.

More ships passed through the Ellice Islands as D-day for Operation Galvanic approached. The people of Funafuti were asked to entertain with traditional dancing. In addition to performing at the main base and the islets of Amatuku, Fualefeke and Tepuka where there were American installations, they were requested to put on shows on board the ships. While aboard, they sensed that the Americans were in a highly emotional state and as they left the ships they received even more gifts of food and clothing than was usual. As Pole O'Brien, an Ellice Islands nurse, recalls: 'They didn't tell us that they were leaving the next day for Tarawa, but we could tell that something was up. Next morning all the ships had gone.'

The assaults on the Gilbert Islands involved the largest force of ships yet assembled at that time in the Pacific Ocean: 116 combat vessels and 75 auxiliaries. Several task forces took part in the Battle of Tarawa and they set out at different times from widely scattered points in the Pacific. The landing ships carrying the AMPHTRAC assault vehicles set out from San Diego, picked up their crews in American Samoa and came north through the Ellice Islands. Marine Fighter Squadron VMF-111, based on Nukufetau, provided protection for vessels as they travelled through the Ellice Group.[14]

Southern Carrier Group—consisting of three aircraft carriers, *Essex*, *Bunker Hill* and *Independence*, three cruisers, *Pensacola*, *Salt Lake City* and *Chester*, and five destroyers, *Bullard, Kidd, Chauncey, Erben* and *Hale*—travelled from Espiritu Santo in the New Hebrides. The ships refuelled at sea at a point near Funafuti where they were joined by four more cruisers from Pearl Harbor. The Relief Carrier Group, who had the task of neutralising the Japanese at Nauru, refuelled off Nanumea. The Southern Attack Force, which had three battleships and five escort carriers, refuelled 75 nautical miles east of Funafuti and the hospital ship *Relief* arrived at Funafuti the day that Galvanic commenced.

Tarawa—The Question of Landing

The starting date for Galvanic was set to tie in closely with other US plans. Continuing on from their successes at Midway and the Battle of the Coral Sea, the Americans planned an attack on Bougainville in Solomon Islands for 1 November. They felt that they must take advantage of this advance by also mounting Galvanic as soon as possible after that (provisionally 15 November) and then pushing on to the Marshall Islands, perhaps six weeks later. Making the final decision on 5 October, Admiral Nimitz recommended as D-Day 19 November (which was 20 November, local time, in the Gilberts) and the Chief of Naval Operations, Admiral King, approved the date.[15]

There has been some controversy over this decision, as the choice bound the operation to a particular tide, and the state of the tide was crucial to the success of the amphibious landing on Tarawa. With the dates set, any flexibility of the plan in relation to the tides was lost. Unfortunately, at midnight on 19 November the moon was in the last quarter, producing neap tides. These conditions were the worst possible for the amphibious landing: there would be little water over the reefs and the landing craft would not be able to reach the shore. One week earlier or later, spring tide conditions would have been very suitable for a landing, with high water early in the morning.

In the process of planning, the Americans had consulted British ex-residents of Tarawa and ship captains familiar with the port of Tarawa, who had prepared a paper, 'Notes on Tarawa, tides and working conditions'. One of the consultants who helped compile the paper, Major Frank Holland, had been headmaster of KGV School and lived on Tarawa for 20 years until the Japanese arrived.

Accompanying the US invasion force to Tarawa, he was appalled to learn of the date set to begin the operation. As he records it:

> I now learned for the first time of D-Day, ie the 19th November. This information filled me with distress. The date selected was most unfortunate, as regards height of tide, and the 20th, which ultimately became D-Day was no better. Boats with troops would not be able to cross the reef on those days, however shallow their draft. My warning led to my being called to the Maryland, before Admiral Hill; General Page, Captain Tschaun, Lieutenant Webster and Captain Forbes were called also.
>
> A discussion containing painful surprises to me followed. I drew attention to the official 'Notes on Tarawa', prepared at Pearl Harbor, which gave 3 or 4 feet of water on the reef at Betio for about 4 hours, during high water springs, but only 1 or 2 feet during high water neaps. I added that often during neap tides before the war, Burns Philp on Tarawa could not work cargo, and had to await higher tides. I stressed my 20 years experience of Tarawa conditions. I pointed out that neap tides would be at their very lowest, on the 19th and 20th. Two feet in my opinion was the maximum depth possible, not an inch more, and there was the likelihood of less than this. It was true, I added, that I had not given any special warning beforehand, but sufficient warning was surely contained in the 'Notes on Tarawa…', and the whole emphasis of talks at Pearl Harbor in this matter had been on spring tides. Moreover I had not been consulted as to the actual D-Day.
>
> Admiral Hill then spoke at length, and most interestingly at that, on the natural phenomena that affected tides. He added that while not wishing to doubt my word, he still expected there to be about 4 feet of water on the reef at Betio, and referred finally to his luck, which had never deserted him…
>
> The infantry attack on Betio occurred on the 20th, just before the time of high water. The boats could not take their personnel nearer than the reef, and from there the marines had to wade across the reef, under heavy fire. Newspapers afterwards reported that, 'a sudden wind lowered the water over the reefs, grounding the landing boats and forcing the marines to wade the last 800 yards to the beach'. In plain terms, there was no 'sudden wind', nor any other abnormality…[16]

The Japanese had also expected the Americans to land at high tide. Ensign Kiyoshi Ohta, the only Japanese officer captured in the battle, explains:

> We expected the American assault at high tide and we made the necessary preparation accordingly. We knew the Americans would suffer the least casualties if they landed on high tide. I think that due to the enormous bombardment from the air and from the naval vessels the Americans thought that there would be no Japanese; at least, if there were, they would all be wounded or killed soldiers by this time. We took them by surprise and there was a great confusion among the enemy.[17]

At that time, the Americans were still developing and testing amphibious assault vehicles. For the landing, the Marines wanted the landing vehicle tracked (LVT or AMPHTRAC) commonly known as 'amtracs', but the only assault vehicle tested in the Ellice Islands had been the 'Duck' (DUKW). Moreover, getting enough LVTs was a problem due to production delays, and the Navy favoured landing craft, which it was more familiar with—the landing craft vehicle and personnel (LCVP) and the larger landing craft mechanised (LCM), which was capable of landing tanks. But these landing craft were not amphibious and needed a minimum depth of four feet (1.2 metres) of water in which to float. The commander of the marine landing force, Major General Holland Smith, proposed using amtracs for the first three landing waves, after which the LCVPs and LCMs could bring in supplies and further troops.

The Americans underestimated the strength of the Japanese fortifications on Betio and greatly overestimated the effectiveness of their own 'softening-up' bombing. As discussed in Chapter 12, beginning on 17 September they had flown thousands of sorties against the islet from Canton Island and Funafuti, adding daily raids by carrier-based planes a month later. On the morning of the invasion, in addition to the aerial bombardment, US battleships shelled the island. With nearly every stick of vegetation on the island destroyed, many of the attackers believed that it was impossible for any human to still be alive on Betio. On the contrary, however, the defenders had dug in so well that more than half survived to face their attackers.[18]

When the landing began, many amtracs were knocked out before they reached the shore. Japanese troops opened up with coastal defence guns, sinking some of the amtracs and hitting drivers and passengers of others—in such cases, a higher tide would not have provided assistance. In other cases, a higher tide could have prevented casualties, as when amtracs were stopped by underwater obstacles and barbed wire, and their occupants had to wade ashore under heavy gunfire (**Figure 17**).

A higher tide would also have assisted the amtracs against the coconut log barricade, a seawall the Japanese had built while reclaiming the land behind it. (Years later, when the Betio landowners returned and re-established their land boundaries, they found their island considerably larger than in pre-war days.) Arriving ashore in their amtracs, the US Marines found that much of the lagoon beach of Betio had disappeared and the water went right up to the seawall. If they had arrived at high-water spring tide, they could have driven right over the seawall. As it was, they had to climb out of the amtracs under a hail of bullets and were pinned down under the wall, unable to advance or retreat. Only two amtracs managed to get past that barricade, while others became impaled on it as they tried to climb over.

Landing craft, not amtracs, were used for the fourth and subsequent landing waves. Incapable of passing over the reef in the low tide, they had to discharge their passengers on the edge of the reef, hundreds of metres out. Men were shot down as they attempted to wade ashore. At least 20 amtracs and several landing craft full of dead and wounded marines were stuck on the reef. Tatou Kaburoro of Bikenibeu, who was watching from Bairiki five kilometres away, thought the scene was similar to a new village on the reef, with the vehicles looking like houses.[19]

Securing the Islet—Costs and Benefits

The US plan had been for a speedy victory: landing 18,600 marines against what remained of the 4871 defenders (supposedly much reduced after the bombing and shelling), overwhelming them and capturing the island within 24 hours.

Figure 17. Marines wade ashore at Betio, Tarawa. 20-23 November, 1943

Yet given that many of the marines were killed even before they reached shore and there were problems in landing reinforcements, Sherman tanks and supplies, it actually took them 72 hours to secure the islet.

The Japanese had been ordered to defend to the last man and they almost did. There was no surrender. The Americans had to tackle the bomb-proof bunkers one by one, with flame throwers and grenades, while the Japanese attempted to kill as many marines as possible before they themselves were killed (**Figure 18**). Many preferred to use their last bullet on themselves, rather than suffer the disgrace of being captured.

Admiral Shibasaki was killed in his bomb-proof command bunker (**Figures 19 and 20**). Japanese records indicate that he died about noon on the first day of fighting, when a warship scored a direct hit on his command centre.[20] This report may be true: although most shells that hit the reinforced concrete walls did

Figure 18. Assault on a Japanese bomb-proof shelter opposite Burns Philp pier. Betio, 20 November 1943

little damage, a few penetrated through to rooms on the western side. However, most Japanese inside the bunker were killed the next day, when marines sealed the entrances with TNT charges and fired flame-throwers into the ports.

The final death toll was 1072 marines and 4729 Japanese. In addition, the Americans had 2292 wounded. The Japanese survivors numbered only one officer and 16 enlisted men, plus 129 Korean labourers.[21]

Tarawa was the first amphibious landing that the Americans had conducted in the Pacific against a strongly defended island. In hindsight, given the high losses, some strategists have suggested that the Americans should have bypassed Tarawa. Others believe that they might have suffered much higher losses if their first amphibious landing had been against the stronger defences in the Marshall Islands—especially without the benefit of the lessons learnt on Tarawa, and with Tarawa still in Japanese hands and able to back up the Marshall Islands bases. The main American errors were that their naval bombardment was ineffective

Figure 19. Admiral Shibasaki's command centre

and that they had too few amtracs. They also blundered in their landing decision in relation to the tides, which were as could be expected and as predicted by Major Holland. The Americans' own weather and tide reports show there were no abnormalities on that day.

Forty-four years after the battle, it was calculated that D-Day at Tarawa occurred when the moon's orbit was at the apogee, resulting in tides even more neap than average.[22] However, this aberration should not be taken as a major factor in, nor used as an excuse for, the Americans' miscalculation of the depth of water covering the reefs. Even an average neap tide would have produced the same disastrous result on the landing. Because it put so many men at risk of losing their lives, the landing deserved the highest standards in careful planning and scrutiny. But the planning did not achieve the required high standard. The Marines were locked into a poor decision, forced on them by an arbitrary calendar date—a date set, not by nautical men, but by politicians.

Figure 20. Interior of Shibasaki's command centre

Failure of Radio Communications

Communications failures were a serious problem that weakened the efficiency and effectiveness of the entire Tarawa operation.

The battleship *Maryland* was the communications hub of the operation, yet every time a salvo was fired from her 16-inch guns, it completely knocked out her ship-to-shore radio communications. The *Maryland* had not been equipped as a command and control ship until just before Galvanic and the radios had not been tested under battle conditions prior to the actual assault on Tarawa. The lack of communications between ship and shore complicated the control of naval gunfire and air support. It also kept the Marine Corps officers controlling the operation in the dark as to what was happening ashore. The ship's radio equipment needed constant repairs.

If the problem with the *Maryland* was bad, radio problems were even worse for the Marines on the beaches and at sea in landing craft. The fighting men had two types of radio sets, designated the TBX and the TBY. The TBX was described as a portable High Frequency (HF) transceiver. Yet unlike a modern portable radio, which weighs a few ounces and which can be carried in a shirt pocket, the TBX was carried by four men. In total, the radio, hand-cranked generator, batteries and antenna weighed over 100 pounds (45 kg). A more portable set was the TBY which was a Very High Frequency (VHF), self-contained backpack, weighing less than 50 pounds (23 kg). In the 1940s, the decade before the semiconductor age dramatically miniaturised radio equipment, the TBY was state-of-the-art in small portable equipment. The problem with both radios was that neither type was waterproof and, as a result of the tide miscalculation, the radios became a lot wetter with saltwater than the Marines had anticipated. The TBX was vulnerable because of its multiple interconnected modules, none of which had been designed to be waterproof.

The TBY had been designed especially for US Navy/USMC landing operations. It operated in the VHF portion of the radio spectrum and so could work efficiently with a short vertical antenna. As it had its own internal battery power, it could also be transported and operated by one man, as a backpack. Its weakness at Tarawa was that, although splash-proof to some degree, it was not waterproof. The sheet metal case and front controls were not sealed and there were several screw holes where water could enter the set. Soon after the battle, the officer in charge of one landing party wrote, '... this landing team suffered one-hundred (100) percent failures in the TBY radios due to the fact these sets are not water-proof'.[23]

At Tarawa some TBYs were made functional during the fighting by drying them out on shore but the success rate was low due to the sensitive nature of the VHF radio circuits used. It was difficult to get the circuits dry enough to work correctly. Some Marine radiomen managed to maintain communication for periods but there were occasions when the command post on the *Maryland* had no communications with any of the various units on the beaches or in landing craft.

'Mopping Up' on Tarawa

After the battle on Betio, the Americans moved to mop up the rest of Tarawa atoll. Their first landings outside Betio were at Bairiki and Eita. At Bairiki the Americans found no live Japanese, only the remains of about 15 men from a machine gun unit who had been killed when US gunfire hit a fuel store and it exploded. At Eita the Marines were very fortunate to be taken to Frank Highland, who spoke excellent English and provided much information about Japanese strength and arrangements. He reported that about 50 or 60 Japanese were at Buariki and Naa, at the extreme northern tip of Tarawa, and 17 at Teaoraereke village where there was also a fuel store.

From Eita the marines began their sweep along the atoll on foot. They were accompanied by D C I Wernham, one of the British administrative officers who had been assigned to assist in liaison with the islanders. The following entries come from his war diary:

25.11.43... Bikenibeu had been [occupied] but was now evacuated by the Japanese. Near the village was a 60 foot high watch-tower. We reached the Japanese labour camp at Temaiku which had recently been evacuated.

26.11.43 At Bonriki the natives reported that the Japanese had left their camps and had marched up the island by night to join the detachment at Naa. At Tabiteuea village we met NMP [native medical practitioner] Tutu Tekanene and introduced him to Col Murray, with whom he remained as interpreter. The natives reported that Japanese strength was about 200 and congregated near Noto village.[24]

As they moved north, the Americans required assistance in getting across a channel between two of the islets which was too deep to ford. Tutu arranged for Gilbertese canoes to carry them across. Then two amtracs arrived to carry supplies and these stayed with the Marines. On land, a group of young Gilbertese men helped carry equipment. Among them was Ambo Terenga of Eita village:

We walked behind the Americans carrying their gear. I carried a rifle for a marine, others carried ammunition, a tarpaulin… we heard gunfire nearby… the Americans told us to keep back.[25]

Near Naa, at the extreme northern end of the atoll, they discovered 160 Japanese armed with mortars, machine guns and rifles, in *babai* pits. District officer Wernham's diary reads:

28.11.43 Japanese and marines engaged in battle. Natives assisting by bringing up water and under Tutu's supervision, looking after the lightly wounded. Col Murray gave permission for natives to bury dead Japanese.

Ambo Terenga gives his perspective on the burials:

The Japanese bodies were decomposing and smelt. We used inai [rough mats woven from coconut fronds] to carry the bodies… we dug three big graves near Buariki, the Americans were burying their own dead.[26]

The fighting continued until all the Japanese in the area were either dead or had retreated further north. It was thought that about 50 Japanese were at the end of Naa. FF fighter planes then machine-gunned the islet and when the marines moved in they found only one Japanese, who had been killed. The final account in lives for the possession of north Tarawa was 164 Japanese (**Figure 21**) and 34 marines. Only one Japanese and one Korean prisoner were taken. Fifty-six Americans were wounded.

Attack on Abemama

On Abemama, south of Tarawa, a small amphibious reconnaissance unit of 68 marines, under Captain James L Jones, was sent to reconnoitre in preparation for the landing of a larger assault force. Travelling on the submarine *Nautilus* from Tarawa, they landed from rubber boats on the southern end of Abemama on the night of 20 November. The marines made contact with some of the islanders who informed them that about 25 Japanese were on an island further north.

As the Americans outnumbered the Japanese by more than two to one, Captain Jones decided to attack rather than wait for reinforcements. They advanced to the edge of a channel that separated them from the Japanese and shooting broke out across the water. One marine was killed and another wounded. Jones decided that he would not attempt to storm the island without first obtaining supporting fire from the *Nautilus*. That afternoon both the *Nautilus* and a destroyer shelled the Japanese position, then all was quiet during the night. The next day around noon, an islander arrived to report that all the Japanese (named in Appendix F) were dead.[27]

John Reiher (son of William Reiher, the well-known shipbuilder on Abemama: see Chapter 1) remembers the fighting:

> We moved away from the Japanese when the Americans came, to avoid the fighting... The captain of the Japanese barge was going on his bicycle to see his boat which had been reported shot up... he was hit by

Figure 21. Memorial to Japanese dead at Naa, north Tarawa

gunfire and killed… The Japanese asked people how many Americans there were, we replied 'takusan, takusan' ['many, many']…

The Americans were on one side of the passage and the Japanese on the other, they shot and some Americans were killed or wounded. An American submarine or warship then shelled the Japanese position. The Japanese got drunk and shot themselves through the mouths with their rifles, their leader shot himself in the side of the head with his pistol.[28]

So ended the Japanese resistance on Abemama and the marines moved quickly to develop air and naval bases there.

Japanese Slowly Expelled from Butaritari

On Butaritari, the principal Japanese defences were between Ukiangang village and the NBK wharf (**Map 10**). They were contained within two tank traps, one just west of On Chong's wharf and the other east of the NBK location. It was in this area that Carlson and his raiders had landed and fought in August 1942 (Chapter 9), but since then the Japanese had increased their defences considerably and moved the command centre underground. Their force totalled approximately 948 men—284 garrison troops of the 3rd Special Naval Landing Force, 140 Japanese and 414 Koreans from the 4th and 11th Naval Construction Units, and an aviation force of 110 men, who were detachments of the 802nd Navy Air Group operating 'Emily' flying boats (Kawanashi patrol bombers) and 952nd Navy Air Group, which flew Nakajima 98 float reconnaissance planes.[29] Set against them was the American attacking force; not marines as for Tarawa and Abemama, but 6472 army assault troops of the 27th Infantry Division.[30]

In preliminary softening-up action, American carrier planes carried out a bombardment and naval guns began shelling. Most local people had previously moved away from the area of action; of those still in the area, nine were killed in the shelling. Many residents of Ukiangang and Butaritari villages lost property. The European or part-European families suffered the greatest property losses, as they had European-style houses which were destroyed along with their

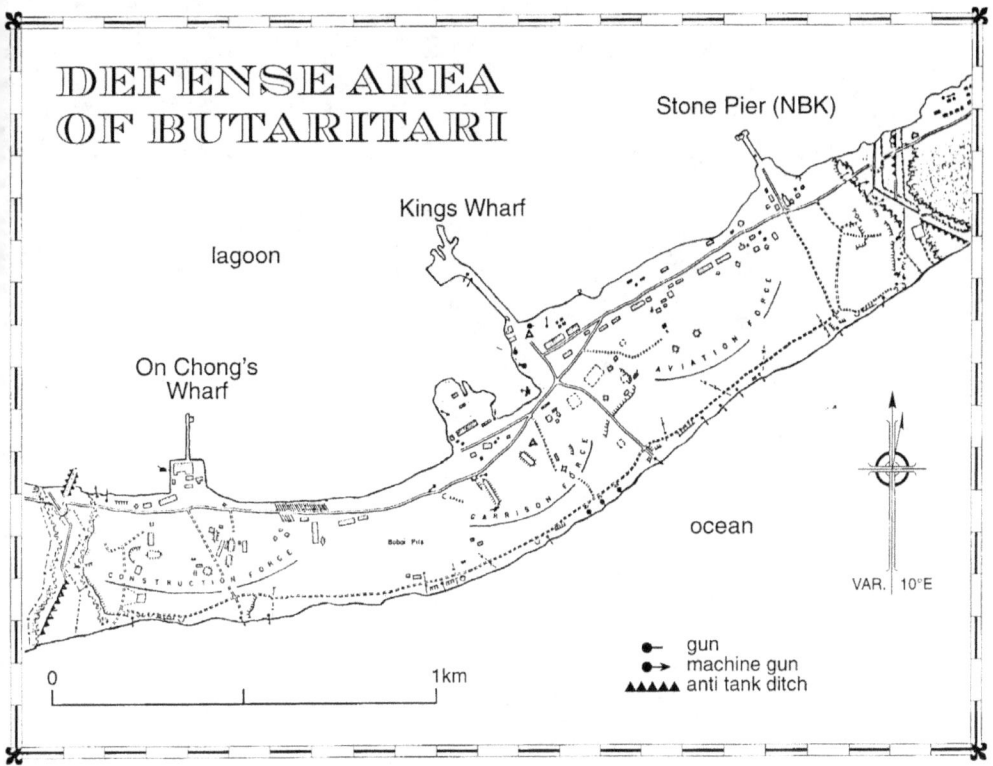

Map 10. US intelligence map of the Japanese defence area of Butaritari

contents—furniture, gramophones, stoves, clocks and, for Robert Narruhn, a piano.[31]

The Americans landed from the west, over the ocean reef at 'Red Beach One and Two' (near Ukiangang), as well as from the north on the lagoon shore at 'Yellow Beach One, Two, and Three' (the area around King's and On Chong's wharves). Opposed by only small arms fire from the Japanese, the two landings were successful. One amtrac actually ran up the Japanese seaplane ramp at the end of King's Wharf. Thirteen Sherman tanks also landed without difficulty. However, the infantry failed to take advantage of their successful landings and ten-to-one superiority on the weakly-defended island. The fighting continued for four more days.[32]

During this period the Americans were assisted by local knowledge. Although they moved most islanders in the Ukiangang and Butaritari village areas—approximately 480 people—to a safe location near Flint Point, several

Figure 22 American landing-craft at Abemama

stayed with the Americans to provide information and act as guides. Prominent among them were Beriki (who had been an On Chong radio operator in 1939 and then government radio operator on Butaritari before the Japanese arrival), Joseph Muller, Joe Narruhn, Taberanteatu and Kiantongo.[33]

Fred Narruhn, son of Robert, had been working overseas when war broke out and had joined the Fiji Infantry Regiment. For the invasion of Butaritari, he was attached to the US Army as an interpreter. For his services, he earned a Silver Star, as described in the following citation:

Headquarters US Army Forces, CP AREA, APO 958, General Order No 192, 16 June 1944.

Award of Silver Star
A Silver Star is awarded by the Commanding General, US Army Forces, Central Pacific Area to:
Private FRED CHARLES NARRUHN (Ser No R-898), First Battalion, Fiji Infantry Regiment. For Gallantry in action at Makin atoll, Gilbert Islands, 20–22 November 1943. Private NARRUHN, attached to the US Army Forces as an interpreter, landed with the second assault wave on Butaritari Island and guided leading elements in establishing contact with another of our landing forces. Later, learning that it was urgent to obtain prisoners for questioning, Private Narruhn voluntarily and under hostile fire pursued and captured an enemy soldier. Subsequently, he accompanied a reconnaissance patrol to a nearby island where he searched out friendly natives to secure urgently needed information concerning enemy strength and disposition. In providing accurate information for the land force commander and by his excellent judgement and conduct under fire, Private Narruhn contributed materially to the success of the Makin operation. (AG 200.6) by Command of Lieutenant General Richardson.[34]

Also assisting the Americans was Lieutenant Bruno von Reymond, originally from Butaritari. After working for On Chong in Sydney, Bruno joined the Royal Australian Navy when war broke out. He was seconded to the US Navy as a special member of the intelligence staff, and his knowledge of Butaritari atoll and its lagoon was a great help. It was only after four days with fighting troops on the island that he found time to search for his parents, whom he had not seen for several years. The Japanese had allowed Captain Moritz von Reymond and his wife Helena to remain in their house in Butaritari village unharmed. The old man was 80 years old and did not recognise his son Bruno when at last they were reunited.[35]

Others liberated on Butaritari were Bishop Octave Terraine, Fathers Pierre Guichard and Marcel Viallon, and Brothers C Webster and H Engelhardt of the Catholic mission (**Figure 23**).

Figure 23. Bishop Terrienne and priests liberated at Butaritari, November 1943

Finally, the Americans overpowered the Japanese. The last stations to be defeated were the lookouts on isolated islets around the lagoon, which were wiped out on 26 November. Of the 948 defenders, only 106 remained alive, mostly Korean labourers. There were only two Japanese prisoners, one of whom had been captured by Fred Narruhn. The US Army had 66 dead and over 100 wounded.

Of still greater loss to the Americans was the sinking of the *Liscome Bay*, one of the aircraft carriers providing air support to the Butaritari invasion. At 5:30 am on 24 November, the *Liscome Bay*, in the company of two other carriers, was steaming at 15 knots about 20 nautical miles southwest of Butaritari when she was hit amidships by a torpedo from the Japanese submarine I-175. Rear Admiral H M Mullinnix, commander of the task group, was lost with the ship, as were 52 other officers and 591 enlisted men.[36]

Figure 24. Site of Shinto shrine at Betio

The Japanese defeat on Butaritari ended the longest period of Japanese occupation in the Gilbert Islands, just short of two years (although before the war ended, this record was surpassed on Ocean Island, where the Japanese were in control for more than three years before surrendering). A new era of occupation, this time by US forces, was beginning.

14

US occupation

It might be said that the US military occupation of the Gilbert and Ellice Islands started in the Line Islands in October 1941, when 30 army engineers established a base on Christmas Island and began constructing an airfield there (Chapter 2). They also established a presence on Canton Island the following month and on Fanning Island in April 1942 (Chapter 3). However their large-scale occupation began on Tarawa after US forces wrested the Gilbert Islands away from the Japanese in Operation Galvanic in November 1943.

After the battles were over, the US priority in the region was to develop Tarawa, Butaritari and Abemama as air and naval bases for the assault on the Marshall Islands. For their part, the British wanted to reclaim possession of their former colony as soon as possible so that, even if the US established bases there, it would not dispute ownership.

The islanders' focus was different: they wanted to normalise their disrupted lives, to go fishing again and to rehabilitate and use their land for traditional agriculture. When the Americans arrived, many Gilbertese were barely surviving, with only enough food to sustain life. Fishing had been banned because all the military activity in the area made it dangerous. When people from the south of the atoll relocated to north Tarawa, resources there became strained, aggravated by the Japanese Navy commandeering much of the food produced by the islanders. The Americans distributed C-rations and medical supplies among the needy islanders. Soon learning that the Americans were rich and generous, the Gilbertese became keen to trade with or be employed by them.

Figure 25. Arrival of Resident Commissioner, Vivian Fox-Strangways and senior local administrative officers at Tarawa, soon after the battle

Establishing a Labour Corps

Immediately after the Battle of Tarawa there was an urgent need for a large, well-disciplined unit of labourers to bury the dead and to help the Americans with construction projects. In addition to the immediate tasks, labour was needed to support the US forces in general labouring duties, for salvage, laundry, mess and other duties.

The resident commissioner designate of the colony was Lieutenant Colonel Vivian Fox-Strangways (**Figure 25**). Although appointed in 1941, by the time he made his way from Nigeria to the Pacific, the Japanese had already taken over part of the Gilbert and Ellice Islands; so, after working for a time in Solomon Islands, he had set up his headquarters in Funafuti in the Ellice Islands. He now moved to Tarawa, to re-establish a British presence and to organise the formation a local labour unit.[1] The US Marines felt there was only one purpose behind his arrival: to show the British flag and thus forestall any possible US claim to

Figure 26. Barracks of the Gilbert and Ellice Islands Labour Corps. Betio

Tarawa which had been won at great expense of US lives. An article in *Time* facetiously reported that the only baggage Fox-Strangways brought with him was 'a Union Jack and a spare pair of underpants'. He did fly his Union Jack on Tarawa but the Marines shot it full of holes; the only solution was to fly both the Union Jack and the Stars and Stripes together.[2]

The Gilbert and Ellice Islands Labour Corps was formed at the end of November 1943 (**Figure 26**). A new colony regulation—the Military Units Ordinance, 1943—constituted it as a unit of the British forces. Although not a combat unit, the men would be trained to defend themselves. In a further move for the solidarity of its empire, the British enlisted the New Zealand government to provide officers and noncommissioned officers for the corps. They stressed the importance of having garrison troops from 'empire sources' for British islands in the Pacific that had been recaptured from the Japanese.[3]

Lieutenant Colonel E Finney, a former British Army officer who had immigrated to New Zealand, was appointed as commanding officer.[4] Further New Zealanders were recruited from Trentham Army Camp in Wellington and other European officers were appointed from among serving colonial administration officers. Harry Maude, a civilian, was in charge of recruiting (he was later appointed the first post-war resident commissioner, replacing Fox-Strangways). Raymond Marsack, a New Zealander seconded from the Royal New Zealand Air Force (RNZAF) in Suva, was moved up from the Ellice Islands where he had been administrative officer on Nanumea.[5]

Early in November the High Commissioner for the Western Pacific and US Commander in Chief, Admiral Nimitz, had agreed that military considerations were of paramount importance now that both British and Americans were present in the reoccupied colony. Supreme authority in the islands was to be vested in the military commander for the Gilbert Islands area, who would determine the timing and extent of the British colonial administration's authority in civil affairs. In practice, however, it is said that, because of Fox-Strangways' strong stance, he was given almost total control of civil matters, including the labour corps.[6]

Because the battle had made a complete mess of Betio, it was decided to establish the headquarters of the labour corps in Abaokoro, the centre of the north Tarawa district. The WPHC ship *Viti* departed from Suva on 28 November with Colonel Finney and supplies for the labour corps on Tarawa. After delivering stores to the coast-watchers in the Ellice Islands, the ship arrived at Tarawa on 6 December, and made her way across the lagoon to Abaokoro to discharge cargo and passengers.[7]

The station in Abaokoro became a boot-camp for the 'bootless soldiers' as they were sometimes known. Army boots would have been extremely uncomfortable for local men who had never worn any form of footwear, so they went barefoot (**Figure 27**). Nonetheless, they were smartly turned out in a working uniform of khaki shorts and shirts or a dress uniform in which khaki *be* replaced shorts. Noncommissioned officers wore shoulder titles, or badges of rank, on

Figure 27. Labour Corps workers on the wharf at Betio. November 1944

shirt sleeves. With both shorts and *be*, they wore a brown leather belt, while officers had a Sam Brown belt which included the over-shoulder strap.[8]

Members of the labour corps were recruited as raw material. They were paid two pounds five shillings (about US$5) per month as privates, and were fed, clothed and trained into a well-disciplined unit, under Sergeant Major Manuela, a retired colony police officer from Nanumea. A former regimental sergeant major himself, Commanding Officer Finney believed in 'spit and polish'. Ray Marsack remembered that the men in the labour corps were always well presented and proud of it:

> … they regarded the American garrison troops as rather an undisciplined lot. The real leatherneck, no, they admired him as we all did, as a fighting man but the occupation troops were a scruffy lot… and frankly

the Gilbertese troops looked down their noses at them and thought… 'This bloody mob don't even know how to march properly.'[9]

However, a more favourable assessment comes from another European, John Dennan, who was a district officer and a major in the Gilbert and Ellice Islands Defence Force on Tarawa. He thought that the general standards of dress and behaviour among the Americans were quite good.

With a roll of 652 men by the end of 1943, the labour corps continued to grow to battalion strength. In January 1945, it peaked at 1524 men, with companies at Abaokoro, Bonriki, Eita, Bairiki and Betio on Tarawa and also on Butaritari and Abemama. Company strengths varied between 100 and 200 men, with each man initially signing on for a one-year term of service. Overseas there were 400 men from the colony working as stevedores for the Americans on Guadalcanal and 140, mostly Ellice Islanders, on Funafuti.[10]

The authorities—the native magistrates, the US military and the British administrators—all attempted to keep Gilbertese who were not working directly for the Americans away from their camps. There were also rules placing the villages out of bounds to the US troops. These rules were enforced with varying degrees of strictness and success (**Figure 28**). For example, in December 1943 the *kaubure* (local government elders) in Eita village on Tarawa were requested to take immediate action against islanders looting the US supply dump there.[11] Moreover, on Abemama in January 1944 there was 'trouble over the question of troops and native women, troops could not be kept out of the native houses'.[12] In contrast, at the same time on Tarawa, native villages were strictly out of bounds and the local commander's discipline was said to be excellent.

In March 1944 the *kaubure* of Eita, Bikenibeu and Buota villages on Tarawa were warned that their people would be moved to another location if the women and children did not stop visiting the US camps.[13] Some islanders were fined in local courts for breaking this regulation.

In June, faced with the task of granting permission for enlisted men to attend dances in Eita, the island commander on Buota granted permission to a maximum of 30 men per night, after numerous 'incidents' and 'disturbances'.[14]

Figure 28. Gilbertese girls pose with US Marine officers at Tarawa

Early in 1944 the island commander on Tarawa issued island orders that forbade all women and children under 16 years from entering US camps and the Bairiki and Bonriki/Temaiku areas. If not enlisted in the labour corps, local people could not be employed, and all Army, Navy and Marine officers and enlisted men based on Tarawa were forbidden from visiting the neighbouring atolls of Marakei, Maiana and Abaiang without permission.[15]

Marine Fighter Squadron VMF—422 Goes Missing

An air disaster occurred early in 1944, when, but for a single plane, a complete squadron of Marine Corsair fighters went down between Tarawa and Funafuti in the Ellice Islands. Twenty-two planes crashed into the sea, six pilots dying in the incident.

Figure 29. Change of dress from traditional to American sponsored clothing

On 25 January Marine Fighter Squadron VMF-422 was to fly from Hawkins Field, Tarawa, to Funafuti via Nanumea, both in the Ellice Islands. The squadron consisted of 24 new Vought Corsair F4U fighter planes just built in California and to be stationed at Funafuti until required for Operation Flintlock—the invasion of the Marshall Islands. The plan for the first leg of the flight was to take off at 1000 hours and fly directly to Nanumea at between 1000 to 2000 feet at a speed of about 200 knots, estimated time of arrival at Nanumea being 1230 hours. Each aircraft carried enough fuel for six hours' flying and therefore had a large reserve for the estimated 2.5 hour flight. However, the Corsair's navigation equipment was only elementary and, as the flight lay entirely over open sea, the squadron leader, Major J S McLaughlin, had requested a navigational escort plane. The request was refused: the escort would have been a PV-Lockheed or a PBY seaplane which carried a navigator. It is unclear as to exactly why the escort was refused: it appears that it was not a case of it being considered unnecessary, but rather that correct procedures were not followed—the request had not been made in the correct manner. The engine on one plane failed to start but the remaining 23 took off and the group departed at 1000 hours as planned.

The en-route weather forecast was for scattered showers and rainsqualls in the Ellice Group, which would be likely to cause problems with navigation. It should be noted that this was the hurricane season in the South Pacific, the time of westerly storms, intense wind and rain, and low visibility. However, the weather initially proved perfect, and all went well until 1215 hours when the squadron should have been close to Nanumea. At this time they flew into an area of dark clouds stretching as far as the eye could see. After descending as low as 200 feet, there was still no break in the cloud and Major McLaughlin ordered the group to fly in close formation. Even so, one pilot, John Hansen, lost visual contact with the others and flew on alone using the compass and the Funafuti Radio Range to set his course.

Both Nanumea and Funafuti airfields had Aural Radio Ranges. These were a type of long-range radio navigational beacon, which allowed pilots to home-in on suitably equipped air bases. Complex radio-direction-finders, the kind that operate like radio-compasses, had not yet been developed and the fighter planes were fitted with only simple, non-directional receivers. Experienced pilots were able to home-in on a radio range by listening to its signal in the headphones of an ordinary receiver. Different tones were perceived depending on whether the plane was in the beam, or to the left or right of it. However, none of the pilots of the VMF squadron had experience of flying by radio range. More important was that they had not been provided with the beam directions of the Funafuti Range or the identification signals of the Nanumea Range. Nevertheless, pilot Hansen managed to tune in to the Funafuti Range and to follow the beam. He landed safely, the only member of the group to do so.

Several more planes became separated from the main body; Lt Walter 'Jake' Wilson broke out of the storm over Niutao island, which lies about 120 kilometres from Nanumea. There was no landing strip on Niutao and he decided to make an emergency landing on the beach, being worried about his ability to locate Nanumea or any other island under the bad prevailing conditions. After he had made a couple of passes over the island and it became apparent that he intended to land, the people flocked to the beach on the western side where there was a lee and the surf was less rough. The radio operator/coastwatcher on Niutao was Maheu Naniseni who had received training at Tarawa and Funafuti. He took the initiative and ran out to the reef where there were submerged rocks and stood there making an X sign with his arms to show that the area was unsuitable. Then he hastened to the place he judged the most favourable for putting the plane down and stood there with arms raised in a 'U' sign. The plane landed safely in very shallow water, alighting on a flat area between beach and surf. The propeller was bent but the body of the plane suffered only moderate damage.

When Maheu went out in a canoe to assist Wilson he encountered the barrel of a pistol and the pilot asking, 'Are you a friend?' While answering that the people were British subjects and friends, Maheu noticed that Wilson also had an automatic rifle slung across his back. The only weapon on the island was the sword that Maheu had brought to Niutao; that was safely stowed in a trunk in his house. Wilson was soon convinced that the people were friendly and completely unarmed. The plane was hauled up the beach by a huge crowd of strong men and, when on high ground, concealed under a pile of coconut fronds.[16] Radio messages were sent and the next day the destroyer *USS Hobby* arrived and sent a whale-boat ashore to pick up Wilson.

The balance of the formation, 20 aircraft, broke out of the bad weather at about 1400 hours with two hours of fuel remaining. They were able to identify Nui Atoll below them and their commander then plotted a new course to take them on directly to Funafuti, bypassing Nanumea. Only briefly into their journey to Funafuti, they again encountered bad weather and it was decided to return to Nui.

About this time they established radio contact with Nanumea Air Base. Nanumea radar had tracked the planes to within 30 kilometres of the island but, because of bad visibility, the fliers had not seen the island. Because Nanumea had not been advised of the flight, they were not expecting a fighter squadron with limited navigational equipment and they had assumed that the planes were bombers. The base now plotted their position and gave a new bearing which would bring them to Nanumea.

One plane developed engine trouble and had to ditch into the sea. The life raft malfunctioned so a second pilot decided to ditch his plane and bale out in order that they could share a raft. Another aircraft, flown by Lt (Tiger) Moran, was getting low on fuel too, and he had to decide whether to bale out over Nui or attempt a water-landing in the lagoon. His leader advised him by radio that a water-landing should be feasible, but that decision was for the pilot to make.

Gordon Wilson, the coast-watch radio operator on Nui, was fishing in the lagoon in his canoe. He counted the 18 planes flying over Nui and then they disappeared into a rain squall. A single plane returned. He could see the pilot who returned his wave. He raced back to the radio shack and soon they were in contact over the radio. Moran asked Wilson for advice on whether to bale out or crash-land. He opted to bale out. Wilson told him to make sure that he came down close to the beach so that canoes could get to him quickly. His parachute was observed by the islanders to open and land in the ocean, just off the western reef, about a mile north of the village. Before he could separate himself from it, he was plunged into an area of heavy surf and became hopelessly entangled. Wilson's and other canoes could not reach him in time and he drowned. When they got to him they found that he still wore his flying kit and had his Colt revolver in his belt. Even had he not become entangled in his parachute, he would have been weighed down and have had difficulty swimming. Resuscitation was tried immediately in the canoe, and persisted with for a long time on the beach, but Moran did not revive. He was buried on Nui; later the remains were recovered and returned to the United States.

When Wilson reported the accident to Funafuti, he was asked whether he had seen any other planes and he then realised that at least 18 planes were in difficulty. The weather closed in and Wilson saw no more aircraft that day but he heard the droning sound of Catalina flying boats searching near the island. Later that night, alone in the radio shack, he heard on the BBC news that a whole squadron of Corsairs had become lost in the area.[17]

All the remaining planes were now low on fuel and at this time, somewhere near Nui, a further four aircraft disappeared, including that of Major McLaughlin. The group at this stage consisted of 13, Nui was not in sight and it was decided that they should all ditch and tie their life rafts together rather than scatter themselves over a wide area of the Pacific Ocean. Thirteen men survived for three days in twelve rafts under harsh weather conditions, until they were found by a PBY amphibian, 160 kilometres west of Funafuti. The amphibian sprang a leak on landing in the rough sea. With this problem plus the extra load of an additional 13 people on board, it was unable to take off again. Within two hours a destroyer arrived to the rescue; it was the *USS Hobby* with Jake Wilson already aboard.

An inquiry into the incident was held in Tarawa. It was decided that the accident arose because the pilots had not been properly briefed on the use of radio navigation and communication facilities at Nanumea and Funafuti. Also, Nanumea had been neither informed of the flight nor requested to assist with navigation. Not highlighted in the inquiry findings was the fact that there had previously been complaints about the unsatisfactory manner in which communications services functioned at Funafuti. Only 11 days before the disaster, it had been pointed out in a memo that Funafuti Control Tower was using unpublished transmission frequencies and that the unreliable nature of the radio-range and beacon made them unsafe as aids to navigation.

Later Jake Wilson described his adventure as something from a Hollywood script. Perhaps there was exaggeration and embellishment for the benefit of his military buddies. He claimed that he was offered his choice of the virgin maidens on Niutao and that he was treated like a king while on the island. Unfortunately for him, he was rescued before he could partake of all of the island's pleasures.

Some time later a team of Marines went to Niutao, stripped Wilson's Corsair of important equipment and then destroyed the remains of the aircraft.

Curly Lehnert was awarded the Marine Corps Medal for his action in bailing out in order to assist a comrade whose life raft had failed. For his part, Maheu Naniseni was awarded a Brave Conduct Medal by the British and a Silver Fern by the Americans. Not long after this, his first son was born on Niutao. He was named Tie Wilson Maheu.[18]

Comparisons and Unrest

The affluence of life with the Americans contrasted sharply with the starvation experienced under Japanese rule. As one islander put it, 'We fed the Japanese, the Americans fed us.'[19] Life was also a good deal more attractive to some than the previous austere conditions under British officialdom had been. It was very difficult for the handful of British officials to compete with the power and wealth of the Americans. In a report in 1944, the resident commissioner himself recognised that in the context of 'several thousand US troops, 1200 natives and 1 Britisher', it was difficult for him to show the British flag:

> ... especially when the food he distributes (and himself eats), the money with which he pays the natives, and the road and water transport on which he depends, all hail from America... [In these circumstances, it is] easy to persuade the natives... that they would be better off under the flag which flies over such rich resources.[20]

There were two areas in which many Gilbertese found the Americans were refreshingly different from the British: one related to attitude, the other to wealth. First, where the British were very paternalistic and treated the 'natives' like children, the Americans were more prepared to accept them as equals. Secondly, the British kept rates of pay for the islanders low because they were concerned about inflation and about the difficulty of sustaining higher rates over the longer term. In contrast, given that their stay was for the short term only, the Americans had no such concerns. Coming from an affluent society, they could not believe that anyone should be paid at such low rates as the islanders were and constantly tried to increase the approved rates for them.

Thus it is not surprising that some Gilbertese began to support the idea of US sovereignty, and were reluctant to accept the reimposition of British rule. The Americans offered the islanders food, ice cream, cigarettes, movies, friendship and well-paid employment. They had also demonstrated their power and won Gilbertese admiration in capturing Tarawa, then Kwajalein and Eniwetok in the Marshall Islands soon after. These changes in attitude caused discontent which erupted on Tarawa in April 1944.

In addition to repairing the damaged Japanese airstrip on Betio and making it operational again, the Americans had built a new, longer bomber strip on Bonriki, naming it Mullinnix Field, after Rear Admiral Mullinnix who died when the *Liscome Bay* was sunk off Butaritari in Operation Galvanic (Chapter 13). After Bonriki village was demolished to make way for the new airfield, the landless people of Bonriki went to live at nearby Buota village, stretching the food resources there to the limit. There had been several hungry deputations to the district officer, Wernham, requesting assistance in obtaining food. Wernham claimed that he had made every possible effort to obtain food for Buota village from the Americans but could not get any. The people of Buota and Bonriki, to avoid starvation, turned directly to the Americans and obtained relief.[21]

In April 1944 the island commander, Commander Linscott, was preparing to leave Tarawa for a new posting and the people went to bid him farewell. They assembled outside his house, performed traditional dances and presented gifts of handicrafts. When he asked if they had any requests, they asked to be allowed to fish at night along the coast opposite Buota and Bonriki. They further requested that women and children be allowed to see the US movies, and that villagers be allowed to make purchases from the US stores and to sell their handicrafts directly to soldiers, rather than only through the district office (which controlled prices). Further, they said that they did not like British rule and wanted to be under the US flag. Apparently the island commander made some noncommittal reply but made sure that they were given food.

The next month the elders of Nabeina village in north Tarawa decided to present a petition for US sovereignty to the new island commander. Looking for support among others known to be sympathetic to this cause, they held talks in

Eita, Tabiteuea and Bikenibeu villages. On 22 May a party of 200 men visited the district officer and asked for permission to visit the island commander, saying that they wanted to trade directly with the Americans. The district officer told them that he could not grant permission without referring the matter to the resident commissioner.[22]

The deputation was not satisfied with this answer as they no doubt knew that the resident commissioner would refuse their request. Leaving the district officer, they headed in the direction of Bonriki and the island commander's office, even though they were informed that this behaviour made them liable to sentences of imprisonment. The armed constabulary went after them but could not prevent them from entering the US camp. There the deputation told the commander of their wish for US sovereignty. New to the job, Commander Massic replied that it would take him four or five days to have an answer for them.[23]

As a result of this unrest, the resident commissioner imprisoned 30 supposed ringleaders among the 200 men. He also issued an order forbidding processions on Tarawa and meetings of more than seven people in the villages of Buota, Tabiteuea and Nabeina. For his part, the island commander informed the elders of Nabeina that the issue of sovereignty had nothing to do with him. From the district officer, they heard that if they wished to proceed, their submission should go first to the resident commissioner, who would then pass it on to the High Commissioner in Suva, and eventually the British and US governments would discuss it. Because both these powers were busy in a great war, the elders were advised, they would probably not look at the question until after the war ended. Largely because 30 of their men were in prison, the people of Nabeina decided not to proceed with the sovereignty issue and apologised for the incident.[24]

At about the same time, there was similar unrest on Butaritari. Labourers there were refusing to work under British rule and wanted to deal directly with the Americans. At a meeting in Keuea village, with the Butaritari Island commander present, the *uea* (high chief) made a statement, on behalf of the people of Makin and Butaritari, that the people were hungry and were willing to work but wanted to be placed under the control of the US government. The island commander explained that the question of sovereignty was for the heads of the British and US governments, but he offered food in exchange for labour. A spokesman for the younger men then stated that they were willing to join the labour corps but wanted the Americans to run it. The main reason that they wanted to break with Britain was that 'the pay is too low' and British rule 'prevented wealth'. The *uea* explained that they had experienced British rule, then Japanese, and now saw that the US way was best for them.[25] Again the British deferred the matter with a statement about following correct procedures and emphasised there was little hope of any change before the end of the war. The island commander, however, did forward the petition to Washington; thereafter apparently nothing was heard of it.

On Butaritari the district officer reported that there were problems with US visits to Ukiangang village where they engaged in all-night drinking parties which he claimed were encouraging prostitution, drunkenness and thieving. It was said that the island commander had little control over this behaviour because some of the Americans involved, visitors in overnight transit, held high rank.[26]

In general, US employment of Gilbertese was very successful and kept them fully occupied if they wanted to be. Men worked in general labouring and construction, women did laundry work (**Figure 30**) or produced handicrafts or local materials for which there was a great demand. US purchase orders were often for thousands of *ba* (coconut frond midribs, used in light construction of walls, fences etc), sleeping mats for the troops, fans, swords or brooms, or hundreds of pounds weight of coir string. For example, one 1945 order was for 31,000 pieces of thatch and 30,250 *ba*, plus a further 500,000 pieces of thatch for use in the Marshall Islands which were now in Allied control. US aircraft visited almost all of the Gilbert Islands in search of materials to fill these orders. Prices were good; for example, sleeping mats sold for US$1.25 and most small handicraft items for US$1.00 each.[27]

Figure 30. Many women and girls were busily engaged in laundry work for the Americans

Development of Abemama

On 26 November 1943 the 3rd Battalion of the 6th Marines left Tarawa to capture Abemama from the Japanese, following on from the reconnaissance unit led by Captain Jones (Chapter 13). They travelled on the transport ship *Harris*, accompanied by battleship *USS Maryland*, four destroyers and a submarine-chaser. Among them was Major F Holland who had been appointed district officer; his role was to organise local labour and see to the islanders' welfare during the US occupation of their island. He took with him Rota, a former assistant master from KGV School, and Domingo, a former student of the school.[28]

When the ships arrived off the southern end of the island, Captain Jones met them, reporting that his unit had dealt with the few Japanese who had been on the island, so the task force was not required. The *Harris* then moved to the northern part of the atoll to put ashore troops there. The garrison group—consisting of transport ship *President Monroe* and three chartered steamers, escorted by two destroyers—also arrived and began unloading.

Next day, 28 November, the Union Jack was raised at the government station, on a coconut tree as the Japanese had cut down the flagstaff. Holland immediately began arranging for 100 men to clear a site for the airfield. Rota and Domingo went to work as interpreters for the island commander, Captain W P Cogswell.[29]

Then 2 December saw the arrival of a landing ship tank (LST)—very large and designed for transporting tanks and other heavy vehicles—which brought more material and earth moving machines. By 6 December every able-bodied man on Abemama (about 150 in total) was doing regular war work and every able-bodied woman was busy with laundry work, while even old men were employed on a casual basis. It was now apparent that meeting US demand would require drawing labour from other islands as well. Visiting Nonouti, Kuria and Aranuka, Holland recruited 287 labourers as well as hoisting the Union Jack again on each island.[30]

Abemama airstrip was used for the first time on 20 December 1943, less than one month after work on it had begun **(Figure 31)**. Soon after, on 3 and 4 January 1944, the Japanese bombed it, destroying one B-24 bomber and killing two crew of a gun emplacement.[31]

As on other occupied islands, rules declared certain areas out of bounds for Americans and Gilbertese, and prohibited the manufacture of sour-toddy (fermented coconut sap). Here, though, the only unrest among the locals resulted from bad behaviour of the visiting troops. Among the complaints were that Americans stole from islanders' houses and molested local women. Moreover, on 13 February 1944 a group of Marines arrived in a truck at the government station and cut down the Union Jack for apparently no other reason than to make a show of power. Two days later, men of Abemama asked the district officer for permission to use force against Americans when they invaded their houses at night. Another unpleasant, culturally insensitive incident related to an American request for island dancing on a Sunday, at a farewell concert for one of their units. On being informed that the islanders forbade dancing on Sundays, the American reply was 'If the missions object, inform them that the island commander **orders** the dance.'[32]

Figure 31. The first aircraft to land on the airfield at Abemama arouses much local interest

However, considering that at one point there were more than 8000 troops on Abemama and similar numbers on Butaritari and Tarawa, the conflicts between the islanders and the occupiers were not many. When conflicts did occur, in most cases they did not have serious consequences.

A Late Development—LORAN Stations

In the Phoenix Group, the United States Coast Guard (USCG) was responsible for one of the last US developments before the war ended, when it constructed and operated stations for long-range radio aid to navigation (LORAN) on Baker, Canton and Gardner Islands. This new navigation system had a reliable range of more than 1000 kilometres over the sea. Designed primarily for maritime use but with an application to air navigation as well, it underwent full-scale trials in June 1942. The LORAN system required the land stations to be synchronised, which they achieved by a master–slave relationship. For reliable navigation, the ships and aircraft using the system had to receive at least two of the stations simultaneously. The master station in the Phoenix Islands was on Gardner Island, with slave stations on Baker and on Atafu (the northernmost of the three atolls of Tokelau), while a monitoring station was based on Canton Island.[33]

Construction of the Gardner Island station began in July 1944 with the arrival of the USCG Construction Detachment on the *USCG Balsam*. Work there continued while thousands of kilometres away the Americans were fighting their way closer and closer to Japan, capturing the Mariana Islands and Palau. Commissioned on 29 September, the Gardner Island station was operated by 25 men of the USCG Unit 92, with an ensign in command.

The Phoenix stations were used mostly by aircraft on the South Pacific ferry flight route between California and Australia. The last of these flights through Canton Island was on 3 December 1945.[34] The LORAN stations were decommissioned soon afterwards.

A Gradual end to Occupation

Gradually, the US troops began to leave the Gilbert and Ellice Islands Colony. As mentioned in Chapter 3, the US garrison on Fanning Island saw no action in the war; it departed for Honolulu on 9 July 1944, after the fighting in the Pacific had shifted far away to the Mariana Islands.[35] The last US personnel on Abemama left on 19 December the same year.[36]

On 4 June 1945 Betio airstrip was decommissioned.[37] By the end of the year there were only token forces of three or four officers and less than 50 men on each of Tarawa, Butaritari and Christmas Island.[38] The last US serviceman to actually leave Tarawa was Lieutenant John Peck, a supply officer responsible for selling and handing over US stores and materials to the colonial government. He flew out on a C-47 transport plane bound for Kwajalein on 24 January 1948.[39] The naval installation on Canton Island was handed over to Pan American Airways for civil use in October 1946.[40]

On 15 October 1948 the US occupation of Christmas Island finally ceased.[41] It had been seven years since the first Japanese occupation of the colony, beginning on Butaritari in 1941. The period of foreign military occupation of various parts of the Gilbert and Ellice Islands was now at an end.

15

Surrender on Ocean Island

Since August 1942 when the Japanese captured them, Ocean Island and Nauru had been left by the Allies to 'wither on the vine'. When the Allies regained control over the rest of the Gilbert and Ellice Islands in November 1943, they finally learned something of events there from islanders whom the Japanese had evacuated from Ocean Island to Tarawa (chapter 10). Speaking of the conditions they experienced a year or more before, they reported that Ocean Island was bare, lacked food and water, and was suffering under a brutal Japanese regime.

This information was later updated from a different source. In April 1944 a group of seven friends escaped from Ocean Island in three canoes and tried to reach the Gilbert Group. One of the canoes disappeared in a storm on the first night out from Ocean Island. The other two were blown to the west, away from the Gilbert Islands, and were eventually separated from each other. On the third canoe, Nabetari, originally of Nikunau, and Reuera continued on until the canoe overturned and Reuera was drowned. Nabetari was the sole survivor, as nothing was heard again of either of the other canoes. Drifting ashore on the island of Ninigo, in the Admiralty Group near New Guinea, in November, he reported that most of the Pacific islanders on Ocean Island (Banabans, Gilbertese and Ellice Islanders) had been removed to other islands to relieve the famine conditions, leaving only about 150 young men to work for the Japanese.[1]

The British Phosphate Commission wanted Ocean Island and Nauru under Allied control again as soon as possible, so that it could reactivate its phosphate mining operations. Thus it put pressure on the governments of Britain, Australia and New Zealand to invade the islands. However, invasion would require US assistance. In response, Admiral Nimitz did ask the British for three volunteers for a parachute landing to reconnoitre Ocean Island, prompting 250 men to volunteer when the request was forwarded to the RNZAF. But the Americans dropped the plan, because such an operation would cost many US lives, detract from their main drive through Micronesia to Japan, and serve no military purpose. The islands remained under siege.[2]

Seeking Japanese Surrender

In May 1944 the US Navy Bombing Squadron, VB-142, based on Tarawa, flew over several Japanese-held islands in the Marshalls, as well as Ocean Island and Nauru, and dropped leaflets which were attached to cans of food by rubber bands (**Figure 32**). These leaflets explained how the Imperial Japanese Navy had not come to the assistance of ground troops on New Guinea or in Solomon Islands, and would similarly desert the Japanese on these islands. If the Japanese here wanted to save their own lives, the leaflets said, they should surrender.[3] Although they made no response to the Americans, the Japanese told the starving islanders not to eat the canned food as the Americans had poisoned it, intending it as a trick to kill them.[4] They did not surrender Ocean Island and Nauru until October 1945, one month after the formal Japanese surrender in Tokyo Bay.

The documents of the formal Japanese surrender were signed in Japan on 2 September 1945, with representatives of Australia, Britain, Canada, France, the Netherlands, New Zealand, Russia and the United States signing on behalf of the Allies. The Australian government then suggested to the United States that Australian forces might accept the surrender on Ocean Island and Nauru, given that Australia had administered Nauru under a League of Nations mandate before the war. Admiral Nimitz replied that the United States regarded the two islands as of relatively low priority and had no objection to the use of Australian forces and ships there, provided that they accept the surrender in the name of the Commander in Chief, US Pacific Fleet and Pacific Ocean Areas.

Australia and New Zealand accepted these terms, recognising that the surrender was of low priority from a military standpoint but urgent to their

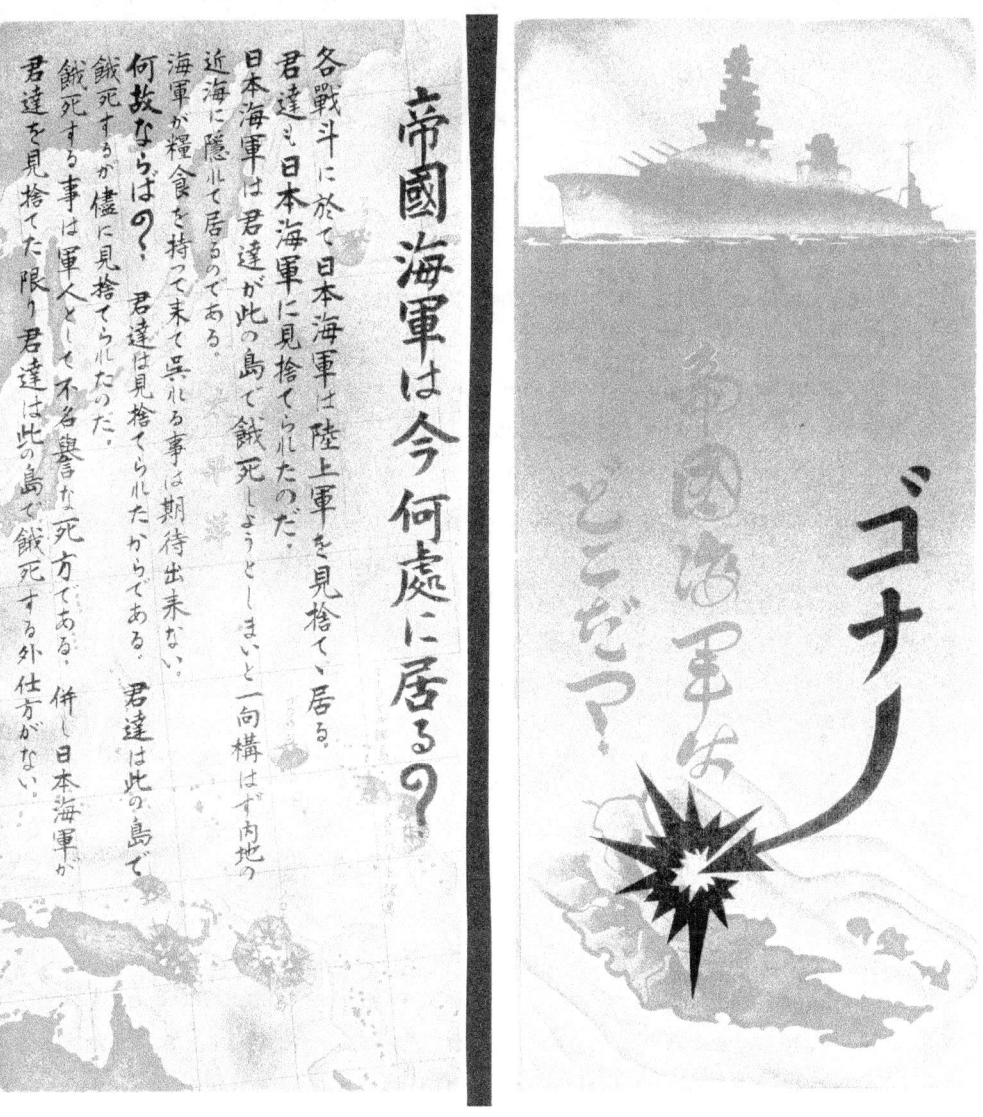

Figure 32. Surrender leaflets dropped at Ocean Island early in 1944

governments in relation to the phosphate industry. Representatives of both governments, along with those from the WPHC, were to attend the surrender on the islands.[5]

As there were no radio communications with the Japanese on Ocean Island or Nauru, more leaflets, signed by Lt General V Sturdee, Officer Commanding the First Australian Army, were dropped over both islands in September. These leaflets advised the Japanese commanders that Japan had surrendered and ordered them to lay down their arms. They also advised of the approximate dates when the Allies would arrive on the islands to accept their surrender.

An Atrocity Unfolds

The surrender on Ocean Island took place on 1 October. When the Allies arrived, they found the only occupants of the island were the Japanese, who said that the islanders had all been evacuated. Although aware that all women and children and most men had been evacuated, the Allies also knew from Nabetari's testimony that approximately 150 young men had remained with the Japanese on Ocean Island. Where were these islanders now? When confronted with this question by Brigadier J R Stevenson, the Japanese commander, Lieutenant Commander Suzuki Naoomi, changed his story:

> One night early in 1944, three natives left in a canoe. They each took a rifle and ammunition. After that on four or five occasions, canoe-fulls natives [sic] left. Food was short at the time and we had been giving them grenades to fish with. They became dissatisfied and attacked us. This was early in December 1944 when there were between 90 and 100 natives on the island. All natives were killed in the fighting.[6]

On another occasion, Suzuki provided a different version of the deaths of the islanders. He alleged that after the islanders had committed repeated thefts, they were warned that death was the punishment for theft. When those warnings had no effect, he claimed, the punishment was carried out under the military code.

However, the truth was revealed when Kabunare Koura, a 28-year-old Gilbertese from Nikunau, came out of hiding. He told how the islanders had worked in gardening, toddy-cutting and fishing for the Japanese and how some had volunteered for service as infantrymen. Issuing them with rifles, the Japanese told the volunteers that they would help repel any attempted landing by the Allies. But in August 1945, after the surrender, the Japanese took away the rifles, split the islanders into nine groups, and marched them to the cliffs over the sea. There, the Japanese blindfolded and shot the island workers. Kabunare had not been hit by the bullets, but fell over the cliff with the others. After feigning death for some time, he hid in a cave near the beach and then in the bush for more than three months, venturing out only under cover of darkness to search for food. One day he heard his own language being spoken and realised that the Japanese had gone.

At first, it was thought that the Japanese had murdered the islanders while the war was still underway, so it was assumed that their purpose was simply to gain all the scarce food and water resources for themselves. But when it was learnt that the executions occurred after the declaration of peace, it became clear that a more likely purpose was to eliminate all witnesses to other atrocities committed on Ocean Island.

Suzuki claimed that on or about 15 August—the date the Japanese government announced the surrender—he heard a radio announcement from Truk that had only mentioned that the terms of a surrender were being discussed and that it had urged all Japanese forces to obey the Emperor's orders to 'fight to the finish'. According to Suzuki, he was then expecting an Allied invasion and feared that the islanders would turn against him when it happened. As they knew the locations of the Japanese defence positions on the island, he believed that he was justified in executing them all. He was unaware of Japan's capitulation, he claimed, until later when he heard the news over the radio on 24 August.

In the case against Suzuki for the mass killing of between 100 and 160 men, after the known declaration of peace, it was necessary to base the total evidence for his crime solely on Kabunare's testimony. Accordingly, the survivor's statement was assembled after many hours of careful questioning on the actual ground of the massacre, walking the very paths, sitting on the cliff on the spot where he had fallen and inside the cave in which he had first hidden on the beach.[7]

At war crimes trials convened by the Australian military in Rabaul, New Guinea, in April 1946, Suzuki stood trial for murder along with his adjutant Lt Nara Yoshio, four company commanders, nine sub-lieutenants, five ensigns and three noncommissioned officers (NCOs). While it was not possible to provide the names or the exact number of all those killed (the figure is now believed to be approximately 142), the murder charges related to two natives named (a Gilbertese, Ueanteiti, and an Ellice Islander, Falailiva), and certain natives unknown, on or about 20 August 1945.

All the accused pleaded not guilty. However, Kabunare's evidence was convincing and all but two were found guilty. Nine were sentenced to be hanged, seven received 20 years imprisonment, three 15 years, and two 7 years. One ensign and one NCO were acquitted. In a petition, Suzuki accepted full responsibility for the killing and made a plea for leniency for Nara, whom he claimed had only been carrying out orders. Suzuki's sentence was upheld and he was hanged but the death sentences of Nara and the others were commuted to 20 years imprisonment.[8]

Nauru's Experience of the War

The situation on Nauru during the war was similar to that on Ocean Island, although Nauru was larger and supported a greater population. From being part of the German Protectorate of the Marshall Islands in 1881, the island had changed hands in World War One. At that time, although the Japanese planned to capture the phosphate-rich island along with the rest of Micronesia, they arrived too late, after the Australians had taken it unopposed. Thereafter, the League of Nations granted a mandate to Australia, New Zealand and Britain, leaving Australia to administer the island. In 1921 the BPC took charge of all phosphate mining operations there; by 1940 it employed approximately 50 Gilbertese and Ellice Islander workers.[9]

As related in chapter 10, in August 1942 Japan seized Nauru along with Ocean Island and for a while tried to mine the phosphate, but US control of the sea and air made shipping it out impossible. However, while they saw Ocean Island as merely an isolated fortress, the Japanese had bigger plans for Nauru. Namely, they developed the island as an air base, from which they planned to expand into the southwest Pacific.

A Japanese School on Nauru

It is obvious that the Japanese believed that Ocean Island and Nauru were going to remain permanent additions to their Micronesian empire, for they introduced Japanese education on both islands. Later, Pacific island children who were evacuated from Ocean Island to Kosrae continued their education in Japanese schools there. One aim of the Japanese wartime government for the Pacific islands was to introduce Japanese as a common language. This had already been done in the Japanese territories in Micronesia to overcome the difficulties that Micronesians had in communicating with each other because most of their languages were mutually unintelligible. Japanese language teaching on Ocean Island and Nauru was also considered a means of creating loyalty towards Japan among the Banabans, Gilbertese, Nauruans and Ellice Islanders on the islands.[10]

A school was opened on Nauru on 19 September 1942 for young Pacific island children of all nationalities, where they were taught spoken and written Japanese, etiquette, numeracy, Japanese history and patriotic Japanese songs.[11] The teachers were Japanese and two Micronesians, a Marshallese woman and a Kosraean man. The school was in operation for nearly three years and closed two days after the Japanese surrender. Many of the students who attended this school and the one on Ocean Island maintained basic spoken Japanese for the rest of their lives.[12]

Under Japanese occupation, the population of Nauru increased to over 4000 Marines, labourers and phosphate workers, plus 750 islanders from Ocean Island. As on Ocean Island, food resources became strained and were strictly rationed. For example, rationing rules allocated three coconut trees to each Japanese, two per islander, and one per Chinese; such distribution reflected the Japanese views of status, including the superiority of the islanders over Japan's ancient enemy. At least a dozen Chinese died on Nauru at the hands of the Japanese, as did all five Europeans who were there when the Japanese arrived. Among the islanders, Nauruans were treated the worst. When the effects of the overcrowding worsened, 1200 of them were sent to Truk, where 460 died of malnutrition and ill treatment by the Japanese.

Along with some Chinese, several Nauruans were beaten to death for stealing pumpkins. Although the relatively high status of Banabans, Gilbertese and Ellice Islanders meant they fared somewhat better, life on Nauru was still tough for them. For example, Ruka Kauaba, a Gilbertese toddy collector, was beaten and tied up for three days then executed for the crime of watering down the toddy supplied to the Japanese. Another Gilbertese man was executed for his part in assisting Japanese soldiers to rape island girls.[13]

Unlike Ocean Island which was spared Allied aerial bombing because it was not a Japanese air base, Nauru was regularly attacked by US Army Air Force bombers and US Navy aircraft carrier planes. Beginning in April 1943, these attacks increased as the date of the US landing on Tarawa drew closer and became a daily occurrence in November, aimed at the specific targets of the air base and the phosphate plant. On 20 November the greatest concentration of bombing occurred during Operation Galvanic, when waves of 50 or more planes bombed the island repeatedly. A later raid in August 1944 killed 19 Nauruans. Altogether, approximately 30 Nauruans died as a result of these US bombing raids.[14]

There were Gilbertese casualties too. In total 60 Gilbertese died on Nauru during the war. Twenty died in the US bombing, mostly men but including at least one woman; 14 from complications arising from malnutrition or outright starvation; 11 were executed by the Japanese for minor crimes,[15] most commonly for stealing food that often belonged more rightly to them than the Japanese. Three men were killed while unloading drums of fuel for the Japanese at the boat harbour. The launch they were on caught fire and exploded, killing also a number of Japanese.

A Catalyst for Relocation

Along with other islanders at the end of the war, Banabans had been rendered destitute and dispersed widely by the events of the war: 250 were now on Kusaie, 346 on Nauru and 107 on Tarawa. It was decided to temporarily accommodate the entire community on the island of Rabi (pronounced 'Rambee') in Fiji, until they could be rehabilitated on Ocean Island.[16]

BPC officials had planned this emigration before the war, because mining was already destroying the island and they wanted the freedom to mine the whole of Ocean Island. In 1941 Rabi had been purchased for £25,000 from its Australian owners, Lever Brothers, as a potentially suitable alternative home. The purchase money came from the Banaban Resettlement Fund, money set aside from the royalties the Banabans received from the phosphate company. Now the destruction and famine of the war rendered Ocean Island uninhabitable and precipitated the planned resettlement on Rabi. Although concerned about the possible fate of their island when it was under the sole control of the phosphate miners, the Banabans felt there was really no other option and agreed to go for a two-year trial period.

Of course, the BPC hoped the Banabans would consider themselves better off on Rabi and decide to stay permanently. The company would then be free to mine the whole island without any interference from the landowners. Moreover, Rabi appeared attractive, with 10 times the land area of Ocean Island, as well as lush vegetation and flowing rivers—quite a contrast to the Banabans' drought-stricken homeland.

On 9 December 1945 the surviving 703 Banabans, along with 300 Gilbertese friends and a handful of Ellice Islanders whom they had invited to accompany them, departed from Tarawa on the BPC ship *MV Triona*. The ship arrived at Rabi five days later.[17]

However, the island failed to meet Banaban expectations. The photographs that they had been shown dated back to the time when it had been an operational copra plantation, with well-maintained houses and orderly gardens. In December 1945 Rabi was overgrown and suffering from several years of neglect, with its remaining buildings in a poor state. It was summer, so the climate was not much cooler than on Ocean Island but it was very much wetter. Those who had not known what mud was on dusty Ocean Island soon experienced too much of it on Rabi.

So life on Rabi began inauspiciously with no houses, no canoes for fishing, no gardens. Banabans were forced to live in tents with only mud as the floor, sleeping on ex-army camp stretchers. They tried to establish a school with no books, paper or pencils. The medical clinic lacked a trained doctor and had few medical supplies. The first winter on Rabi brought influenza, pneumonia and several deaths.

The newcomers also had to become accustomed to a quite different diet. The staple food crop on Rabi was cassava, which Banabans had not grown or eaten on their home island. The reef contained different fish to those they knew— and some of them were poisonous. They also had to learn to cut and dry copra which was to become their main economic occupation.

But slowly life on Rabi improved and eventually the Banabans decided to settle there permanently, while retaining their land rights on Ocean Island and the freedom to travel between the two islands. They re-created the four villages that had disappeared from their homeland through mining: now Tabiang, Uma, Tabewewa and Buakonikai sprang to life on Rabi. The administrative centre on Rabi was established at Nuku, the former headquarters of Lever Brothers.[18]

Initially, Fiji authorities placed some restrictions on the Banaban community. Banaban families had to pay a bond of £40 for each Gilbertese adult they had invited to Rabi, to cover good behaviour and the expense if the guest decided to return to the Gilbert Islands. However, only 51 of the invited Gilbertese were ever covered by bonds, as the other 249 had been associated with the Banaban community for so long that they were regarded as a part of it. Similarly, authorities tried to restrict Banaban movements and ensure that they lived only on Rabi, but abandoned this policy so that the Banabans became free to move from island to island as much as any other resident of Fiji.[19]

Thus over the next 50 years, from their founding population of 1003 in 1945, their number grew to more than 4000 on Rabi. A further 1500 of these Banabans and Gilbertese—or 'Rabians' as they are sometimes now known in Fiji—have settled in other parts of Fiji. At first they maintained little contact with their mined-out and deserted island of Ocean Island, but recently a small Banaban community has re-established itself there.

16
Conclusion

The war in the Gilbert Islands had a profound effect on many people there. Of course, there was loss of life among both islanders and combatant forces. Much property was destroyed and many islands experienced physical changes through the building of airfields, wharves and roads. With the arrival of inter-island and international radio communications, as well as foreign occupation, islanders' eyes were opened to a bigger world than they had previously known.

Dead and Wounded

We will probably never know exactly how many Gilbertese and others died in the Gilbert Islands, nor how many Gilbertese died elsewhere, as a result of the war. However, available records allow a close approximation. About 730 Gilbertese men, women and children died in the Gilbert Islands, and on Ocean Island, Kusaie, Nauru, the Marshall Islands, and at sea. The majority of these deaths occurred at: Ocean Island (462), Butaritari (82), Nauru (60), Tarawa (37) and Kusaie (35). Some of these deaths were a result of Japanese or Allied military action; others resulted from famine, disease, punishment by the Japanese, or murder. The combatant nations lost the greatest numbers: first the Japanese with 6194 deaths, including 4599 at the Battle of Tarawa and 524 at Butaritari; Okinawans 661; and Koreans 410. Next come the Americans with 1900. Sixty Ellice Islanders and a handful of New Zealanders, British, Australians and other Europeans were killed. Thus the estimated total reaches approximately 8906.[1]

In addition, many people were wounded, with some permanently disfigured or disabled due to loss of limbs. A 1996 Government of Kiribati report states 321 Gilbertese were wounded during the war. The greatest number of these

(116) were wounded on Butaritari as a result of the Japanese bombing of Keuea, while many were also wounded on Ocean Island (82) and Tarawa (52).[2]

Destruction and Compensation

Abemama, Ocean Island, Butaritari and Tarawa experienced much destruction of property, and the Japanese burnt a large area of productive land on Kuria. Much destruction of the environment was associated with clearing of land for airfields, as well as with the bombing attacks. A total of 60,000 registered trees were on the land then cleared for airfields on Abemama, Butaritari and Tarawa and an estimated 2000 *babai* pits were likewise destroyed.

In 1947 the British Secretary for State for the Colonies set up a claims commission to register and assess claims for property lost or damaged as a result of the war. In the Gilbert Islands, a commission of inquiry also considered the matter of rehabilitation of damaged lands. It comprised the magistrates and *kaubure* of Abemama, Butaritari and Tarawa, the islands most affected. There was a huge list of claims in the Gilbert Islands for items destroyed by Japanese and Americans; the largest items were trees, houses, *babai* gardens, and fishponds and traps. While individuals made most of the claims, the LMS and Catholic missions, and the cooperative society also made some. In addition, Burns Philp claimed for the destruction of: the *Helena A* and work boats; its wharf, wireless station and staff quarters on Tarawa; and stores and copra sheds on 11 other islands in the Gilbert Group.[3]

It was impossible to establish the exact number of trees that had been lost. Moreover, the British administration did not want replanting to be hampered by complications associated with compensation. They were fearful that if lands were not replanted quickly, islanders would not have sufficient food resources ready when they ran out of the money that they had earned from the Americans. So it was decided that compensation would be paid based on proof that replacements had been made or trees planted, rather than direct payment for gardens and trees lost. Trees must be replanted at the correct spacing for maximum production. Some landowners were not happy with the scheme because it meant they would end up with fewer trees than they owned before the war. Also they felt the rate of compensation for *babai* pits was too low, in view of the extremely hard work involved in digging a pit. The following are some of the comments the commission received from landowners:[4]

> I had more trees on my land before the war than what I will be paid for now, according to the spacing of trees. It seems unfair that I should not be paid full compensation.
> (Tekinano of Noto, Tarawa)

> The government is offering only what she thinks she is able to pay.
> (Annaua of Abaokoro)

> I say three pounds compensation for a babai pit.
> (Tibwe of Noto)

> To dig a babai pit is no joke! I suggest six pounds.
> (Mote of Buariki)

> Let the government or whoever is responsible re-dig our pits, we did not destroy them.
> (Karotu of Teaoraereke)

> To dig a pit on an airfield is impossible, we must be paid compensation.
> (Iokara of Bonriki)[5]

The commissioners were not persuaded by the landowners' arguments. The following response from Nabatiku, a native magistrate, is typical:

> It is impossible to know the exact number of trees… one can easily say 300 when he had only 90… or he might estimate 50 when actually there were 120… The government has worked out a most fair way… you replant according to the correct spacing and whatever the number you plant, that number will be compensated.[6]

The amount of £28,406 was approved for tree compensation on Abemama, Butaritari and Tarawa, including compensation for compacted areas such as airfields which were impossible to replant. Payments were spread over two years (1947–1948) on Tarawa, where the majority of the money (£17,181) went, while compensation was paid in full in 1947 on the other two islands. All landowners receiving compensation were encouraged to save it in the Post Office Savings Bank; for those who opened bank accounts, the compensation was paid directly to their accounts.[7]

In addition to claims for trees and gardens, many filed for compensation for thousands of other personal and household items. The wide variety of items destroyed is reflected in the claims for camphor-wood chests, clothing, food and kitchen utensils, sewing machines, furniture, many bicycles and canoes. On Ocean Island, compensation was requested for a few cars and motorcycles, a truck and a cave that had been a source of fresh water. Personal items plundered by the Japanese included jewellery, watches and binoculars.[8]

It had been envisaged that there would be a pool of Japanese reparation money for distribution but, when it was found that the available Japanese assets were few and the money derived from their sale would very small, it was decided not to form a pool of funds. Instead the Japanese assets in a particular territory would become available to that territory. In the Gilbert and Ellice Islands, no compensation was paid for loss of personal property and all the colonial government got was a few Japanese vehicles and other small items found on Ocean Island. There were three Daihatsu barges, two Nissan cars that had belonged to the island commander, three trucks, a motorcycle and a jeep, and three cases of stationery and some tools.[9]

The Question of Ownership

Although the fighting was over and the British colonial administration was working on rehabilitation, there was renewed attention to the question of sovereignty in a number of Pacific islands. For example, the Americans and the British both claimed sovereignty over several of the same islands in the Line and Phoenix Groups and four in the Ellice Group. The Cook Islands were under New Zealand control but the United States claimed ownership of four of those islands, while both colonial powers also claimed the three atolls of Tokelau.

With plans to develop naval bases in the Pacific islands, in early 1946 the US government suggested to Britain that the US should take back the bases on Canton Island, Christmas Island and Funafuti, on the grounds that, as they had paid to build them, they should own them.

The United States did not dispute the British ownership of Tarawa, although its defence had cost many American lives, but it wanted exclusive rights to use the island as a military base, for 99 years. In the Line Islands, the Americans claimed the small and uninhabited islands of Caroline, Flint, Malden, Starbuck and Vostok. They also made a more significant claim for Christmas Island. The British believed Gilbertese might be resettled on the island, so maintained a presence there, even if it was only a handful of men working the copra plantation. More Americans were based there, and even though the number dwindled to four officers and 79 enlisted men by the end of 1946, they considered that the island belonged to them. It was a situation that the British had little power to change, as the Western Pacific High Commissioner acknowledged to the colony's resident commissioner on 23 January 1947:

> The island commander remarks how he could starve the natives and us out if he so wished. Unfortunately it is perfectly true. It is only by keeping on the right side of him that we get any water… our claim though historically strong is steadily weakening through reliance on the Americans.[10]

The impending dispute over the islands was averted when the US President directed his navy to curtail its expenditure. As a result, the United States abandoned a number of Pacific bases, and did not pursue its claims for the British islands. However, it did not drop them formally until the mid-1970s when it realised that continuing to make claims to sovereignty, by now with very weak justification, would harm its attempts to establish friendly relations with newly independent countries in the Pacific. Nonetheless, its treaties of friendship with Pacific countries provided that the countries would consult with the US over any plans for third parties to use any of the islands for military purposes.[11]

Japanese in Hiding?

After the Americans left Butaritari in April 1946, the colony still had to deal with the problem of Japanese nationals who, it was suspected, were hiding on the island. There were reports of sightings of supposedly Japanese men at a distance and of food stolen from villages at night. The Americans had tried to kill any hiding Japanese by laying poisoned food, but this tactic had tragic consequences. In February and March 1945, three Gilbertese had died from eating the poisoned rice; one of the victims, Kaue Baraniko, was a six-year-old girl.[12]

In September 1946 someone heard two men talking in what they thought was Japanese, north of Ukiangang village. The island police searched the area thoroughly—not an easy task because it was dense mangrove swamp. After two days, the party discovered an empty hide-out made of tarred paper, built two metres up in the mangrove roots, and hid nearby, waiting for the owners to return. When the two men arrived, they surrendered without a fight. They were Korean labourers who had lived on coconut and raw fish for nearly three years after Butaritari had been captured from the Japanese. Although one of their first questions for their captors was how to make fire without matches, they were nonetheless in good physical condition. They were elated to hear that the war was over and that they would soon be returning to Korea. They left for Kwajalein on a US Army Air Force plane.[13]

The Future of the Colonial Administration

The colonial administration also faced several questions in regard to its own future in the short and long term.

An immediate practical question was where to locate a new colony headquarters. Ocean Island was no longer suitable because so many of its buildings and utilities had been destroyed during the war. Even before the war, Sir Harry Luke, High Commissioner from 1938 to 1942, and his predecessor Sir Arthur Richards had both urged moving to a more suitable location, on the grounds that it might serve the interests of the islanders better. After his first tour of the colony, Luke concluded that the administration was too concerned with the BPC on Ocean Island and he wanted more attention given to expanding education and health. In April 1940 he asked the New Zealand government to undertake hydrographic surveys of several islands, in particular Abemama, with a view to establishing new headquarters.[14] After the war, Resident Commissioner Harry Maude also favoured a move to Abemama. Finally, however, Tarawa was selected because the US military was there, the reconstruction of the island needed to be supervised and its lagoon facilities were superior to those of Abemama.

More deeply, the war experience changed attitudes of both the islanders and the British administration. The colonial government recognised that the islanders had become better equipped to 'run their own show', with greater confidence in speaking English, dealing with foreigners and handling money matters. Perhaps the British also recognised that the islanders would no longer tolerate strict control. According to the British, the islanders had too much money and too little respect for the white man—a change in attitude they attributed largely to the US influence.

Thus the British administration was now ready to relax its paternalistic laws and transfer as many responsibilities as possible to local governments. The new policy is expressed in the 'Policy and administration after the war' issued by the new High Commissioner in Suva, P E Mitchell, on 4 October 1944:[15]

I—Policy
(i) The Colony is to be regarded as a 'native territory'; its inhabitants are now discharging a wide variety of administrative and technical functions and are assumed to be capable of being taught all the others which their society requires, given the necessary time, educational facilities and genuine determination to do so.

(ii) No European or other foreign officer is to be engaged for any post in the islands until it has been conclusively shown that it is impossible to obtain or train an islander for it.

(iii) The main preoccupation of the administration must be to train the islanders to discharge all necessary functions for themselves.

(iv) Such European staff (other than members of the Colonial Administration and other services posted to the Colony) as it is inevitable to employ in the meantime should be engaged on short term secondment conditions so that it may readily make way for trained islanders as they become available.

These principles must be modified in application to Ocean Island as long as the phosphate deposits are being worked and in relation to such special subjects as aviation and wireless telegraphy....

III—Local government

(i) The Native Governments of the islands have been established for many years in a form well suited to their circumstances and to the increasing responsibilities which they must assume as they gain experience and maturity. Each village elects a Headman (Kaubure) and all the Kaubures of an atoll together form the Island council under a Chief Headman appointed by the resident commissioner. There is also on each atoll a Native Magistrate, a Scribe and such numbers of village policemen as circumstances require. These 'Native Governments' are local government bodies, analogous in functions and responsibilities to a County Council, and risk of misunderstanding will be avoided if in future they are called 'Tarawa Island Council', 'Abemama Island Council', and so on.

(ii) It does not appear that this general set up requires any considerable modification but some readjustment of functions may be desirable, especially in respect of finance, for financial responsibilities are an essential part of progress in political and administrative responsibility.

In addition, the resident commissioner was to study the possibility of establishing a consultative or legislative council, composed of representatives elected by each island council. By advising the administration, this elected council would share in the running of the colonial government. When this idea was implemented, it became the first step for the Gilbertese and Ellice Islanders towards gaining control of their own futures, and led eventually to their independence from Britain. One signal of the new outlook was the decision to drop the word 'native' from official titles such as native magistrate and native clerk. The change was justified on the grounds that '… the term is fast becoming an invidious one throughout the South Sea Islands…'[16]

Development of Infrastructure

There were also plans to develop communications to all outer islands and internationally, with the use of local expertise. The Bairiki Wireless Training School established on Tarawa (Chapter 4) would continue to train colony wireless operators. Local operators took over all existing wireless sets in the colony, once the European operators left.

Another matter of great interest to the government was the provision of post-war air services. As early as February 1943, the resident commissioner had asked district officers to consider this requirement, seeking their opinions on what general form air services in the Pacific might take and how the needs of the colony might be met.[17] It was obvious that the Gilbert and Ellice Islands could benefit from linking Fiji, Funafuti and Tarawa, but more viable services would probably be trans-Pacific routes, which might use small Central Pacific islands as refuelling stops.

By the end of the war, much infrastructure for air services was established throughout the Pacific: airfields, refuelling facilities, and radio communications with procedures for weather reporting. In Australia and New Zealand were trained airmen and engineers with experience in the islands. There was a surplus of aircraft such as the Douglas DC-3, which had been designed to carry economic payloads. More generally, there was much interest in air services right across the Pacific. Fiji was a focal point for trans-Pacific routes and regional flights, and businesses there were keen to have a domestic service from Suva to Labasa and Lautoka.

On the other hand, in areas of the Pacific such as the Gilbert and Ellice Islands, developments languished because of the vast distances involved and the lack of sufficient passengers or freight. In October 1945 the resident commissioner proposed that the Betio airstrip should be maintained in the hope that an airline might eventually wish to establish a base there. However, the need for land was too great and it went back to the landowners. Commercial air services in the colony did not begin until 21 years later, in 1966, when Fiji Airways operated de Havilland Heron aircraft from Suva to Tarawa via Funafuti. On Tarawa, the airline used the Bonriki airfield that the Americans had built.

Most of Betio was returned to its landowners in 1947, while the government rented parts of the islet for offices and warehouses. War rents were paid to all landowners on Tarawa and the other islands that had been used as bases. Payment was calculated on land area used and the duration of the occupation.[18]

Contributions to the War Effort

Earnings during the American occupation and payments for rent and compensation brought relative affluence to many Gilbertese after the war. Yet, equally, their contribution to the Allied war effort should not be overlooked. In addition to investing in war bonds and savings certificates, they freely contributed to charities such as the Red Cross. Ironically, the islanders who gave the most money were those who were completely abandoned by the British at the start of the war: the Banabans donated A£12,500, an enormous sum in those days, which they had accumulated in savings from phosphate royalties.[19] At the end of 1946 when the war was over and the Banabans themselves were struggling to establish a new home on Rabi, they made a further gift of A£1000 towards food for the hungry people of Britain.[20]

An accumulated sum of A£5600 from the colony enabled the Royal Navy to purchase two aircraft tenders.[21] Further donations funded a mobile canteen to serve hot food and drinks to the bombed-out people of London.[22] Many more contributions went well beyond financial efforts: as the preceding chapters and Appendix G indicate, many citizens of the Gilbert and Ellice Islands Colony distinguished themselves in their courageous assistance to the Allies during the war.

The extent of the generosity and loyalty of the islanders to the British Commonwealth is impressive. It is especially striking given that all the aid went to support the war in Europe and that Britain failed to provide any defence for her colonies in the Pacific. Moreover, at the time when much of the money was

Figure 33. A well on Butaritari incorporates part of a WWII aircraft as its lining

donated, it was the rich and generous Americans who were driving the Japanese out of the Pacific, without the financial assistance of the islanders.

Aftermath—In Summary

The overall lasting effects of the war in the Gilbert Islands were the environmental changes made by developments such as airfields, roads and passages blasted in lagoons. The war sped up the introduction of radio communications and air transport to the region. The post-war government supported the development of cooperative stores, which meant the end to the big commercial traders who were well-established before the war. Travel and emigration, especially to Fiji, increased after the war. In general, the Gilbertese moved more rapidly along the road to self-determination.

17

Epilogue–Dealing With the Dead

American and Japanese Dead

As soon as possible after capturing Betio from the Japanese, the American Marines began burying the dead. With over 1000 US Marines, 5000 Japanese Marines and Korean labourers dead, the bodies posed a serious health risk to the survivors. The Second Marine Division had not anticipated the enormous losses they would suffer in battle and the task of burying the dead was a challenge they had not prepared for. The climate was hot and humid, flies were plentiful and the decomposing bodies needed to be buried quickly to prevent the spread of disease. Many Marines were buried where they fell, in temporary cemeteries created by their units. As one veteran of Tarawa remembered, 'We buried them where the fighting stopped.'[1]

At least 43 temporary cemeteries were created, perhaps more, scattered all over Betio, with between one and 150 bodies in each. There were also additional graves that were not recorded and became lost. On 26 November 1943, two days after all fighting ceased, a map was prepared which showed the locations of 324 American graves on Betio. By 4 December this number had risen to 622. There were also a number of bodies that were swept out to sea from the invasion beaches, only some of which were recovered. Other Marines had simply disappeared during the violence of the battle, obliterated by exploding shells. After the invasion forces were withdrawn from Tarawa, additional bodies were found and buried by the garrison troops and construction and repair crews of the Navy.

Bulldozers were used to make burial trenches where large numbers of bodies could be quickly buried. The dead were laid side by side in the trenches. Small stick-markers were then placed in the sand above where the bodies lay, giving the names and other information about each man but, because the corpses lay so close together, the position of the markers was not precise. Whatever information available at the time that could be used to identify the bodies was recorded in a register.

The Japanese dead were bulldozed into bomb craters and tank traps and covered over with sand. Those who died in bunkers were left there and the bunkers sealed shut. The Americans made one large mass Japanese burial in the southeast quarter of Betio but many other Japanese burials scattered about the island and if the burial records of the American dead were minimal, records of Japanese burials were non-existent.

Although the Americans seem to have accounted for and buried approximately half of their Marines killed, the number who had been positively identified was far lower and the proportion of bodies successfully identified was to decrease after the fighting force left Tarawa and garrison troops took over.

During 1944 garrison forces under Commodore Earl C B Gould tidied up the cemeteries on Betio and in doing so they moved burial markers, causing the remains of many to become unmarked and lost. In undertaking this 'Reconstruction and Beautification' exercise, Navy Seabees graded literally every square metre of the island, removing as they did so every surface marker above the graves. New lines of crosses were set up so as to run parallel to geographical features such as the coastline or roads but the bodies were not moved along with them. The net result was that the cemeteries looked attractive but the mass burial trenches lay at diagonal angles to the rows of white crosses above them—that is, the crosses bore no relation to where the bodies were truly buried.[2]

A decision on the final repository for the American dead did not come until more than two years after the battle. In December 1943 the British ambassador in Washington had suggested that the King of England should present the whole atoll of Tarawa to the United States of America, as a tribute to the dead and to reinforce American commitment to regaining Britain's Pacific territories. Both the Australian and New Zealand governments were against the idea, believing it might prejudice their own Pacific Islands interests and the High Commissioner of the Western Pacific stated, 'We cannot give away two to three thousand British Subjects without their consent...'³ Against the British and British Commonwealth interests and sovereignty was the US claim that the expense of building bases was justification for keeping them and the Navy's development plans for post-war bases in the Pacific.⁴ A compromise was later proposed that not all of Tarawa, but only Betio, be given to the Americans and that the whole islet could be a massive cemetery. But finally, after the US President directed the Navy to curtail its spending, none of the British territories in the Pacific was transferred to American control.

Lone Palm Cemetery

Perhaps the Americans favoured owning simply a cemetery and memorial rather than a whole island and its entire people, for Washington decided that the 43 war cemeteries on Betio should be concentrated into a single cemetery. Another reason for concentrating the graves was in readiness should the decision be made to transfer all US remains to the United States. Tarawa was the first large-scale war dead concentration operation in the Central Pacific. Fifty men of the US Army's 604th Quartermasters Graves Registration Company travelled from Hawai'i on a small freighter, the *Lawrence Philips*, which arrived at Tarawa on 4 March 1946. A suitable site for the new cemetery was selected at the western end of Betio and named *Lone Palm Cemetery*.

It was a formidable task to disinter, identify and reinter the numerous dead who were scattered all over Betio and on other parts of Tarawa Atoll. Some monuments had bodies directly beneath them but in many cases no remains could be found beneath the markers. At Grave 33 they should have found the remains of 400 bodies but, after several days digging, recovered only 129. At Grave 27, which reportedly contained 40 dead, they found no remains at all. When the concentration operation had completed in May, there were 532 recovered remains from 43 burial sites, resting in Lone Palm Cemetery. A short time later, Robert Sherrod, a war correspondent who had landed with the Marines in November 1943, revisited Betio. He wrote of his disappointment that of the more than 1000 Americans who died at Tarawa, only 532 were buried in Lone Palm Cemetery and, of these, only 265 had been identified.⁵

Disinterment—Removal to Hawai'i

In August 1946 it was announced that disinterment at battlefield cemeteries on Wake Island and in the Gilbert and Marshall Islands would begin by October and be completed by the end of December. It had been decided that all the dead were to be removed to Oahu, Hawai'i, where they would be stored until final burial. They would eventually be interred in either a national cemetery such as the Punchbowl near Honolulu, or in hometown cemeteries, depending on the family's wishes.

In November the 604th Quartermasters Company again departed from Hawai'i to begin the final exhumation of the dead from Lone Palm Cemetery. At Betio the remains were transferred into regular, full-sized coffins. Once returned to America they would each have a full-length grave with a normal-size headstone. The problem for the Army's Graves Registration Company on Tarawa was that they often had few remains to place in the coffins. Charles Williams, the district officer, Northern Gilberts, who had been captured at Butaritari and who spent the war years as a prisoner of war in Japan (see Chapter 7), was back working in the Gilbert Islands in 1946. He reported that in one coffin there were no remains at all, only dog tags, scrap metal and a pile of coral stones.[6] Other British administrative officers stationed at Tarawa at the time reported similar coffins without remains, containing only stones.[7] The British generally felt that the US Army should have been more honest when the remains of the dead could not be found, rather than deceiving the families concerned.

Post-war Discoveries

Doubts about the accuracy of the locations, identification and authenticity of the original American burials grew with post-war discoveries. Workers installing underground electrical and telephone cables and water pipes unearthed the remains of several Marines. Some of these discoveries were identifiable by dog tags found with the bones, yet the person identified already had a grave in the United States. In 1974 an Australian aid project to reticulate water around Betio unearthed an amphibious landing craft (LCV) with the remains of an identifiable US Marine inside. He was recorded as having been buried in one of the

Figure 34. Amphibious landing craft (LCV), uncovered in 1974

original post-battle cemeteries (Cemetery 33), but obviously was not. While Ronald Summers, a British engineer working for the Gilbert Islands Public Works Department, was installing electrical cables in the 1960s, he discovered the remains of several bodies. Some of his discoveries were identified as US Marines who already had graves in the United States.[8] It seems that the families of the deceased were not advised of Mr Summers' discovery of the authentic remains and that these were buried as 'unknowns' in the National War Memorial of the Pacific, in Hawai'i. In the year 2000, the bones of two Marines were found buried in John Brown's garden on the southern coast of Betio. One of the deceased was recorded as having been buried in Cemetery 10, on the other side of the island.[9]

Recent Discoveries

An American non-governmental organisation, History Flight, whose mission is to preserve and honour America's World War Two history, was established in the year 2000. Its executive director, Mark Noah, led a History Flight team to Tarawa in 2008 and made news by locating eight lost American burial sites on Betio. These sites contained the remains of scores of US Marines. The success of the six-week expedition was due largely to the use of modern technology to locate the buried remains. The team included an expert who specialised in the recognition of buried human remains using ground-penetrating radar equipment.

Mark Noah submitted a detailed report of the History Flight findings to the US Department of Defense in 2009, which resulted in a Joint POW/MIA Accounting Command (JPAC) mission to Tarawa in 2010. JPAC excavated six of the grave sites that had been identified by History Flight and material recovered from these sites was taken to Hawai'i for identification.[10]

The Remains of Carlson's Raiders

In 1949 the Defense Department made an unsuccessful attempt to locate the remains of the 19 Marine raiders who died on Butaritari in August 1942 (see Chapter 9). The search was renewed in 1998 by relatives of the deceased and a breakthrough made when the searchers met an elderly Butaritari man who had helped bury the bodies as a young boy. He was able to locate the grave and the remains of 19 bodies were recovered in 1999. The Army's Central Identification Laboratory in Hawai'i made the identifications. The remains of six bodies were returned to the families who had opted for private burials. The remains of the other 13 were buried at the Arlington National Cemetery in 2001.[11]

Japanese Bones

The Japanese have been active in recovering the remains of Japanese World War Two dead since 1952. The Social Welfare and War Relief Bureau, of the Ministry of Health, Labour and Welfare (MHLW), has sent out teams to former battlefields to collect Japanese remains and return these to Japan. To date, the remains of approximately 1.26 million out of an estimated 2.4 million people who died on service overseas have been recovered.[12]

The Japanese initially faced opposition from western colonial governments (the United States, Australia, New Zealand, Great Britain) and from Pacific islanders, who were unwilling to assist them. People of Christian-based cultures did not like the idea of groups of Japanese veterans, with Shinto and Buddhist priests, collecting all the bones in an area and cremating them in situ—their economical and efficient method which contrasted with the American practice of using large coffins for individual remains. Once cremated, of course, there was no way of recovering individual bones from the collected ashes, giving rise to the concern that American, Micronesian and Polynesian bones could be collected in error and mixed in with Japanese ones, never to be returned.[13]

The Japanese considered it their duty to collect and honour the remains of their war dead. There were far more Japanese bones than those of other races and they did not intentionally include non-Japanese remains, but inevitably some bones of other nationalities must have been collected, cremated and the ashes taken to the Chidorigafuchi National Cemetery and other memorials in Japan. However, reports that foreign remains were also taken to the Shinto shrine, Yasukuni Jinga at Kudan, are incorrect.[14] Shinto shrines are places for the spirits of the deceased not for the remains of their bodies. At Yasukuni only the names of the deceased are kept. There is also a small shrine at Yasukuni for the souls of all war dead, including Japan's former enemies, but there is no name list for this shrine and no physical remains are kept there.[15]

Since 2003 the Japanese have used DNA analysis to help identify war remains properly.

Accidental Japanese Discoveries

Japanese remains have also been discovered accidentally on Tarawa. The History Flight team, looking for the remains of Americans, has found many Japanese graves which have since been notified to the Japanese authorities. Any Japanese remains unearthed by History Flight have been treated with respect and have been left with the Republic of Kiribati Police.

In 1989 Yoshinori Kori, a Japanese Navy aviator in the Pacific during World War Two, was working on a government of Japan aid project at Betio. During the construction of a new building, a coconut palm was removed and beneath it Mr Kori found a complete skeleton with skull. He was sure the bones were Japanese because he also found and identified 25 Japanese bullets for a model 38 rifle with the bones. He received instructions from Japan to cremate the bones and send the ashes to Japan for enshrinement in the Chidorigafuchi National Cemetery. While stationed at Tarawa he heard that other workers from the Japan International Cooperation Agency (JICA) had found bones which had been cremated and sent to Japan.[16]

Buariki, North Tarawa

The last fighting in the Battle of Tarawa took place near Naa, the extreme northern end of the atoll. The Japanese dead were reportedly buried in three pits near Buariki village (see Chapter 13). An attempt to recover the remains of 173 men was made by the Japanese MHLW in 1999. But because of opposition from the Buariki villagers, no bones were collected.[17]

Butaritari

The MHLW team recovered bones from Butaritari in February 1999. The remains of 20 men were recovered from: Ukiangang (9); near Ainenkarawa School (1); Onomaru (1); near Nanteinaura School (1); and north of the airport (8).[18]

Korean Bones

There had been up to 100 Koreans on Betio at the time of the American attack. Only 15 servicemen and 25 civilian war workers were captured alive. At Butaritari, there were 414 Korean civilian war workers. Unknown to the Americans, the Korean civilians had been separated from Japanese military personnel and were all sheltering in the concrete NBK warehouse. The US Army soldiers killed most of the Koreans; only 104 survived.

It seems that there has been no attempt to locate and collect the remains of the Korean men who died on Betio and Butaritari and it would be a difficult task to locate, identify and separate Korean remains from all the Japanese and American bones. However, a memorial group of Koreans from North and South Korea, plus Koreans living in Japan, made a pilgrimage to Tarawa in November 1991 and installed a stone monument at Betio Memorial Peace Park (see Appendix E).[19]

Gilbertese Burials

There has been far less fanfare in dealing with the Gilbertese war dead. Where possible, family members claimed the bodies of those killed during the war and buried them in graves on land of their own or of the extended family. Such bodies were interred within hours of death. Those who died while working overseas at Ocean Island or Nauru were generally buried in the island graveyards. The bodies of the last Gilbertese and Ellice Islands men executed by the Japanese at Ocean Island were merely thrown over the cliffs into the sea.

Coast-Watcher Bones

The initial search for the coast-watchers' remains and the inquiry into their deaths took place in 1944 (see Chapter 11). In 2008 the History Flight team, while searching for remains of US Marines, identified two sites that could possibly contain the coast-watchers' bones, along with those of the other executed British subjects. Mark Noah of History Flight advised the New Zealand High Commission on Tarawa that radar searches had located two sites where bodies and heads had been buried separately from each other. Because the coast-watchers had been beheaded, either of the two sites could possibly be their graves. However, Noah has also pointed out that the skulls and the headless skeletons could belong to Japanese killed in the American bombardment of Betio, or to Americans who died in the lagoon landing. Some American bodies were not recovered from the sea for some time after the battle and were so decomposed that the heads had fallen off.

The sites will first need to be carefully excavated and the human remains subjected to forensic analysis to identify them. History Flight is assisting the New Zealand Department of Defence in this task and the New Zealand Government has requested the technical assistance of JPAC. However, at the time this book goes to print, it is not known when this matter might come to some conclusion.

Appendix A
Contributors

The following people provided first-hand information on their war experiences. (Names using the Gilbertese system are listed with given name first; those using European system, given name last.)

Alan, Peter
Alolae Cati
Ambo Terenga
Bing, John Carter
Brown, S B
Buariki Tekateke
Cheng, Christopher Wing
Christopher, Frank Airu
Drennan, D J (John)
Fakatene Pili
Gresham, J J
Hardy, C D
Iabeta Tarakai
Iaonibure Unaia
Ituaso Laafai
Jones, John M
Kiantongo
Kum Kee, Ang
Laing, N M
Lau, George J
Maatusi Nofoaiga (Peniamina)
Maheu Naniseni
Marsack, Raymond O
Maui Teonea
McQuinn, Maxwell P
Mela (Sister, OLSH)
Metusela Neeia
Milne, John
Murdoch, Otebina
Namonaterara Wiriam
Narruhn, Bob
O'Brien, Pole
O'Leary, George
Pall, Tom
Pedro, Jack
Peleti Lauti
Penitala Teo
Powell, Winnie
Prentice, Margaret
Pulekai Sogivalu
Reiher, Florence and Karl
Reiher, John
Reiher, Tom
Reita Tekateke
Reymond, Oscar
Roberts, R G
Robuti
Sale, Louise
Schutz, Henry and Mary
Tabakea
Tatou Kaburoro
Tebanini
Tetaua
Teveia Ntiua
Teweka
Tikaouti Bonabati
Usher, Sir Len
Vaughan, D L
Wilson, Gordon

Appendix B
Coast-Watchers in the Gilbert Islands

Island	NZ radio operators	NZ soldiers	Colony radio operators
Makin	M P McQuinn	Pte L B H Muller	
		Pte B L Were	
Butaritari	J M Jones	Pte J M Menzies	Beriki
		Pte M Menzies	
Abaiang	S R Wallace		Telavi Faati
Tarawa			R G Morgan
			John Milne
			Willie Schutz
			Bob Narruhn
			Domingo Muller
Maiana	A C Heenan	Pte C J Owen	Ruotake Iantin
		Pte L B Speedy	
Abemama	J J McCarthy	Pte R J Hitchon	Taukiei
		Pte D H Howe	
Kuria	H R C Hearn	Pte R A Ellis	Maatusi Peniamina
		Pte R Jones	
Nonouti	A E McKenna	Pte C A Kilpin	Kapoa
		Pte J H Nichol	
Beru	A L Taylor		Falavii Sosene
	Tom C Murray		Irata Kaisala
			Tekarara (Stephen Brechtefeld)

Island	NZ radio operators	NZ soldiers	Colony radio operators
Tamana	C A Pearsall	Pte R M McKenzie	
		Pte W A R Parker	
Ocean	Rupert S Bastin		Fred Resture
	R Third		Maui Teonea
	P B Thorburn		Peleti Lauti
			Reuben Uatioa
Canton	F R Dayman		Metusela Neeia
	J M Lee		Tito Homasi
	Allan M Wilde		
Hull			Arnold Cookson
			Faasamata O'Brien
Christmas			Flemming
			G V Langdale
			F H Rostier
Gardner			Reuben Uatioa
			Frank Christopher
			Robert Resture (also at Hull and Canton Islands

Appendix C

Chinese in the Gilbert Islands in World War Two

One difficulty in writing about the Chinese and Chinese-Gilbertese who were in the Gilbert Islands during the war is that often they were known by several different names. Some had a Europeanised name and a Gilbertese name as well as a formal Chinese name. In addition, Europeans often used the Chinese given name as a family name. For example, **Foon** was originally the given name of a family member, but the whole family became known as the Foon family. Similarly, the **Kum Kee** family is well known in the Gilbert Islands, yet the name originates from Jong Kum Kee whose family name was Jong.

Chinese traders have operated in the Gilbert Islands since the 1880s; there is a record of an Ah Sam trading on Butaritari in 1883. On Chong and Company, a trading and shipping company founded in Sydney by the Yip family, arrived in the Gilberts in about 1880. From a base on Butaritari, they branched out to eventually have 13 or 14 stores on different islands of the Gilbert Group, and five major shareholders all originally from the same village in China. In its heyday, when the price of copra was high, On Chong's headquarters on Butaritari had 50 or more Chinese staff. They had their own clubhouse with food, wine and opium specially imported from China, and ran gambling sessions every night. On Chong were general merchants, shipowners and island traders, importing general trade goods and exporting copra and shark fin.

The first Chinese to arrive in large numbers in the colony were those recruited by the BPC to work in the phosphate industry on Ocean Island. The BPC had been unable to recruit all the labour it required from the Gilbert and Ellice Islands Colony (which at the time included Tokelau, and a few Tokelauans were recruited). It felt also that Asians were better suited to the more technical jobs of mechanics, carpenters and boat builders, than were Pacific islanders. After recruiting some Japanese workers, in 1920 the BPC recruited 500 labourers from British Hong Kong. Initially, there were frequent disputes between the Chinese and Gilbertese workers, with serious race riots in 1920 and 1925. But over time the antagonism declined. In 1938 there were 665 Chinese BPC workers on Ocean Island compared with 700 Gilbertese and Ellice Islanders and 87 Banabans. Although Chinese workers were supposed to be repatriated at the end of their three-year contracts, some managed to find their way to the Gilbert Islands, start businesses and marry into local families.

Returning to 'Safety'

Shortly before the New Zealand coast-watchers arrived in the Gilbert Islands in 1941, a group of 17 Chinese-Gilbertese were returning to the islands from Hong Kong and mainland China, where they had been for education, business or family reasons. With the Japanese takeover of parts of China, they believed that they would be safer back in the Gilbert Islands. Ironically, some of them went to Butaritari, little knowing that it would be the first Pacific island to be occupied by the Japanese in World War Two. Others went to Abemama which was also to become a Japanese base.

A significant leader within the group was John Carter Bing, born on Butaritari and educated in China. At the start of the war, he was a gunner in the Hong Kong Volunteer Defence Corps. Although only 20 years old, he was instrumental in securing permission for the group to travel as passengers on the maiden voyage of the new touring ship for the High Commissioner of the Western Pacific, the *Viti*, which had been built in Hong Kong. All had been born in the Gilbert Islands and therefore were British subjects, although some had been forced to leave Chinese-born family members behind in China. They travelled as war refugees from Hong Kong to Suva; some remained in Fiji while others went on to the Gilbert Islands on the colony ship *Kiakia*. Their names are listed at the end of this appendix.

On Butaritari, Jong Kum Kee was manager of On Chong and was about 55 years old when war broke out. He had arrived in the Gilbert Islands in 1910, after working on the On Chong ship *SS Macquarie,* and had married Mary Sing

Figure 35. John Carter Bing (left) and an Ellice Islander crewman, *RCS Viti*, 1940

(daughter of Joe Sing and Nei Kareke) on Betio in 1917. After the war, Jong stayed in the Gilberts and died in Abaokoro, north Tarawa, in 1946.

One of Jong's daughters, Miria, was married to Willie Foon, who had an Gilbertese mother, Nei Timake, and Chinese father. Willie and Maria were among those who returned to Butaritari on the *Viti*. Willie then obtained work as a mechanic and wireless operator with On Chong. He was gifted in his work, which was to his advantage when the Japanese invaded soon after. When the Japanese could not start the only seaplane on the island, Willie fixed it and thereafter received gifts of food and cigarettes from them. He also undertook translating work for the Japanese officers; they wrote instructions which, because the Japanese and Chinese share some of the same written script, he could then translate into Gilbertese.

Later, when the Americans took control of Butaritari, Willie assisted them with his mechanical skills as well. On one occasion, the USCG unit on Bikati islet called on him when they could not repair a faulty water desalination plant and he fixed it for them. In his spare time, he made model canoes and shell necklaces which he sold to the US troops, and he also worked for the US Marine garrison forces on Tarawa. After the war he emigrated to Fiji.

Chinese Traders Present During the War

Prior to the Japanese occupation, the Chinese in the Gilbert Islands were representatives of trading firms or were engaged in private trading. The Japanese occupation took away their livelihood and they moved away from settled areas to survive by subsistence living. A list of some of the Chinese traders known to be in the Gilbert Islands during World War Two follows.

Makin

- Nei Ketia (daughter of Nei Tibe and Siu Akam); her husband Lau Man Jack (Man Tiaki) could not return to the Gilbert Islands from Hong Kong as he had been born in Tong Mei village in Guangtung, China, and therefore was not a British citizen.
- Their son George Lau, also known as 'Manti' (born on Makin on 3 June 1927 and named George after King George V, with whom he shared the same birthday). Wesley Van Nattan, a US medical corpsman and assistant chaplain, met George on Butaritari when stationed there during the war and encouraged him to emigrate to the United States.
- Siu Waiang, whose wife was Turia (father European, mother Gilbertese), was stationed at Kiebu at the southern tip of Makin.

Butaritari

- Jong Kum Kee (manager of On Chong) from Zhengcheng, China. Willie Foon, (also known as Atauea) and wife Miria (daughter of Jong Kum Kee).
- Yee Pung Chong Gum (ex BPC, Ocean Island).
- Lau Sam, Adam (cook for On Chong), Cheng Kwo Yang (assistant manager and accountant for On Chong), with his wife Ruth and family who stayed at Kuma as did all other Chinese on Butaritari after the Japanese took over the On Chong compound.

Kuria
- Ah Lim

Abemama
- Carter Bing (Ah Nga) and wife Yuan Lon Mei.
- Louis King, manager of On Chong.
- The six Chinese who returned on the *Viti* (see list below).

Nonouti
- Ben Kum Kee, son of Jong. Government trade scheme representative and his wife Wong Day. Went to Nauru after the war to work for the BPC and died in Hong Kong in 1967.

Tabiteuea
- Pak Ming (also known as Ba Ming, Li Pak Ming), resident of Terikiai village and government trade representative; his wife, Nei Marewe.
- Yee Kum On (senior) lived near Tanaeang village.
- Yee Kum On (also known as Yee On Bonto), son of Yee Kum On (senior) above, was part of the *Nimanoa* crew and escaped from Tarawa with the first mate on a small boat in February 1942 (Chapter 8).

Beru
- George Kwong, son of Kwong Choy. He moved to Nonouti, home of his wife, in 1942.
- Kwong Choy or Kong Choy, of Shung Shue, Canton; his wife, Eren Redfern.

Onotoa
- Mak King (son of George King and Nei Rerebati Lanyon) and his wife Tung Ang were in Buariki village, Onotoa in December 1941. After the war Mak went to Ocean Island as an interpreter for the BPC; he died in Vancouver, Canada.

Passengers on the maiden voyage of the *Viti*, 1940

The following 17 Chinese-Gilbertese travelled from Hong Kong to Fiji on the *RCS Viti* in 1940. The first 10 listed travelled on to Kiribati; the others remained in Fiji.

1. Willie Foon (Butaritari)
2. Miria Foon, née Kum Kee (Butaritari)
3. Nei Nanoa Low Gee Leong (Abemama)
4. Agnes You Fook, née Gee Leong (Abemama)
5. Tai Moong Chai, son of Agnes You Fook (Abemama)
6. Joseph Low Gee Leong (Abemama)
7. Emeri Low Gee Leong (Abemama)
8. Toma Low Gee Leong (Abemama)
9. Nei Ketia Man Jack (Makin)
10. George Lau, son of Nei Ketia and Lau Man Jack (Makin)
11. John Carter Bing
12. James Bing
13. Willie Lau Gee Leong
14. Ioteba Kee Yang
15. Nei Rerebati Lanyon
16. Mosley King
17. Beri King

The above information was kindly supplied by John Carter Bing of Honolulu, George Lau of California and Christopher Wing Cheng of Vancouver.

Appendix D

Victims of the Bombing of Keuea, 18 August 1942

Aata Powell
Anna Tekateke
Aokitawa Tebarine
Areieta Toare
Ata Kabukitaake
Atanibeia Rabuna
Atara Tata
Bakai Tabaka
Baraiti
Baraniko
Beia Tiribo
Birirake Takateke
Buretau Tekautu
Ekeieta Tebarine
Ioteba Tebarine
Iotua
Itinneita Tiribo
Kairake Teerua
Kaitamakin Tekatoa
Kaneaka Tetaake
Karaba Tekateke
Karubea Nikaroo
Katungaa Maraiti
Kaua Ru
Kauae Timoe
Kawatu Nabwebwe
Kiantetaake Babarua
Kiaua Tiribo
Marewenua Manoku
Mikaere Tiribo
Okitawa Tebarine
Rabuna Bakuea
Rekareka
Takentarawa Katokauea
Tarekaua Tokamatawa
Teabo Koreia
Teaiauea Teburita
Tebarine Nanuatun
Teburita
Tekateke Bureieta
Temane Tiribo
Terabata Noa
Tiakuan Timoe
Tibe (boon Tebarine)
Toare
Tokantetaake Bakarawa
Tokarake Nantebwebwe
Witiotio Tioti

Appendix E

Memorials

American

On the 25th anniversary of the Battle of Tarawa, in November 1968, the US Marines erected a stone marker at the end of Betio mole, overlooking Tarawa lagoon. Attached was a brass plate with an inscription remembering the Marines who fought and died:

"Follow Me" 2nd Marine Division, United States Marine Corps, Battle of Tarawa November 20, 1943. To our fellow Marines who gave their all. The world is free because of you. God rest your Souls. 1,113 killed, 2,290 wounded.

When the Marines' monument needed to be moved because of development to the wharf area, another memorial plaque was added to it and it was placed near the Betio Post Office in November, 1987 with the additional inscription:

In Memory to those men who paid for liberty with lives, Sailors, Airmen, Chaplains, Doctors and especially to Navy Corpsmen, 30 killed, 59 wounded. To the crews of supporting United States ships, carriers, battleships, cruisers and destroyers, submarines, transports, and landing craft.

An additional small plaque was added to the memorial in 2008 commemorating the 65th anniversary of the battle.

British

Soon after the Battle of Tarawa, the Americans erected a memorial on Betio to the 22 British subjects, mostly New Zealand coast-watchers, executed there by the Japanese. The temporary structure was later made permanent by the British (see **Figure 15**). The Betio tablet reads:

In memory of twenty two British Subjects murdered by the Japanese at Betio on the 15th of October 1942. Standing unarmed to their posts, they matched brutality with gallantry and met death with fortitude.

R G Morgan	C A Pearsall
B Cleary	L B Speedy
I R Handley	C J Owen
A M McArthur	D H Howe
A L Sadd	R J Hitchon
A C Heenan	R Jones
J J McCarthy	R A Ellis
H R C Hearn	C A Kilpin
A E McKenna	J H Nichol
A L Taylor	W A R Parker
T C Murray	R M McKenzie

Gilbert *and* Ellice Islanders

No memorial has been made to the 780 Banabans, Gilbertese and Ellice Islanders, who also died and who were also British subjects. The one exception is a tablet on Ocean Island with the following inscription:

This tablet commemorates the loyalty and bravery of the natives of the Gilbert and Ellice Islands Colony during three years of Japanese occupation of Ocean Island, 1942 to 1945. Some died of privation and many were brutally put to death by the Japanese.

A separate memorial to the Europeans who died on Ocean Island was also erected:

In memory of:
C G F Cartwright, L W H Cole, A H Mercer, Rev Father V J Pujebet, Bro H Brummel, R Third

Figure 36. Last surviving coast-watcher in the Gilbert Islands, John M. Jones, at the memorial at Betio

On Butaritari, the people of Keuea Village erected their own memorial to the 48 people who died when Japanese planes bombed their village (see Chapter 9, **Figure 11**) and at the Ainen Karawa School, the Kiribati Japan Friendship Association installed a monument in February 1988, with the following inscription:

To console the spirits of those who died irrespective of nationality in this area in November 1943

Betio Memorial Peace Park
Japanese

In the Peace Park there is a concrete monument built in 1982 by bereaved Japanese families who lost men in the Marshall Islands and at Tarawa. This is watched over by a standing figure of Kannon, the Buddhist Bodhisattva of Compassion (sometimes described in English as the Goddess of Mercy), who is oriented to face to the northwest, towards Japan. There has been widespread use of Kannon in the post-war period, at sites dedicated to those who died in Japanese military conflicts and the role of Kannon seems to have become more social than exclusively Buddhist. The Tarawa monument actually represents 'Maria-Kannon', the amalgamation of the Christian, Mother Mary, with the Buddhist Kannon, as indicated by the large cross on the back of the figure. Maria-Kannon figures originated in the mid-17th century when Christianity was outlawed in Japan and Christians worshiped in secret. The statues were really the Virgin Mary disguised as a Kannon figure. A Christian cross was hidden within the image or as a small cross on the back. On this post World War Two monument, the cross is no longer hidden and can be seen as a conspicuously large cross at the back. The statue represents both Buddhism and Christianity. Kannon, as described in Buddhist scripture, can exist in many guises both male and female. Like Mother Mary in Christian traditions, the female form of the Japanese Kannon, especially Jibo Kannon, embodies the absolute love and compassion of a perfect mother. It was obviously decided therefore that

Figure 37. The Maria-Kannon monument at the Betio Peace Park

Maria-Kannon would be an appropriate symbol to use in a Christian country such as Kiribati (Gilbert Islands).

The park also contains a poem by Umeko Shimozato, a Japanese tanka poet whose husband died in the battle. An English translation of the poem is:

> Where have you gone my dear in this lagoon? Standing on sand with my shoes burning, I feel your spirit coming.

Korean

A Korean memorial stone was installed in the park in November 1991 when a group of Koreans from North and South Korea, plus Koreans living in Japan, made a pilgrimage to Tarawa. The group consisted of nine Koreans and eight Japanese, a priest, four journalists and three government representatives. The leader of the group, Mr You Heedon, was a Korean from Osaka, Japan. He had landed at Tarawa on 26 December 1942 as a civilian construction worker and worked building radar installations at the eastern and western ends of Betio. He had been seriously injured in the chest during one of the US bombing attacks of September 1943 and was evacuated to Japan. The inscription on the stone reads:

> In commemoration of our people who lost their lives in this land. May their souls rest in eternal peace. November 25, 1991.

Naa, north Tarawa

There is a stone monument at Naa, north Tarawa, to the 173 Japanese who died and are buried near Buariki village (see Chapter 13, **Figure 21**).

Figure 38. Korean monument at the Betio Peace Park

Appendix F

Japanese Dead on Abemama

Kimura, warrant officer in charge
Yamauke, launch captain
Fujimaju, wireless operator
Kirabaiaje, wireless operator
Kurotaki, wireless operator
Isava, signalman
Takisava, launch driver
Kampe, truck driver
Inoue, medical orderly
Inoue, machine gunner
Kujita, machine gunner
Ono, machine gunner

Tanaka, machine gunner
Ape, cook
Itoa, cook
Izi, cook
Numayama, cook
Onota, cook
Saito, cook
Saito, cook
Siva, cook
Suzuki, cook
Toyi, cook
Watanape, cook

Appendix G

Honours and Awards

A number of citizens of the Gilbert and Ellice Islands Colony were given awards or commendations for gallantry or distinguished service. Some have been mentioned already in this book; others are listed below.

Beriki

For exceptional loyalty and devotion to duty on Butaritari. During the initial Japanese landing in December 1941, in the raid of Carlson and the US Marines in August 1942, and in the US landing in November 1943.

George Brechtefeld

For outstanding skill, courage and service in undertaking a series of voyages between islands to distribute supplies to the coast-watchers.

Telavi Faati

For his instrumental role in hiding much of the wireless equipment on Abaiang and later handing it over to the British.

Frank Highland

For communicating with and supplying food to Europeans who were confined on Betio.

Iaokiri

For courage in hiding a party of Americans who landed on Tarawa before the invasion in November 1943.

John Milne

For carrying out his duties as wireless operator on Tarawa in September 1942, while enemy aircraft were over the island, and for attempting to transmit messages after the enemy occupation of Tarawa, and for communicating with and smuggling food to European government officers who were confined as prisoners on Betio.

Moanimarewe
For assisting three US airmen who had landed on Butaritari in October 1943, while the Japanese occupied the island.

Domingo Muller
For loyalty and courageous service in operating a secret wireless station on Tarawa in 1942.

Ben Randolph
For loyalty and bravery in the face of the enemy. On 6 September 1942, when the Japanese had already occupied Abemama, he sailed in a canoe from Kuria to Abemama for reconnaissance purposes. He returned to the coast-watching station on Kuria with valuable information on enemy forces and movements.

William (Willie) Schutz
For carrying out his duties as a wireless operator and continuing transmissions from Betio on the morning of 10 December 1941, after enemy troops had landed.

Tekai
For outstanding loyalty in the face of the enemy. When the Japanese landed at Kuria in September 1942, they interrogated Tekai as to the location of the hidden wireless equipment of the coast-watching station. He was beaten, and a shot was fired towards him, but he refused to give any information.

Charles Williams
The King's Commendation. As administrative officer on Butaritari, he was captured by the Japanese and sent to prison in Japan. Along with a number of other prisoners, he was ordered to participate in Japanese propaganda radio broadcasts and was told that refusal would mean execution. In spite of this threat,

he steadfastly refused and was punished with solitary confinement. Williams returned to work in the Gilbert and Ellice Islands Colony in 1946.

For Services to Coast-Watching

The following wireless operators were awarded for their services to coast-watching:

Ruotake Iantin
Kapoa
Peleti Lauti
Maatusi Peniamina
Peni O'Brien
Reuben
Taukiei
Maui Teonea

Falavii Sosene was awarded the Brave Conduct Medal for repairing and operating a radio transmitter on Beru when the area was within the Japanese occupied area.

New Zealanders

New Zealand coast-watchers who had been stationed in the Gilbert Islands and Ocean Island were recognised. All those captured in the northern Gilberts survived the war and received the award of mention in despatches for distinguished service, while the remainder received a posthumous mention in despatches. Temporary Corporal P B Thorburn, who had been evacuated from Ocean Island for medical reasons before the Japanese invasion, and D L Vaughan, who had been in charge of the Ellice Islands operation, were mentioned for devotion to duty.

Three members of the Royal New Zealand Navy were awarded the Bronze Star Medal by the United States Navy. These officers acted as pilots for US warships entering Tarawa lagoon while under fire from the Japanese.

Lieutenant J Forbes, RNZNR
Lieutenant S S Page, RNZNR
Lieutenant G J Webster, RNZNR

Appendix H

Chronology

1939 **30 August**
First New Zealand Army contingent departs Auckland for Fanning Island, to protect cable station.

3 September
Britain and its colonies and Australia, New Zealand and France, declare war on Germany.

10 September
Coast-watching organisation formed throughout the Gilbert and Ellice Islands.

1940 **6 December**
British Phosphate Commissioner's ship *Triona* sunk by German raiders while on route to Ocean Island and Nauru. Four other phosphate ships also sunk by raiders.

1941 **4 April**
New Zealand team begins survey of airfields at Christmas Island.

13 July
Ship *Matua* departs Auckland with NZ coast-watchers for Gilbert and Ellice Islands.

17 July
European women and children evacuated from Ocean Island.

29 October

USS Ellet arrives Christmas Island to establish US Army base.

12 November

US Army engineers arrive Canton Island to commence construction of airfield.

8 December

Japanese bomb Ocean Island; raid Singapore, Malaya, Manila, Hong Kong, Guam, Midway Island, Wake and Pearl Harbor.

10 December

Butaritari and Tarawa first visited by Japanese Navy; Japanese base established at Butaritari.

1942   **28 February**

Majority of European workers and Chinese evacuated from Ocean Island and Nauru.

17 August

Carlson's Marine raiders attack Butaritari. Keuea bombed.

26 August

Ocean Island captured by Japanese forces.

3 September

Japanese occupy Tarawa.

1943   **20 November**

Amphibious landings at Tarawa and Butaritari by US Marine Corps.

1944 **3 April**
Nabetari escapes from Ocean Island in canoe.

9 July
US garrison departs Fanning Island.

1945 **4 June**
US naval base at Betio decommissioned.

20 August
Banabans, Gilbertese and Ellice Islanders executed at Ocean Island.

1946 **18 April**
US naval forces depart Butaritari.

14 October
All US naval facilities on Canton Island disestablished.

1948 **15 October**
US occupation of Christmas Island ceases.

Appendix I

Abbreviations

Sources are identified by the following abbreviations in the notes:

AA—Australian Archives
AWM—Australian War Memorial
ANU/ABL—Australian National University/Archives of Business and Labour.
KNA—Kiribati National Archives
MONO—Japanese Monographs. Japanese Research Division, Military History Section, Headquarters, Far East Command, Washington: Office of the chief of Military History, Department of the Army, 1952. 4. Vol 5, The Naval Armament Program and Naval Operations (Part II), Monograph 161, Inner South Sea Islands Area Naval Operations, Part I, Gilbert Island Operations.
NAF—National Archives of Fiji
NANZ—Archives New Zealand
NATUV—National Archives of Tuvalu
NAW—National Archives, Washington DC

The sources for each chapter are listed below:

NOTES

Chapter 1. The Arrival of the German-Marshallese
1. Mark R Peattie, *Nanyo, The Rise and Fall of the Japanese in Micronesia 1885–1945*. Honolulu: University of Hawaii Press, 1988. *Isla: A Journal of Micronesian Studies,* Vol. 3 No. 2, 1995, University of Guam Press.
2. Karl and Florence Reiher, pers comm, 29 October 1996.
3. Sister Maria Talaima, *Go Forth, 1895–1995, OLSH Missionary Experience in Kiribati*. Tarawa: Maria Printing Office, 1995.
4. Catalogue of foreign contacts, KNA. John Carter Bing, pers comm,17 January 1997.
5. Intelligence Report on the Gilbert Islands, compiled in Funafuti, December 1942 to February 1943. NATUV
6. Lou Sale, pers comm, 30 September 1994.
7. Genealogies of the Narruhn, Muller, Reiher and von Reymond families, compiled by Winston Thompson of Suva.
8. Tom Reiher, pers comm, 18 August 1994.
9. Oscar Reymond, pers comm, 10 April 1997.
10. Robert Narruhn, pers comm, 28 January 1995.

Chapter 2. Airfield Surveys in the Phoenix and Line Islands
1. NANZ, NAVY, Series 1, 8/10/7.
2. KNA, HM 410 How the US resolved disputed South Sea Island Claims.
3. NANZ, AIR, Series 1, 109/6/11.
4. KNA, HM 93 Report on the colonisation of the Phoenix Islands.
5. Ian H Driscoll, *Airline, The Making of a National Flag Carrier*. Auckland: Shortland Publications, 1979.
6. NANZ, AIR, Series 1, 103/2/5.
7. *History of the Aerodrome Services Branch of the Public Works Department (N.Z.) 1939–1945*. Wellington: Department of Internal Affairs, 1947.
8. Ibid.
9. KNA, HM 410 How the US resolved disputed South Sea Island Claims.
10. TIGHAR Tracks, Vol. 12, No 2/3, Sept 1996, Wilmington, TIGHAR.
11. NANZ, NAVY, Series 1, 8/10/7.

12. NANZ, AIR, Series 1, 103/2/9 and E. J. Paton, *Unconventional Journeys*. (Airfield surveys in Fiji and Line Islands), unpublished manuscript.
13. Erwin Thompson, *Pacific Ocean Engineers History of the U.S. Army Engineers in the Pacific, 1905–1980*. p87.
14. *Historical Review, Corps of Engineers, Vol. 1, Covering Operations During WWII, Pacific Ocean Area*. Honolulu: US Army, 1946.
15. Ibid.
16. Ibid. and Metusela Neeia, pers comm, 23 January 1991.
17. Erwin Thompson, op cit.
18. Ibid.
19. Harold D Mendelson, pers comm, 25 September 2002.
20. *Historical Review, Corps of Engineers, Vol. 1*, 1946, op cit.
21. Ibid.
22. *Life*, Vol. 14, No 4, 25 January 1943, pp24–25.
23. Accounts of the flight and subsequent events are given in: James C Whittaker, *We Thought We Heard the Angels Sing*, New York: EP Dutton, 1943; and Vernon E Rickenbacker, *Seven Came Through*, New York: Doubleday, 1943.
24. Robert J. Buckley, *At Close Quarters, PT Boats in the United States Navy*, Washington: Naval History Division, GPO, 1962, p 169.
25. Vaughan, Part 19, p2.
26. Quoted in Buckley, op cit, p170
27. *Honolulu Advertiser*, 23 November 1942, p 5.
28. This detail supplied by Salvador D'Amico, who interviewed Richard Seither's sister, Johanna Seither.
29. *Life*, Vol 14, No 4, 25 Jan; No 5, 1 Feb; No 6, 8 Feb.
30. Vernon E Rickenbacker, *Rickenbacker*, London: Hutchinson, 1968.

Chapter 3. Fanning Island Garrison

1. Oliver A Gillespie, *Official History of New Zealand in the Second World War 1935–1945, The Pacific*. Wellington: War History Branch, Department of Internal Affairs, 1952.
2. *Documents Relating to New Zealand in the Second World War 1939–1945*. Vol. III, Wellington: War History Branch, Department of Internal Affairs, 1963.

3. *The Men That Beat the Gun.* unpublished manuscript by C. D. Hardy, copy in Kippenberger Military Archive, Queen Elizabeth II Army Memorial Museum, Waiouru.
4. NANZ, Navy 2, 030/12/2.
5. J J Gresham, pers comm, 7 July 1997.
6. NANZ, Log of H.M.S. Leander, August/September 1939.
7. J J Gresham, op cit.
8. C D Hardy, pers comm, 5 July 1997.
9. NANZ, Navy 30, 30/61/1.
10. Margaret Prentice, pers comm, 10 January 1997.
11. NAF, F31/280.
12. Oliver A Gillespie, op cit.
13. George O'Leary, pers comm, 25 August 1997.
14. KNA, List 28 II, F1/J Coast-watching Fanning Island.
15. KNA, List 28 II, F1/k.
16. E J Paton, *Unconventional Journeys.* (Airfield surveys in Fiji and Line Islands), unpublished manuscript.
17. Ibid.
18. KNA, List 28 II, F1/k.
19. NANZ, Air 1, 132/7/7.
20. KNA, List 28 III, SF 1/6.

Chapter 4. Coast-Watching
1. NAT, Intelligence Report on the Gilbert Islands, compiled in Funafuti December 1942 to February 1943.
2. August Karl Muggenthaler, *German Raiders of World War II.* London: Robert Hale, 1977.
3. Ibid.
4. KNA 3 I, SF 3, Coastwatching.
5. KNA 11/I, F3/3/2.
6. D L Vaughan, *Report on Coastwatching Radio Stations in the Gilbert and Ellice Islands, 1941–45.* Wellington: Vaughan, 1990.
7. NAT, Intelligence Report on the Gilbert Islands, op cit.
8. Frank Christopher, pers comm, 1 February 1997.

9. Numerous personal communications: Don Vaughan, 1990 –1997; John M Jones, 1994–97; Gordon Wilson, 1993–97.
10. NANZ EA 1, 86/26/1.
11. New Zealand Post Office War History, NZPO Chief Engineer's Office – Radio Section, Wellington, 1949.
12. Ibid.
13. Ibid.
14. NATUV, Intelligence Report on the Gilbert Islands, op cit.
15. Metusela Neeia, pers comm, 23 January 1991.
16. NATUV, Intelligence Report on the Gilbert Islands, op cit.
17. John Milne, pers comm, 29 December 1992.
18. Metusela Neeia, op cit.

Chapter 5. German Raiders

1. August Karl Muggenthaler, *German Raiders of World War II*. London: Robert Hale, 1977.
2. AA MP1587/1, 153M, Loss of the *Triona, Triadic* and *Triaster*.
3. AA MP1185/8, 2021/5/518, Manoora's report on the loss of shipping at Nauru.
4. AA MP1587/1, 153M, op cit.
5. Ibid.
6. Albert Ellis, *Mid-Pacific Outposts*. Auckland: Brown & Stewart, 1946.
7. NANZ, N1,16/8/30, Raider Activity Nauru and Ocean Island 1940–41.
8. NANZ, N1, 16/12/21, Wireless Communications Ocean Island.
9. R H Garvey, 'The Ocean Island Defence Force', *History of Events in the Gilbert and Ellice Islands Connected with the War with Japan, Dec 41–March 42*. Suva: WPHC, 1942.
10. Ibid.
11. Herman G Gill, *Royal Australian Navy 1939–1942*. Canberra: Australian War Memorial, 1957.

Chapter 6. After Pearl Harbor —Ocean Island and Tarawa

1. R H Garvey, 'The Ocean Island Defence Force', *History of Events in the Gilbert and Ellice Islands Connected with the War with Japan, Dec 41–March 42*. Suva: WPHC, 1942.
2. Ibid.

3. Quotations from the account of the Japanese occupation of Tarawa by Lloyd Sinclair are from the unpublished letters of Percy Lloyd George Sinclair, held in the private collection of the Sinclair family and quoted here with permission of Mr G Sinclair and Mrs D Sinclair.
4. Bob Narruhn, pers comm, 28 January 1995.
5. John Milne, pers comm, 29 December 1992.
6. ANU/ABL, Burns Philp South Sea Co. Ltd, Tarawa Branch correspondence, 1942–48.
7. Sister Maria Talaima, *Go Forth, 1895–1995, OLSH Missionary Experience in Kiribati*. Tarawa: Maria Printing Office, 1995.
8. ANU/ABL, Burns Philp South Sea Co. Ltd, Tarawa Branch correspondence, 1942–48.
9. Ibid.
10. Ibid.
11. The declaration document is preserved in the records of the Catholic Mission at Teaoraereke, Tarawa.

Chapter 7. Butaritari Captured

1. NATUV, Intelligence Report on the Gilbert Islands, compiled in Funafuti, December 1942 to February 1943.
2. MONO, Monograph 161.
3. John M Jones, pers comm, numerous 1994–1997.
4. Ibid.
5. Ibid.
6. Ibid.
7. Christopher Wing Cheng, pers comm, October 1997.
8. Maxwell McQuinn, pers comm, 18 December 1994.
9. KNA 1 II, F1/9/3.
10. John M Jones, op cit.
11. KNA 1 II, F1/9/3.
12. John M. Jones, op cit.
13. NANZ AD 1, 339/1/64.
14. John M Jones, op cit.
15. Pers comm, 16 April 1997.
16. Pers comm, 10 April 1997.
17. Pers comm, 12 April 1997.
18. Winnie Powell, pers comm, 15 April 1997.

Chapter 8. Launch Escape

1. NANZ AIR 1, 132/3/5, Evacuation of Ocean Island and Nauru.
2. Accounts of the loss of the *Donerail* can be found in: NAF F41/290, M. V. *Donerail* loss through enemy action; *Fiji Times and Herald*, 18.3.42 and 20.3.42; and ANU/ABL, Burns Philp South Sea Co. Ltd, Tarawa Branch correspondence, 1942–48.
3. R H Garvey, *History of Events in the Gilbert and Ellice Islands Connected with the War with Japan, Dec 41–March 42*. Suva: WPHC, 1942.
4. Documentary accounts of the escape voyage in: R H Garvey, op cit, and ANU/ABL, op cit. Oral accounts through personal communication with: Tom Pall, 8 April 1997; Maatusi Nofoaiga, 2 December 1990; Bob Narruhn, 28 January 1995.
5. Pers comms: Doug Hunt, February 2011, John Ragg and Margaret Cleary, February 2012.
6. Pers comms, Tom Pall, Maatusi et al, op cit.
7. NATUV, Intelligence Report on the Gilbert Islands, compiled in Funafuti, December 1942 to February 1943.
8. ANU.ABL BPCo, N115/439. Letter to Trotter, BP Suva, from Manager, Tarawa Branch, 15 March 1942.
9. Copy of letter supplied by Doug Hunt of Auckland and also held in the Sinclair family archive.
10. Unpublished letters of Percy Lloyd George Sinclair, held in the Sinclair family archive.
11. Stan Brown, pers comm, 22 March 1991.
12. NAW, Record Group 59, US State Department, file 819.857/150.
13. Murray Chambers, *Merchant Man*. Radio interview broadcast 10 May 1943 on station 2FC Sydney. Transcript held at National Archives of Australia.

Chapter 9. Carlson's Raid and the Bombing of Keuea

1. Samuel Eliot Morison, *History of United States Naval Operations in World War II, Vol. IV, Coral Sea, Midway and Submarine Actions May 1942 – August 1942*. Boston: Little, Brown & Co., 1958.
2. MONO, Monograph 161.
3. Morison, op. cit.
4. NAW, deck log *USS Nautilus*, 16–19 August 1942.
5. Personal communications: Iaonibure Unaia, 12 April 1997; Oscar Reymond, 10 April 1997; Winnie Powell, 15 April 1997.

6. NAW, op cit. Morison, op cit.
7. Morison, op. cit.
8. Pers comm, 16 April 1997.
9. Pers comm, 15 April 1997.
10. Morison, op. cit.
11. Details of the deaths are contained in: *Ana Ribooti te Komete are Kateaki ibukin Kakaean mwin Mate, Ikuaki, Uruaki, ao Kabuanibwai ake a riki imwin te Kauoua ni Buaka n te Aonaaba,* Tarawa: Maneaba ni Maungatabu, 1996. [A report on deaths, injuries, damages and losses caused by the Second World War, published by the Kiribati Government, 1996.] [Gilbertese language.]
12. Pers comm, 17 April 1997.
13. Pers comm, 14 April 1997.
14. Pers. comm, 18 August 1994.
15. Morison, op cit.

Chapter 10. Occupation of Ocean Island and Abemama
1. MONO, Monograph 161.
2. R H Garvey, 'Evacuation of European and Chinese from Ocean Island', *History of Events in the Gilbert and Ellice Islands Connected with the War with Japan, Dec 41–March 42.* Suva: WPHC, 1942.
3. NANZ AIR 1, 132/3/5, Evacuation of Ocean Island and Nauru.
4. NANZ NAVY 2, 020/14/11.
5. Peleti Lauti, pers comm, 25 September 1997.
6. Personal communications: Tikaouti Bonabati, 4 January 1993; Teveia Ntiua, 22 March 1997; Ituaso Laafai, 7 January 1991; Maatusi Nofoaiga, 2 December 1990; Fakatene Pili, 15 November 1992; Pulekai Sogivalu, 10 March 1997.
7. NATUV 8 I, F: 19/1/8, Japanese files captured at Ocean Island.
8. Peleti Lauti, op cit.
9. Pers comm, 7 January 1991.
10. Pers comm, 4 January 1993.
11. Pers comm, 22 March 1997.
12. Pers comm, 7 January 1991.
13. Pers comm, 22 March 1997.
14. NATUV 8 I, F: 1/9/1.
15. KNA 1/II, F: 1/11/1 and KNA 3 II, SF: 41/2/1.

16. Taukiei was awarded for his bravery (see appendix G).
17. Statement, 29 May 1944, KNA 21 II, F: 5/1/2.
18. Statement, 19 October 1944, KNA 3 II, SF: 12/4/3.
19. Statement by Nateri, KNA 21 II, F5/1/2.
20. Ibid.
21. Ibid.
22. Statement, 4 October 1942, KNA 3 I, SF: 3.
23. Statement 7 January 1944, KNA 1 III, F: 1/9/3, Vol. 1.
24. Ibid.
25. Pers comm, 2 December 1990.
26. KNA 2 (1) I, F: 79/4/9, Lands compensation Kuria Island.
27. NANZ Navy 2, 30/33/17, part 3, W T Communications, South Pacific.
28. F Jones, Minister of Defence, responding to S G Holland, member parliament, 23 March 1944. NANZ Army Department 1, 339/1/64.

Chapter 11. Occupation of Tarawa and fortification of Betio

1. William H Bartsch, 'Operation Galvanic', *After the Battle*, 1977, no 15, pp 1–33.
2. NAW, Report of the 5th Antiaircraft Battalion, USMC, 1 December, 1940 – 30 April 1944, Washington DC: Department of the Navy, Headquarters US Marine Corps.
3. The contract between the Imperial Japanese Navy and Vickers Sons and Maximum is held by Vickers Limited, London.
4. Ian H Nish, *Anglo-Japanese Alliance: the Diplomacy of Two Island Empires,* London: Athlone Press, 1966.
5. Pulekai Sogivalu, pers comm, 10 March 1997.
6. Fakatene Pili, pers comm, 15 November 1992.
7. KNA 1 II, F1/9/3 vol. 1, Alleged execution of Europeans.
8. NAW, deck log of *USS Portland*, 15 October 1942, and William Generous Jr., *Sweet Pea at War : A History of USS Portland*, pp 66–68.
9. KNA 1 II, op cit.
10. Ibid.
11. Otebina Murdoch (wife of David Murdoch), pers comm, 7 February 1996.
12. Sister Mela, pers comm, 2 May 1997.
13. John R Grigg report. Copy held by his son, Murray Grigg, 31B Lomond St, Takapuna, Auckland.
14. NANZ AD1, 339/1/64, Atrocities by Japanese at Tarawa.

15. Ibid.
16. William H Bartsch, op cit.
17. Pers comm, 1 April 1997.
18. MONO, Monograph 161.
19. Charles T Gregg, *Tarawa*, New York: Jove, 1991. p 133.
20. Ibid.

Chapter 12. Bombing

1. *Operational History of the Seventh Air Force 7 December 1941 to 6 November 1943*. Army Air Forces Historical Studies: No 41, Washington: Headquarters Army Air Forces, 1953.
2. NAW, Report of the 5th Antiaircraft Battalion, USMC, 1 December, 1940 – 30 April 1944, Washington DC: Department of the Navy, Headquarters US Marine Corps.
3. USMC5, p 8.
4. Ibid, pp 9–10.
5. Harold D Mendelson, pers comm, 25 September 2002.
6. MONO, Monograph 161.
7. *Operational History of the Seventh Air Force 7 December 1941 to 6 November 1943*, op cit.
8. NAW, Report of the 5th Antiaircraft Battalion, op. cit.
9. Oto Degener and Edwin Gillaspy, 'Canton Island', *Atoll Research Bulletin*, no 41, Washington DC: National Academy of Sciences, 1955.
10. *Operational History of the Seventh Air Force 7 December 1941 to 6 November 1943*, op cit.
11. NAW, Report of the 5th Antiaircraft Battalion, op cit.
12. MONO, Monograph 161.
13. *Operational History of the Seventh Air Force 7 December 1941 to 6 November 1943*, op cit.
14. Wesley Frank Craven and James Lee Cate, Eds, *The Army Air Forces in World War Two, Vol. 4, The Pacific, Guadalcanal to Saipan, August 1942 – July 1944*, Washington DC: Office of Air Force History, 1983.
15. Ibid.
16. Pulekai Sogivalu, pers comm, 10 March 1997.
17. Pers comm, 10 March 1997.
18. Pers comm, 17 March 1997.

19. *The Capture of Makin (20 Nov – 24 Nov, 1943)*, American Forces in Action series, Washington DC: Historical Division, War Department, 1946.
20. KNA 21 II, F: 4/1/8.
21. Tebanini, pers comm, 20 April 1997.
22. KNA 21 II, F: 4/1/8.

Chapter 13. Operation Galvanic

1. William H Bartsch, 'Operation Galvanic', *After the Battle,* 1977, no 15, pp 1–33.
2. Wesley Frank Craven and James Lee Cate, Eds, *The Army Air Forces in World War Two, Vol. 4, The Pacific, Guadalcanal to Saipan, August 1942 – July 1944,* Washington DC: Office of Air Force History, 1983.
3. USMC5, p 11.
4. Ibid, p 15.
5. Philip A Crowl and Edmund G Love, *United States Army in World War Two: Seizure of the Gilberts and Marshalls,* Washington DC: Department of the Navy, 1955.
6. Frank Wesley Craven and James Lee Cate, Eds. 1983, op cit, p 295.
7. E P Forrestel, *Admiral Raymond A Spruance USN,* Washington DC: GPO, 1966, p 71.
8. Ibid, p 78.
9. Worrall Reed Carter, *Beans, Bullets and Black Oil,* Washington DC: GPO, 1953, pp 91–93.
10. James L Mooney, Ed, *American Naval Fighting Ships,* Washington DC: Naval Historical Center, Department of the Navy, 1981, p 107.
11. Irving Johnson, 'Adventures with the Survey Navy', *National Geographic,* July 1947, p 140.
12. Charles Wilkes, *Narrative of the United States Exploring Expedition During the Years 1833–42,* 5 vols and atlas, Philadelphia: Lea & Blanchard, 1845.
13. Irving Johnson, op cit, p 141.
14. Samuel Eliot Morison, *History of United States Naval Operations in World War Two: Vol VII Aleutians, Gilberts and Marshalls, June 42 – April 45,* Boston: Little Brown & Co, 1953, p 97.
15. Ibid.
16. KNA, 21 II, F: 12/4/6, *War Diary F. G. L. Holland, Period August – November 1943,* entry for November 1943.
17. Quoted in: Charles T Gregg, *Tarawa,* New York: Jove, 1991, p 183.
18. Morison, op cit.

19. Tatou Kaburoro, pers comm, 17 March 1997.
20. MONO, Monograph 161.
21. A discussion of casualties is found in chapter 16 and also in: Charles T Gregg, op cit.
22. Donald W Olson, 'The Tide at Tarawa', *Sky and Telescope*, November 1987, pp 526–29.
23. Capt L C Hays Jr, Lt 1/8, 1st Battalion, 8th Marines. In FMFRP 12-90, Second Marine Division Report on Gilbert Islands Tarawa Operation.
24. KNA 21 II, F: 12/4/6, War Diary, D C I Wernham.
25. Ambo Terenga, pers comm, 1 April 1997.
26. Ibid.
27. An account of the capture is given in: Morison, op cit. A list of Japanese dead on Abemama is contained in: KNA 21 II, F: 4/1/8, vol 1, War Graves Abemama.
28. John Reiher, pers comm, 28 April 1997.
29. MONO, Monograph 161.
30. *The Capture of Makin (20 Nov – 24 Nov, 1943),* American Forces in Action series, Historical Division, War Department, Washington DC: 1946.
31. KNA 2 (1) I, F: 79/3/1. Loss due to enemy action.
32. Capture of Makin, op cit.
33. KNA 21 II, F: 5/1/2, Honours and Awards—War Graves.
34. KNA 21 II, F: 5/1/3, Honours and Awards—US Awards
35. Stories praising Lt Bruno von Reymond and describing the family reunion are contained in: *Pacific Islands Monthly*, January 1944, p 39 and June 1944, p 10.
36. Morison, op cit, p 140.

Chapter 14. US Occupation
1. KNA 5, Item 6, War Diary D C I Wernham, 1943–45.
2. KNA 1 II, F: 1/5/12.
3. NANZ AD 12, 28/19 Garrisons for British Pacific Islands Captured from the Enemy.
4. KNA 5, Item 6, op cit.
5. Raymond Marsack, pers comm, 26 November 1992.
6. John Drennan, pers comm, 25 October 1997.
7. KNA 5, Item 6, op cit.
8. Ray Marsack, op cit.
9. Ibid.
10. KNA 1 II, F: 1/6/10 Labour Corps Strength.

11. KNA 1 II, F: 1/5/3 Native relations with Allied Forces, 1943–47.
12. Ibid.
13. Ibid.
14. Ibid.
15. KNA 1 II, F: 1/5/10 Island Orders Tarawa.
16. Maheu Naniseni, pers comm.
17. Gordon Wilson, pers comm.
18. Published sources on the loss of VMF-422 are: Marine Fighter Squadron 422 is Missing, *Air Classics*, vol 12, no 8, August 1976; and Robert Sherrod, *History of Marine Corps Aviation in World War Two*, Washington DC: Combat Forces Press, 1952, pp 228–230.
19. Iaonibure Unaia, pers comm, 12 April 1997.
20. KNA 1 II, F: 1/11/2 Labour Force Butaritari.
21. KNA 1 II, SF: 1/5/7 Nabeina Incident.
22. Ibid.
23. Ibid.
24. Ibid.
25. KNA 1 II, F: 1/11/2 op cit.
26. KNA 1 II, F: 1/5/3 op cit.
27. KNA 2 (1) I, F: 79/2/2 vols I & II War Compensation.
28. KNA, 21 II, F: 12/4/6 War Diary F G.L Holland.
29. Ibid.
30. Ibid.
31. Ibid.
32. Ibid.
33. The Coast Guard at War, Loran IV, Vol. II, Washington: USCG Historical Section, 1946.
34. KNA 3 I, SF: 2 Allied Occupation 1942–47.
35. KNA 28 III, SF: 1/6 Evacuation of US Forces 1944–45.
36. KNA 3 I, SF: 10 US Claims to Hull Island 1943.
37. Ibid.
38. KNA 3 I, SF: 2 op cit.
39. Peter Alan, pers comm, December 1995.
40. KNA 3 I, SF: 2 op cit.
41. KNA 2 (1) I, F: 7/1/1 Christmas Island, US Claims.

Chapter 15. Surrender on Ocean Island

1. KNA 17, F: 16/2/1 Cumulative Interrogation of Nabetari; also John Drennan, pers comm, 25 October 1997.
2. NANZ Navy 2, 020/14/11 Defence of Pacific, Ocean Island and Nauru.
3. Ralls C Clotfelter, US Navy Bombing Squadron VB-142, pers comm.
4. Teveia Ntiua, pers comm, 22 March 1997.
5. AWM 54 615/5/1 Intelligence Report 2 Part II, Covering the Surrender and Occupation of Ocean Island, September 1945.
6. KNA 17 F: 16/2/2 Japanese Activities on Ocean Island, [Suzuki's interrogation on 1/10/45].
7. KNA 17 F: 16/7/1 Atrocities on Ocean Island.
8. AA: MP742/1, 336/1/1397 Record of Military Court, Japanese War Criminals. 1975/273, Box 1, Copy of transcript of War Crimes Trial of Lt Cmdr Suzuki and L Nara.
9. Ralph Shlomowitz and Doug Munro, 'The Ocean Island (Banaba) and Nauru Labour Trade, 1900–1940', *Journal de la Societé des Oceanistes*, 1991, vol 94, no 1, p10.
10. Toru Okamura, 'Japanese Teaching in Nauru', *People and Culture in Oceania*, Society for Oceanic Studies, 2009, vol 18, pp 65–76.
11. AA (ACT) A518 DV118/6, The War Diary of Patrick Cook, and AWM 54 615/5/1 Narrative of Japanese Occupation of Ocean Island, Nauru, diary of Nai Fai Ma.
12. Pers comms: Teveia Ntiua, 22 March 1997; Miliagi, 13 January 1993; Tikaouti Bonabati, 4 January 1993.
13. AA (ACT) A518 DV118/6 and AWM 54 615/5/1 op cit.
14. Patrick Cook, Ibid. and MONO monograph 161.
15. *Ana Ribooti te Komete are Kateaki ibukin Kakaean mwin Mate, Ikuaki, Uruaki, ao Kabuanibwai ake a riki imwin te Kauoua ni Buaka n te Aonaaba*, Tarawa: Maneaba ni Maungatabu, 1996. [A report on deaths, injuries, damages and losses caused by the Second World War, published by the Kiribati Government, 1996.] [Gilbertese language.]
16. AWM 54 615/5/1 Intelligence Report 3 Aust Inf. Bn.
17. KNA 1 II F: 1/9/1 Prisoners of War, Internees and Missing Persons.
18. NAF F128 Settlement of Natives of Ocean Island on Rabi Island Fiji.
19. NAF F128/1 Banabans and Gilbertese on Rambi Island, Control of Movements.

Chapter 16. Conclusion

1. Main US casualties in Operation Galvanic were members of the Marine Corps. The Marines' casualty figures were revised several times after 1943 until the final number was settled on in 1952. The source for this is: 'Final Report on Tarawa Casualties', Casualty Division, Headquarters, USMC, 1952.

Records of US Army and Navy, and Japanese casualties can be found in the many published books on the Battle of Tarawa (see Bibliography).

The source for Japanese dead on Abemama (Appendix F) is KNA 21 II, F: 4/1/8.

Records of other Japanese casualties and those of the British (including Australians and New Zealanders), Gilbertese and Ellice Islanders can be found in the following:

Taniura 2000 and Kori 1996 (Japanese and Korean casualties).

KNA 21 II, F: 12/4/12, Japanese Peace – War Dead 1964–65 and F: 4/1/4 Census and vital statistics, War Ocean Is. (includes translations of Japanese files captured at Ocean Is.).

KNA 1 II, F: 1/9/3 vol. 1 Alleged Executions of Europeans.

Death records Butaritari, Registrar General's Office, Tarawa.

Ana Ribooti te Komete are Kateaki ibukin Kakaean mwin Mate, Ikuaki, Uruaki, ao Kabuanibwai ake a riki imwin te Kauoua ni Buaka n te Aonaaba, Tarawa: Maneaba ni Maungatabu, 1996. [A report on deaths, injuries, damages and losses caused by the Second World War, published by the Kiribati Government, 1996.] [Gilbertese language.]

2. *Ana Ribooti...*, op cit.

3. KNA 1 II, F: 79/3/1 War compensation – Losses Due to Enemy Action, F: 79/2/2 War Compensation, F: 79/4/9 Land Compensation Kuria Is., F: 79/4/2 Land compensation Abemama Is., F: 79/4 Vol. I Land Compensation and Rehabilitation - General Policy, F: 79/4 Vol. II Land Compensation.

4. KNA 2 (1) I, F: 79/4, vol. I. op cit.

5. Ibid.

6. Ibid.

7. Ibid.

8. KNA 2 (1) I, F: 79/1/1 Reparations Looted Property.

9. Ibid.

10. KNA 3 II, SF: 7/1/1, Christmas Island, US Claim to Sovereignty.

11. KNA H. M. 410, How the US Resolved Disputed South Pacific Island Claims.

12. Death records Butaritari, op cit.; *Ana Ribooti...*, op cit.

13. KNA 3 I, SF: 15, Intelligence Report Gilbert Islands.
14. NANZ Air 1, 109/6/7, Operations Gilbert and Ellice Islands.
15. NAF F128/52, Gilbert and Ellice Islands Colony, Policy and Administration After the War, SF 82/3, 4 October, 1944.
16. NATUV TUV 8 I, Gilbert and Ellice Islands Colony memo on post-war reorganisation and administration policy.
17. NATUV TUV 8 I, F: 2/1, letter dated 10/2/43
18. KNA 1 II, F: 155/13 Areas occupied – rentals.
19. Sir Harry Luke, *Cities and Men vol. III,* London: Geoffrey Bles, 1956.
20. KNA 1 II, F: 7/6/5
21. NATUV TUV 8 I, F: 7/6/2
22. Solomon Islands National Archives, F: 9/17/1, Mobile Canteens, 1940–41.

Chapter 17. Epilogue—Dealing with the Dead

1. Marvin Strombo, a 6th Marines Division veteran, quoted in: Mark Noah, *The Lost Graves of Tarawa.* Florida: History Flight, 2009. [Unpublished report.]
2. Information on the initial burials are found in: Mark Noah 2009, op cit; Edward Steere and Thayer M. Boardman. *Final Disposition of World War II Dead 1945–51.* Department of the Army, Quartermaster Corps, QMC Historical Studies, Series II, No. 4, Washington DC: Historical Branch Office of the Quartermaster General, 1957.
3. Mitchell to Secretary of State, 20-12-1943, DO35/2124, National Archives of Gt. Britain. Cited in: Judith A Bennett, *Natives and Exotics—World War II and Environment in the Southern Pacific*, Honolulu: University of Hawaii Press, 2009, p 276.
4. Dorothy Richard, *US Naval Administration of the Trust Territory of the Pacific Islands*, vol III, Washington: Office of the Chief of Naval Operations, 1957. p 21.
5. Robert Sherrod, 'Tarawa Today', *Life*, 5 August 1946, pp 19–20.
6. Charles Williams, pers comm to John Jones.
7. Raymond Marsack, pers comm, 1993.
8. Ronald Summers, pers comm, 1969.
9. Noah, 2009, op cit.
10. Ibid.
11. http://wwwarlingtoncemetery.net/raiders-1942 and *Honolulu Advertiser*, 11 March 2002.

12. MHLW website: http://www.mhlw.go.jp/english/wp/wp-hw4/08.html.
13. Bennett, 2009, op cit.
14. Bennett, 2009, op cit, p280, quotes an *International Herald Tribune* article and states that remains of Japanese from the Pacific were taken to Yasukuni shrine.
15. Hiroshi Nakajima, pers comm, 2011.
16. Yoshinori Kori, *Mauri Kiribati*, Tokyo: Kindaibungeisha, 1996. [Japanese language.]
17. Kiribati Tomonokai [Kiribati Friendship Society]. *Tarawa & Makin Tokusyu* [A special issue on Tarawa & Makin]. Tokyo: 31 July 1999. [Japanese language.]
18. Ibid.
19. Kori, 1996, op cit.

BIBLIOGRAPHY

Ana Ribooti te Komete are Kateaki ibukin Kakaean mwin Mate, Ikuaki, Uruaki, ao Kabuanibwai ake a riki imwin te Kauoua ni Buaka n te Aonaaba. Tarawa: Maneaba ni Maungatabu, 1996. [A report on deaths, injuries, damages and losses caused by the Second World War, published by the Kiribati Government, 1996]. [Gilbertese language].

Bailey, Eric. *The Christmas Island Story*. London: Stacey International, 1977.

Bartsch, William H. 'Operation Galvanic', *After the Battle*. 1977, no 15, pp 1-33.

Bennett, Judith A. *Natives and Exotics—World War II and Environment in the Southern Pacific*. Honolulu: University of Hawaii Press, 2009.

Bevington, Eric. *The things We Do For England: If Only England Knew*. Burley: Eric Bevington, 1990.

Buckley, Robert J. *At Close Quarters: PT Boats in the United States Navy*. Washington: Naval History Division GPO, 1962.

Carter, Worrall Reed. *Beans, Bullets, and Black Oil*. Washington: GPO, 1947

Cooper, Harold. *Among Those Present: The Official Story of the Pacific Islands at War*. London: HMSO, 1946.

Craven, Wesley Frank, and James Lee Cate. Eds. *The Army Air Forces in World War Two*. Vol. 4., Washington: Office of Air Force History, 1983.

Crowl, Philip A, and Edmund G Love. *United States Army in World War Two*. Washington: Department of the Army, 1955.

Driscol, Ian H. *Airline-The Making of a National Flag Carrier*. Auckland: Shortland Publications, 1979.

Eastman, Rev G H. *Frontline Islands – the Gilbert and Ellice Islands in Wartime*. London: The Livingstone Press, 1944.

Forrestel, E.P. *Admiral Raymond A Spruance USN*. Washington DC: GPO, 1966.

Generous, William Thomas. *Sweet Pea at War: A History of USS Portland*. Kentucky: University Press of Kentucky, 2003.

Gill, Herman G. *Royal Australian Navy 1939-1942*. Canberra: Australian War Memorial, 1957.

Gillespie, Oliver A. *Official History of New Zealand in the Second World War*. Wellington: Internal Affairs, 1952.

Gregg, Charles T. *Tarawa*. New York: Berkley Publishing, 1984.

Hall, D O W. *Coastwatchers.* Wellington: Internal Affairs, 1951.

Howard, Clive and Joe Whitley. *One Damned Island After Another, the saga of the 7th Air Force in W.W.II.* Washington D C: Zenger Publishing, 1946.

Hoyt, Edwin P. *Storm Over the Gilberts.* New York: Van Nostrand Reinhold, 1978.

Johnson, Irving. 'Adventures with the Survey Navy.' *National Geographic*, July 1947.

Kiribati Tomonokai [Kiribati Friendship Society]. *Tarawa & Makin Tokusyu* [A special issue on Tarawa & Makin]. Tokyo: 31 July 1999. [Japanese language.]

Kori, Yoshinori. *Mauri Kiribati*, Tokyo: Kindaibungeisha, 1996. [Japanese language.]

Life, vol 14, no 4, 25 January, 1943, pp 24–25.

Macdonald, Barrie. *Cinderellas of the Empire.* Canberra: ANU, 1982.

Maude, H E. *Of Islands and Men: Studies in Pacific History.* Melbourne: ANU, 1968.

McQuarrie, Peter. *Strategic Atolls-Tuvalu and the Second World War*. Christchurch: Macmillan Brown Centre for Pacific Studies, University of Canterbury and Suva: Institute of Pacific Studies, University of the South Pacific, 1994.

Mooney, James L. Ed. *American Naval Fighting Ships.* Washington: Naval Historical Center, 1981.

Morison, Samuel Eliot. *History of United States Naval Operations in World War Two, Vol. II: Aleutians, Gilberts and Marshalls.* Boston: Little, Brown, 1953.

Muggenthaler, August Karl. *German Raiders of World War II.* London: Robert Hale, 1977.

Noah, Mark. *The Lost Graves of Tarawa.* Florida: History Flight, 2009. [Unpublished report]

Okamura, Toru. 'Japanese Language Teaching in Nauru', *People and Culture in Oceania, 18*, 30.09.2009, pp 65–75. Tokyo: Japanese Society for Oceanic Studies.

Olsen, Donald W. 'The Tide at Tarawa', *Sky and Telescope*: Nov 1987, pp 526–29.

Peattie, Mark R. *Nanyo The Rise and Fall of the Japanese in Micronesia 1885–1945.* Honolulu: University of Hawaii Press, 1988.

Richard, Dorothy. *United States Naval Administration of the Trust Territory of the Pacific Islands.* Washington: Office of the Chief of Naval Operations, 1957.

Shaw, Henry I. *Tarawa: A legend is Born.* New York: Ballantine, 1969.

Sherrod, Robert. *Tarawa: The Story of a Battle.* New York: Duell, Sloan and Pierce, 1944.

────── 'Tarawa Today', *Life*, 5 August 1946, pp19–20.

Shlomowitz, Ralph and Doug Munro. 'The Ocean Island (Banaba) and Nauru Labour Trade, 1900–1940', *Journal de la Societé des Oceanistes*, 1991, vol 94, no 1, p 110.

Smith, Holland M and Percy Finch. *Coral and Brass*. New York: Scribner, 1949.

Steere, Edward. and Thayer M. Boardman. *Final Disposition of World War II Dead 1945–51*. U.S. Army, Quartermaster Corps, QMC Historical Studies, Series II, No. 4, Washington DC: Historical Branch Office of the Quartermaster General, 1957.

Stanley, David. *Micronesia Handbook-Guide to the Caroline, Gilbert, Mariana and Marshall Islands*. Chico: Moon Publications, 1992.

Taniura, Hideo. *Tarawa Makin no Tatakai* [Battle on Tarawa & Makin]. Tokyo: Soushi Sha, 2000. [Japanese language.]

Umeko, Shimozato. *Tarawa Lagoon*. Hokkaido Shimbun, 1988. [Japanese language.]

Vaughan, D L. *Report on Coastwatching Radio Stations in the Gilbert and Ellice Islands. 1941–45*. Wellington: D L Vaughan, 1990.

Whittaker, James C. *We Thought we Heard the Angels Sing: the complete epic story of the ordeal and rescue of those who were with Eddie Rickenbacker on the plane lost in the Pacific*. New York: E P Dutton, 1943.

Wilkes, C., *Narrative of the United States Exploring Expedition during the years 1838, 1839, 1840, 1841, 1842*. Philadelphia: Lea and Blanchard, 1845.

Index

Symbols

1st Battalion, Fiji Infantry Regiment 160, 161
1st South Seas Garrison 123
1st South Seas Garrison, Japanese 123
2nd Marine Division, United States 209, 229
2nd Raider Battalion, United States 91
3rd Battalion of the 6th Marines, United States 181
3rd Special Naval Landing Force, Japanese 158
4th Fleet Construction Department, Japanese 123
4th Naval Construction Unit, Japanese 158
4th South Seas Garrison, Japanese 123
7th Army Air Force, United States 127, 130-132
8th Gunboat Division, Japanese 67
11th Naval Construction Unit, Japanese 158
13th Army Air Force, United States 139
19th Air Group, Japanese 93
24th Air Flotilla, Japanese 103
27th Destroyer Division, Japanese 103
27th Infantry Division, United States 158
51st Naval Garrison, Japanese 67, 72
62nd Naval Garrison Unit, Japanese 91
63rd Naval Garrison Unit, Japanese 104
111th Construction Unit, Japanese 123
111th Naval Construction Unit, Japanese 122, 123
604th Quartermasters Company, United States 212
604th Quartermasters Graves Registration Company, United States 211
802nd Navy Air Group, Japanese 158
804th Army Engineer Aviation Battalion 16
952nd Navy Air Group, Japanese 158
955th Naval Air Group, Japanese 123

A

Abaiang Island 7, 38, 71, 97, 220, 237
Abaokoro Islet, Tarawa 168, 170, 224
Abatao Islet, Tarawa 132
Abbott, Wainwright, US Consul in Fiji 90
Abe, Kose, Vice Admiral 100
Abemama Island 6, 8, 40, 61, 80, 83, 100, 101, 103, 108, 109, 115, 118-120, 129, 134, 137, 141, 156, 158, 165, 170, 181, 182, 183, 198, 199, 203, 220, 223, 226, 236, 238
Achilles, HMS 11
Adamson, Colonel 20, 21, 22
Ah Lim 226
Ah Nga. *See* Bing, John Carter (Ah Nga)
Alan, Peter 219
Alolae Cati 219
Amalgamated Wireless Australia Limited 36
Amatuku Islet, Funafuti 144
Ambo Terenga 155, 219
amphibious landings x, 129, 131
amtracs (LVT) 147, 148, 151, 155, 159
Annaua 199
Antares, USS 17
Aorangi, New Zealand ship 14, 29
Aranuka Island 182
Argonaut, USS, submarine 92
Asanagi, Japanese destroyer 57, 123
Asiatic Petroleum Company 26
Atafu Atoll, Tokelau Islands 184
Atauea. *See* Foon, Willie (Atauea)
Atholdike, US ship 29
Azuchi Maru, Japanese warship 107

B

B-17 (Flying Fortress) bomber aircraft 19-22

265

B-24 (Liberator) bomber aircraft 128-132, 138-140, 182
Bairiki Islet, Tarawa 63, 117, 132, 148, 154, 170, 171
Bairiki Wireless Training School 36, 205
Baker Island 10, 130, 183, 184
Balsam, USCG 184
Ba Ming. *See* Pak Ming
Banaba. *See* Ocean Island
Banaban Resettlement Fund 195
Banabans 100, 103, 107, 187, 193-196, 206
Bangao 106
Bangkok Maru, Japanese auxiliary cruiser 123
Bastin, Rupert Stanley, Chief Wireless Officer 50, 221
Battle of Tarawa 138, 142-144, 197, 216, 229, 237, 258
Belleau Woods, USS, aircraft carrier 132
beriberi at Ocean Island 106
Beriki, radio operator, Butaritari 67, 93, 160, 220, 236
Beru Island 8, 34, 36, 41-43, 80, 83, 109, 111, 129, 220, 226, 239
Beru Mission Station 36
Betio Islet, Tarawa 34, 36, 56-58, 61, 63, 65, 81, 100, 115-121, 123, 124, 127, 129, 131-133, 139, 146-150, 154, 163, 167-170, 178, 205, 206, 209-211, 214, 216, 217, 224, 229, 234, 237, 238
Betio Memorial Peace Park 217, 232, 233, 235
Bevington, Eric, District Officer 56
Bikati islet, Butaritari 224
Bikenibeu village, Tarawa 148, 154, 170, 179
Bing, James 227
Bing, John Carter (Ah Nga) 219, 223, 224, 226, 227
Bonriki, Tarawa Atoll 155, 170, 171, 178, 179, 206
bootless soldiers 168
Bougainville, Solomon Islands 123, 145

BPC. *See* British Phosphate Commission (BPC)
Brechtefeld, George 8, 83, 237
Brechtefeld, Lina 74
Brechtefeld, Stephen (Tekarara), radio operator, Beru 8, 42, 111, 220
Brechtefeld, W Maximilliam 8
British Phosphate Commission (BPC) 45, 46, 48, 50, 56, 104, 108, 187, 192, 195, 202, 222, 223
Brown, S. B. 219
Brummell, H. (Brother), Sacred Heart Mission 103, 230
Buariki Tekateke 97-99, 219
Buariki village, Tarawa 132, 154, 155, 216, 226, 234
Bubu, radio operator Nimanoa 61
Bullard, USS, destroyer 145
Bunker Hill, USS, aircraft carrier 144
Buota village, Tarawa 170, 178, 179
Burnie Island 10
Burns Philp South Seas Limited 5, 7, 11, 26, 34, 36, 37, 41, 56, 61-63, 65, 79, 80, 81, 84, 103, 146, 150, 198
Butaritari Island 4-7, 33, 41, 57, 65-70, 72, 74, 75, 77-79, 91, 92, 95, 99-101, 107, 115, 128, 129, 131, 133, 134, 138, 140, 141, 158-163, 165, 170, 178-180, 183-185, 197-199, 202, 207, 212, 214, 216, 217, 220, 222-225, 232, 237, 238

C

Cable and Wireless, Ltd. 25, 28
cables cut, Fanning Island 25
cable station, Fanning Island 25-28
cannibalism 89
Canton Island 10, 11, 13, 14, 17, 18, 20, 34, 42, 43, 127-131, 147, 165, 183, 184, 201, 221
Carlson, Evans F., Lt. Colonel 6, 92, 94, 95, 101, 158
Carlson raid 6, 91, 102, 131, 158
Carlson's Raiders 214, 237

Caroline Island, Southern Line Islands 201
Carpenter, W. R., trading company 74
Cartwright, Cyril George Fox, administrator of Ocean Island 102, 103, 230
casualties 87, 132, 147, 148, 194, 197, 209, 210, 211
Catholic Church 4, 56, 77, 103, 120, 121, 161, 198. *See also* Sacred Heart Mission
Chambers, Murray, crew of Donerail 80, 90
Charlotte, convict ship vii
Chauncey, USS, destroyer 145
Cheng, Christopher Wing 219
Cheng Kwo Yang 225
Cheng, Ruth 225
Cherry, William, Captain 21, 22
Chester, USS, cruiser 144
Chidorigafuchi National Cemetery, Japan 215, 216
Chinese traders, workers 4, 28, 49, 56, 70, 74, 102, 103, 108, 193, 194, 222, 223, 225
Christmas Island 10, 11, 13-17, 19, 29, 30, 34, 165, 184, 185, 201, 221
Christopher, Frank Airu, radio operator, Christmas Island 37, 43, 219, 221
Clark, T. L., Burns Philp employee, Tarawa 62, 81
Cleary, P. B. A. (Basil), Government Dispenser, Tarawa 60, 81, 118, 230
coconut log guns 29, 30, 105
coconuts 21, 28, 72, 79, 107, 118
Cogswell, W. P., Captain 182
Cole, L. W. H., BPC employee, Ocean Island 103, 230
contributions to the war effort 206
Coode, James, district officer 80, 83
Cookson, Arnold, radio operator, Hull Island 34, 42, 221
Copeland, Leslie A., Burns Philp employee, Tarawa 62, 110
copra 7, 10, 11, 34, 195, 196, 201, 222

Coral Sea, Battle of the 101
Corrie, Robert 106
Croydon, Christmas Island 14

D

dances 144
Davis, Colin 22
Dayman, F. R., radio operator 221
DeAngelis, John, Second Lieutenant 22
de Brum, Rosa 5
Degei, Fiji government ship 42, 43, 80, 83, 84, 90
dengue fever 41
Dennan, John, Major, District Officer 170
disease, deaths from 197
Domingo, student, KGV School 181, 182
Donerail, Norwegian ship 78, 89, 112
Doughty, Captain T. C., Helena A 63, 65, 81, 86
Drennan, D. J. (John) 219

E

Eadie, Lieutenant 21
Earhart, Amelia 9
Eastman, G. H., Reverend 34, 80, 83, 88
Eita village, Tarawa 154, 170, 179
Ellet, USS 15
Ellis, R. A., Private, New Zealand soldier 112, 220, 230
Enderbury Island 11, 13
Engelhardt, H. (Brother), Sacred Heart Mission 4, 74, 161
English Harbour, Fanning Island 28, 30
English, Pat, government sub-accountant 59, 63, 65, 81
Eniwetok, Marshall Islands 178
Enterprise, USS, aircraft carrier 101
Erben, USS, destroyer 145
Espiritu Santo, New Hebrides 145
Essex, USS, aircraft carrier 144
executions, at Betio 118-120
executions, at Ocean Island 106

F

Fakatene Pili 118, 219
Falailiva, Ellice Islander 192
Falavii Sosene, radio operator, Beru 41, 111, 220, 239
Fanning Island 11, 13-15, 24-27, 29-31, 33, 34, 45, 105, 165, 184
ferry route, aircraft 9, 16, 18
Fiji 5, 14, 223, 227
Finney, E. J. C., Lieutenant Colonel 168, 169
Fleming, British representative at Canton Island 42, 43
Flint Island, Southern Line Islands 201
Foon, Miria 224, 225, 227
Foon, Willie 227
Foon, Willie (Atauea) 224, 225
Forbes, Captain 146
Forbes, J., Lieutenant, RNZNR 240
Fox-Strangways, Vivian, Lieutenant Colonel, Resident Commissioner 166-168
Frank Highland 154
Fualefeke Islet, Funafuti 144
Funafuti Atoll, Ellice Islands 20-23, 39, 77, 113, 115, 127-131, 138-145, 147, 166, 170-176, 201, 205, 206

G

Gardner Island 9, 11-13, 34, 42, 43, 183, 184
Garvey, R. H., Resident Commissioner 38
Gee Leong. *See* You Fook, Agnes
German raiders 33, 45, 46, 48, 49, 50, 52
Germans, people of German descent 3-5
Gibson, E. A. 12
Gibson, Herbert D., Colonel 18
Gilbert and Ellice Islands Labour Corps 167
Gould, Earl C. B., Commodore 210
graves 100, 107, 155, 209-215, 217
Gresham, J. J. 219

Gridley, USS 31
Grigg, John R., Captain, New Zealand 121
Guadalcanal, Solomon Islands 91, 102, 115, 170
Guam Island 100
Guano Act of 1856 10
Guichard, Pierre (Father), Sacred Heart Mission 70, 74, 161

H

Haleakala, US ship 16
Hale, USS, destroyer 145
handicrafts 178, 180
Handley, Isaac R., retired mariner, Tarawa 118, 230
Hansen, John, pilot 173
Hardy, C. D. 219
Harness, E. W., Captain, Nimanoa 40, 56, 59, 61, 64, 77, 81, 86
Harris, USS 181
Hawai'i 23
Hawaiian Constructors 16
Hearn, H. R. C., coast-watcher 83, 112, 113, 220, 230
Hector, HMS 29
Heenan, A. C., coast-watcher 82, 109, 110, 220, 230
Helena A, Burns Philp ship 56, 63, 65, 70, 198
Henderson, J. A. 12
Higgings, Edwin C., wireless operator 37
Highland, Frank 120, 237
Hill, Admiral 146
Hilo, USS 20-22
Hitchon, R. J., Private, New Zealand soldier 220, 230
Hobby, USS, destroyer 174, 176
Holland, dredge at Canton Island 17, 18
Holland, F. G. L. (Frank), Director of Education 36, 79, 81, 87, 89, 90, 145, 146, 181, 182
Honolulu, Hawai'i 19, 20, 78, 79, 92
Hoover, J. H., Rear Admiral 139, 140

Hornet, USS, aircraft carrier 101
Howe, D. H., Private, New Zealand soldier 220, 230
Howland Island 9, 10
Hull Island 9, 11, 13, 34, 42, 221
Hunt, Walter Lindsay 81, 86

I

I-10, Japanese submarine 78
I-175, Japanese submarine 162
Iabeta Tarakai 69, 75, 219
Iaokiri 237
Iaonibure Unaia 219
Ibuki, Japanese war ship 116
Ikamawa, government district clerk, Beru Island 111
Ikuta Maru, Japanese war ship 107
independence, from Great Britain 88, 204
Independence, USS, aircraft carrier 144
Iokara 199
Irata Kaisala, radio operator, Beru 42, 220
Isaac, Walter Lindsay, Dr. 81, 87
Isabelle, Mother, Catholic Mission on Butaritari Island 4
Ituaso Laafai 106, 107, 219
Iupeli, Samoan LMS pastor, Beru Island 111
Iwarri, Japanese battleship 116

J

Jaluit Gesellschaft 7, 8
Jaluit, Marshall Islands 5, 57, 71, 79, 123, 139
Japan International Cooperation Agency 216
Jarvis Island 10
Jenner, George W., Burns Philp manager, Tarawa 62, 63, 80
John Williams, LMS Mission ship 61
Joint POW/MIA Accounting Command (JPAC) 214, 218
Jonchere (Father), Catholic Mission 70
Jones, James L., Captain 156, 181
Jones, John M., coast-watcher 67, 69, 73, 75, 219, 220, 231
Jones, R., Private, New Zealand soldier 112, 220, 230
Jong Kum Kee, Miria. See Foon, Miria
Jong Kum Kee, On Chong Manager, Butaritari Island 70, 74, 223-225
JPAC. See Joint POW/MIA Accounting Command (JPAC)

K

Kabunare Koura 190-192
Kaczmarczyk, Alexander 20
Kanemitsu, Kyusaburo, Sergeant Major 93
Kannon memorial, Betio 232-234
Kantetaake, Nei 97
Kanton. See Canton Island
Kanzaki, Chosito, NBK manager, Butaritari Island 7, 67, 70, 72, 74, 110, 111, 122
Kapoa, radio operator, Nonouti 81, 83, 88, 112, 220, 239
Karotu 199
Katori Maru, Japanese war ship 110
Kaue Baraniko 202
Kee Yang, Ioteba 227
Kenilworth, Australian ship 52
Keuea village, Butaritari 95-97, 99, 100, 133, 179, 198, 228, 232
KGV. See King George V School
Kiakia, RCS. Government ship 6, 223
Kiantongo 160, 219
Kidd, USS, destroyer 145
Kilpin, C. A., Private, New Zealand soldier 220, 230
King, Beri 227
King, Ernest J., Admiral 145
King George V School 36, 41, 43, 117, 132, 145, 181
King, Louis 226
King, Mak 226
King, Mosley 227
King's Wharf, Butaritari Island 74, 93, 159

269

Kiritimati. *See* Christmas Island
Komata, New Zealand ship 48
Komet, German raider 45, 46, 48, 49
Kong Choy. *See* Kwong Choy
Korambati Aretima 63
Korean labourers 122, 123, 156, 158, 162, 197, 202, 209, 216, 217, 234
Korean memorial, Betio 234, 235
Koreans in hiding at Butaritari Island 202
Korina Takeimoa 37
Kori, Yoshinori 216
Kosrae Island 193. *See* Kusaie
Kulmerland, German raider 45, 46
Kuma village, Butaritari 225
Kum Kee. *See also* Jong Kum Kee
Kum Kee, Ang 219
Kum Kee, Ben 112, 226
Kurama, Japanese battleship 116
Kuria Island 82, 83, 112, 113, 182, 198, 220, 226, 238
Kusaie, Caroline Islands 107, 108, 135, 194, 197
Kwajalein, Marshall Islands 71, 100, 137, 140, 178, 184, 202
Kwong Choy (Kong Choy, Shung Shue) 226
Kwong, George 226

L

Laing, N. M. 219
Langdale, Geoffrey Vavasour, radio operator, Christmas Island 11, 221
Lanyon, Nei Rerebati 227
Lau Gee Leong, Willie 227
Lau, George J. (Manti) 219, 225, 227
Lau Sam 225
Lawrence Philips, freighter 211
Leander, HMS, New Zealand Division, Royal Navy 11, 25, 26, 27
Le Bourget, Christmas Island 14
Lee, J. M. (Mike), radio operator 43, 221
Lehnert, Curly, pilot 177
Leith, HMS 10, 11

Lemuta, Ellice Islander 107
Le Triomphant, French destroyer 102
Lever Brothers 195, 196
Lexington, USS, aircraft carrier 101, 132
Likiep Atoll, Marshall Islands 5, 6
Linscott, Island Commander, Tarawa 178
Li Pak Ming. *See* Pak Ming
Liscome Bay, USS, aircraft carrier 162, 178
LMS. *See* London Missionary Society
London Missionary Society 34, 36, 42, 61, 80, 97, 111, 198
Lone Palm Cemetery, Betio 211, 212
LORAN (Long-range Radio Aid to Navigation) 183, 184
Low Gee Leong, Emeri 227
Low Gee Leong, Joseph 227
Low Gee Leong, Toma 227
Luke, Sir Harry, High Commissioner, Western Pacific High Commission 202

M

Maatusi Nofoaiga (Peniamina), radio operator, Kuria 81, 83, 88, 112, 219, 220, 239
Macquarie SS, On Chong ship 6, 223
Maheu Naniseni, radio operator 46, 174, 177, 219
Maiana Island 40, 61, 80, 82, 83, 97, 109, 118-220
Makin Atoll, Gilbert Islands 6, 7, 41, 57, 70, 97, 161, 179, 220, 225
Malden Island, Southern Line Islands 201
Malekula, New Hebrides 102
Mamo, tug boat at Canton Island 18
Mangarita, Nei 6
Manra Island. *See* Sydney Island
Manti. *See* Lau, George J. (Manti)
Manuela, Sergeant Major 169
Manyo Maru, Komet, disguised as. *See* Komet, German raider
Marakei Island 7
Mariana Islands 184

Marine Fighter Squadron VMF-422, United States 171
Mariposa, S.S. 17
Marsack, Raymond O. 168, 169, 219
Marshall Islands 57, 71, 72, 79, 93, 172, 178, 188, 192, 197, 212, 232
Maryland, USS, battleship 146, 153, 154, 181
Massic, Island Commander, Tarawa 179
Masubusi, Shingo, NBK Manager, Butaritari Island 74, 122
Matai, New Zealand ship 29
mats 155, 180
Matua, MV, New Zealand ship 39
Maude, Harry E., Resident Commissioner 168, 203
Maui Teonea, radio operator, Ocean Island 219, 221, 239
Mavis, flying boat at Butaritari 93
McArthur, A. M. 40, 41, 112, 118, 230
McCarthy, J. J., coast-watcher 83, 220, 230
McKean Island 11
McKenna, A. E., coast-watcher 83, 220, 230
McKenzie, R. M., Private, New Zealand soldier 221, 230
McLaughlin, J. S., Major 173, 176
McQuinn, Maxwell P., coast-watcher 70, 71, 73, 219, 220
Mela (Sister, OLSH), Catholic Church 219
Menzies, John (Jack) M., Private, New Zealand soldier 69, 220
Menzies, Michael, Private, New Zealand soldier 69, 220
Mercer, Arthur H., BPC employee, Ocean Island 103, 230
meteorological stations 37
Metusela Neeia, radio operator, Canton Island 42, 43, 219, 221
MHLW. *See* Social Welfare and War Relief Bureau, of the Ministry of Health, Labour and Welfare, Japanese
Micronesia, Japanese mandate of 3, 5
Mikaere 120

Mili Atoll, Marshall Islands 139
Milne, John, radio operator, Tarawa 36, 43, 59, 61, 219, 220, 237
missionaries 38, 56, 61, 120
Mitchell, Maria 7
Mitchell, P. E., High Commissioner, Suva, Fiji 203
Moanimarewe 238
Monowai, HMS, New Zealand ship 29
Moore, W. A., Captain, New Zealand Army 29
Moran, 'Tiger', Lieutenant 175
Morgan, Reginald G., wireless instructor 36, 63, 118, 119, 220, 230
Mote 199
Muller, Domingo, radio operator, Tarawa 220, 238
Muller, Fritz 6
Muller, Helen Lina 7
Muller, Henry (Heinrich Jelske) 6, 7
Muller, Herman 6
Muller, Joseph 6, 93, 95, 160
Muller, Lewis B., Private, New Zealand soldier 70, 220
Muller, Lina 74
Muller, Paul, radio operator 81, 88
Muller, Rudolph Keakea 6
Muller, William 6
Mullinnix, H. M., Rear Admiral 162, 178
Mullins, Lieutenant Commander, RNR 39
Murdoch, David 120
Murdoch, Otebina 219
Murray, Colonel 155
Murray, Tom C., coast-watcher 42, 43, 111, 220, 230

N

Naa, Tarawa Atoll 154-157, 216, 234
Nabatiku, native magistrate 199
Nabeina islet, Tarawa 178, 179
Nabetari 187, 190
Nagata Maru, 8th Gunboat Division, Japanese Navy 67

271

Namonaterara Wiriam 219
Nantaku Maru, trading ship, Butaritari Island 107
Nanumea Atoll, Ellice Islands 39, 128, 130, 131, 138, 140, 145, 168, 172-176
Nanyo Boyeki Kabushiki Kaisha (NBK) 6, 7, 67, 74, 122, 158, 216
Nara, Yoshio, Lieutenant 191, 192
Narruhn, Bob, radio operator, Tarawa 57, 81, 88, 219, 220
Narruhn, Frederick 5, 7, 160-162
Narruhn, Joe 65, 160
Narruhn, Robert 5, 159
Nateri, Sergeant 110
Nauru Island 33, 45, 46, 48, 49, 50, 52, 100-103, 107, 121, 128-131, 134, 135, 137-140, 145, 187-189, 192-194, 197, 217
Nautilus, USS, submarine 92, 93, 95, 156
NBK. *See* Nanyo Boyeki Kabushiki Kaisha (NBK)
Nei Kaeka, wife of A. M. McArthur 40
Nei Kareke 224
Nei Ketia 225, 227
Nei Marewe 226
Nei Nanoa Low Gee Leong 227
Nei Reibo 6
Nei Ruta 6
Nei Tibe 225
Nei Timake 224
Nei Tita 134
Nell (Mitsubishi 96 attack bomber) 128
New Zealand Meteorological Department 37
New Zealand Post and Telegraph Department 37
Nichol, J. H., Private, New Zealand soldier 220, 230
Nikumaroro Island. *See* Gardner Island
Nikunau Island 78-80, 111
Nimanoa, RCS, government ship 36, 40, 41, 56-58, 61, 63, 64, 226
Nimitz, Chester, Admiral 91, 145, 168, 187, 188

Ninigo Island, New Guinea 187
Niulakita Island, Ellice Islands (Tuvalu) 39, 84
Niutao Island 174, 176, 177
Noah, Mark, History Flight 214, 217
Nonouti Island 4, 7, 8, 40, 41, 80, 82, 83, 112, 182, 220, 226
Nortum, ship 41
Noto Islet, Tarawa Atoll 155
Nui Atoll 39, 174, 175, 176
Nukufetau Atoll 22, 39, 130, 138, 140, 143
Nukunonu, Tokelau Islands 13, 144
Nurnberg, German raider 25

O

O'Brien, Faasamata, radio operator, Hull Island 42, 221
O'Brien, Peni 239
O'Brien, Pole 144, 219
Ocean Island 33-35, 41, 42, 46, 47, 50-52, 55-57, 67, 78, 100-109, 120, 121, 129, 131, 163, 187-198, 200, 202, 204, 217, 221-223, 230, 239
Ocean Island Defence Force 51, 52
Ohta, Kiyoshi, Ensign 147
Okinoshima, Japanese destroyer 67
O'Leary, George P., Captain, New Zealand Army 29, 219
Oliva (Sister) 121
On Chong and Company 6, 67, 70, 74, 158, 159, 161, 222-225
Onotoa Island 226
Operation Flintlock 172
Operation Galvanic 137, 138, 141, 143-145, 153, 178, 194
Operation Grandpass 14
Operation MO 101
Orion, German raider 45, 46, 48
Orona Island. *See* Hull Island
Otsaki, Sergeant Major 106
Owen, C. J., Private, New Zealand soldier 110, 220, 230

P

Page, General 146
Page, S. S., Lieutenant, RNZNR 240
Pagopago, American Samoa 18, 22
Pak Ming (Ba Ming, Li Pak Ming) 226
Palau Island 184
Pall, Tom 81, 87, 219
Palmyra Island 20
Pan American World Airways 9, 184
Parker, W. A. R., Private, New Zealand soldier 221, 230
Paton, E. J. 14
Pearl Harbor, Hawai'i 17-19, 35, 55, 67, 78, 95, 141, 145, 146
Pearsall, C. A., coast-watcher 221, 230
Peatross, Oscar, Lieutenant 94
Peck, John, Lieutenant 184
Pedro, Jack 219
Pedro, Kima 15
Peleti Lauti, radio operator, Ocean Island 41, 103, 106, 219, 221, 239
Pelican, USS, survey of Phoenix islands 13
Peniamina. *See* Maatusi Nofoaiga
Penitala Teo 219
Pensacola, USS, cruiser 144
Petersen, Anton, officer, Donerail 89, 90
Phoenix Island 11
phosphate mining 45, 46, 49, 50, 56, 104, 192, 195
Pii, Niels, Captain, Donerail 78
poisoned rice, at Butaritari 202
Pollack, USS, submarine 123
Portland, USS 118, 119
Port Moresby, Territory of New Guinea 101
Powell, Winnie 94, 219
Prentice, Campbell, Sergeant Major 29
Prentice, Margaret 219
President Munro, USS 181
President Taylor, USS 18, 19
Princeton, USS, aircraft carrier 132
prostitution 180
Prusa, USS 78-80, 83
Pujebet, V. J. (Father), Sacred Heart Mission 103, 230
Pulekai Sogivalu 117, 219, 132

R

Rabi Island, Fiji 195, 196, 206
radar 105, 128, 129, 214, 217, 234
Ramuz (Father), Sacred Hear Mission 61
Randolph, Ben 238
Randolph, Joe 59
rape 107, 194
Reiher, Christopher 5
Reiher, Florence 219
Reiher, Fritz 6, 79
Reiher, Henry 6, 79
Reiher, John 156, 219
Reiher, Karl 219
Reiher, Tom 99, 219
Reiher, William 6
Reita Tekateke 99, 219
Relief, USS, hospital ship 145
Reuera 187
Reymond. *See also* von Reymond
Reymond, Carla Anna 37
Reymond, Oscar 72, 219
Reynolds, James, Sgt 22
Richards, Arthur, Sir 202
Rickenbacker, Eddie, Captain 19, 20, 21, 22, 23
Rigel, USS, destroyer tender 31
RNZAF. *See* Royal New Zealand Air Force (RNZAF)
Roberts, R. G. 219
Robuti, Butaritari Island 72, 94, 219
Roi-Namur, Kwajalein, Marshall Islands 140
Rongorongo, Beru Island 34, 111
Roosevelt, James, Major 92
Rostier, F. H., radio operator, Christmas Island 11, 221
Rota, assistant master, KGV School 181, 182
Royal Australian Navy 7, 34, 161

Royal New Zealand Air Force (RNZAF) 37, 168
Ruka Kauaba 194
Ruotake Iantin, radio operator, Maiana 81, 82, 88, 109, 220, 239

S

Sacred Heart Mission 103, 161
Sadd, A. L. (Reverend), LMS Church 111, 118, 230
Saichiro, Tomanari, Rear Admiral 115, 123
Saipan Island 137
Sale, Louise 219
Salt Lake City, USS, cruiser 144
Santa Teretia, Catholic Mission ship 6, 61
Sasebo Naval Special Landing Force 123
Savage, Michael, New Zealand Prime Minister 26
Scarborough HMS vii
Schutz, Henry 8, 219
Schutz, Mary 219
Schutz, Paul 7
Schutz, William (Willie), radio operator, Tarawa 7, 8, 43, 57, 59, 60, 81, 88, 220, 238
Sea Bees. *See* US Naval Construction Battalion
Seikai Maru, trading at Butaritari and Jaluit 7
Seither, Richard, Sergeant 23
Sherrod, Robert 211
Shibasaki, Keiji, Rear Admiral 123, 149, 151, 152
Shikoku Island, Japan 71
Shosa, Matzu, Japanese Naval Commander 115, 122
Shung Shue. *See* Kwong Choy
Sinclair, P. L. G. (Lloyd), Chief Engineer, Nimanoa 56, 58, 62-66, 81, 84, 86
Sing, Joe 224
Sing, Mary 223
Siu Akam 225

Siu Waiang 225
Skegerak, merchant ship 52
slavery, Japanese 118, 122
Smart, Eric, NZ Public Works Department Engineer 11
Smith, Holland, Major General 147
Social Welfare and War Relief Bureau, of the Ministry of Health, Labour and Welfare, Japanese (MHLW) 214, 216
Solomona, radio operator 41
Solomon Islands 45, 91
sovereignty 11, 42, 178, 180, 200, 211
Speedy, Leslie B., Private, New Zealand soldier 110, 220, 230
Spruance, Raymond A., Vice-Admiral 140, 141
Starbuck Island, Southern Line Islands 201
Stead, Harold, Chief Mate, Nimanoa 63, 64, 79, 80, 86
Steenson, K. R., Dr., Senior medical Officer, Gilbert & Ellice Islands 56, 57, 64, 81, 87
Stevenson, J. R. Brigadier 190
Sturdee, V. A. H., Lieutenant General, Commander, 1st Australian Army 189
Summers, Ronald 213
Sumner, USS, survey ship 143
Suva, Fiji 26, 27, 30, 35, 77, 79, 83, 84, 90, 168, 179, 205, 206, 223
Suva School for Wireless Operators 37
Suzuki, Naoomi, Lieutenant Commander 190, 191, 192
Swan, USS, survey of Phoenix Islands 13
Sydney Island 9, 11, 34

T

Tabakea 219
Taberannang Teuaba 122
Taberanteatu 160
Tabiteuea village, Tarawa Atoll 155, 179
Tabokai, bosun, Nimanoa 81, 87

Tabuaeran Island. *See* Fanning Island
Tagua, NZ auxiliary schooner 15, 30
Tai Moong Chai 227
Takaua (Constable) 120
Takunan Maru, Japanese transport ship 123
Tamana Island 6, 39, 40, 110, 129, 221
Tamoa, Gilbertese 106
Tangitang Cooperative Society 7
Taninta, Japanese civilian 107
tanks 123, 147, 149, 159, 182
Tarawa Atoll, Gilbert Islands 5-8, 34-38, 40, 41, 54, 56, 58, 61, 65, 66, 70, 77-83, 89, 97, 101, 103, 107-109, 112, 115, 116, 118, 120, 123, 127-132, 137-141, 144-146, 149-151, 153-158, 165-168, 170-172, 176, 178, 179, 181, 183, 184, 187, 188, 194, 195, 197-201, 203, 205, 206, 209-211, 214-217, 220, 225, 229, 232, 234, 237, 238, 240
Tarekaua Tokamatawa, LMS pastor 97
Tatou Kaburoro 133, 148, 219
Tauantang 106
Taukiei, radio operator, Abemama 81, 83, 88, 220, 239
Taylor, Alan L., coast-watcher 36, 42, 43, 111, 220, 230
Teaoraereke village, Tarawa Atoll 154
Tebanini 134, 219
Teieta Hugill 134
Tekai 238
Tekarara. *See* Brechtefeld, Stephen (Tekarara), radio operator, Beru
Tekemau, Tamana Island 110
Tekinano 199
Telavi Faati, radio operator, Abaiang 71, 220, 237
Teleradio, radio equipment 36, 39
Temaiku, Tarawa Atoll 154, 171
Tenyo Maru, Japanese destroyer 67
Tepuka Islet, Funafuti 144
Teraina Island. *See* Washington Island
Terrienne, Octave (Bishop), Sacred Heart Mission 120, 161, 162
Terror, USS, minelayer 142
Tetaua 219
Teveia Ntiua 107, 108, 219
Teweka 219
thatch 180
Third, Ronald, radio operator 41, 103, 104, 106, 221, 230
Thorburn, Philip B., radio operator 41, 221, 239
Tibwe 199
Tikaouti Bonabati 106, 219
Till, N. J. 14
Tiriata, Gilbertese clerk 112
Tito Homasi, radio operator, Canton Island 37, 43, 221
Toanikarawa Teaero 106
toddy (*karewe*) 107, 182, 190, 194
Tokelau Islands 10, 184, 200, 222
Tokyo Maru. *See* Kulmerland, German raider
Toma Tonana 63
trans-Pacific air routes 9, 13, 16, 18, 184
Triadic, BPC ship 45, 46
Triaster, BPC ship 45, 48
Trienza, BPC ship 108
Triona, BPC ship 45, 46, 195
Tripartite Pact - Japan, Germany, Italy 4
Truk Islands 101, 137, 194
Tschaun, Captain 146
Tulagi, Solomon Islands 91, 101
Tung Ang 226
Turia Siu 225
Tutu Tekanene, native medical practitioner 155
Tuvalu. *See* Ellice Islands

U

Uatioa, Reuben, radio operator, Gardner Island 42, 43, 221
Ueantabo, Tamana Island 110
Ueanteiti, Gilbertese 192
Ukiangang village, Butaritari 67, 133, 134, 158, 159, 180, 202, 216

Unaia, Iaonibure 72, 74
Union Islands. *See* Tokelau Islands
Union Jack 10, 13, 167, 182
Union Steam Ship Company 29
US Army 5, 6, 15, 16, 18, 19, 127-129, 135, 158, 160-162, 165, 171, 211, 212, 214, 216
US Army Air Force (USAAF) 23, 127, 128, 130, 131, 134, 139, 140, 194, 202
US Coast Guard (USCG) 183
Usher, Len (Sir) 219
US Marine Corps (USMC) 6, 23, 57, 65, 70, 89, 91, 93-95, 97, 100, 115, 122, 123, 128, 129, 131, 132, 135, 139, 140, 144, 146-151, 153-156, 158, 166, 167, 171, 172, 176, 177, 181, 182, 193, 209-214, 217, 225, 229
US Naval Construction Battalion (Sea Bees) 122, 158
US Navy 7, 55, 102, 128, 129, 139, 140, 141-143, 147, 153, 158, 161, 171, 188, 194, 201, 209, 211, 240

V

Vaitupu Atoll 39
Van Nattan, Wesley, US medical corpsman 225
Vaskess, H., Secretary, West Pacific High Commission 90
Vaughan, D. L., radio operator 219, 239
VB-142, US Navy Bombing Squadron 188
Verrier, Walter Lindsay, Dr.. *See* Isaac, Walter Lindsay, Dr.
Viallon, Marcel (Father), Sacred Heart Mission 161
Vickers, 8-inch guns, Betio 116
VII Army Air Force, United States 139, 140
Vinni, Norwegian phosphate ship 46
Viti, HMFS, Fiji ship 39, 41, 42, 168, 223, 224, 226, 227
Vito, phosphate ship 52

VMF-111, US Marine Fighter Squadron 144
VMF-422, US Marine Fighter Squadron 171, 172, 173, 174, 175, 176, 177
von Reymond. *See also* Reymond
von Reymond, Bruno, Lieutenant 7, 161
von Reymond, Helena 161
von Reymond, Maiana 7
von Reymond, Moritz 7, 161
von Reymond, Nikunau 7
Vostok Island, Southern Line Islands 201

W

Wallace. Sydney R., coast-watcher 71, 73, 220
war compensation 198, 199, 200, 206
war crimes 49, 50, 100, 106, 118, 122, 191, 192, 194
war rents 206
war savings and donations 206
Washington Island 30, 34
Webster, C. (Brother), Sacred Heart Mission 161
Webster, Gordon Jack, Captain of ships RCS Kiakia, MV Degei; later made Lieutenant, RNZNR 80, 84-86, 146, 240
Wellington, HMS 9
Were, Basil L., Private, New Zealand soldier 70, 220
Wernham, D. C. I., administrative officer 154, 155, 178
Western Pacific High Commission 50, 90, 102, 168, 189
Westralia, Australian ship 52
Whittaker, James, Lt 21, 22
Wilde, Allan M. (Oscar), radio operator 43, 221
Williams, Charles R. Fulford, District Officer, Butaritari 67, 69, 70, 71, 74, 212, 238
Wilson, Gordon, coast-watcher 175, 219
Wilson, Walter 'Jake', Lieutenant 174, 176

Wong Day 226
WPHC. *See* Western Pacific High Commission

Y

Yamamoto, Isoroku, Admiral 102
Yee Kum On (senior) 226
Yee Kum On (Yee On Bonto) 226
Yee On Bonto 80. *See* Yee Kum On
Yee Pung Chong Gum 225
Yokata, Lieutenant, Japanese Navy 115, 122
Yokohama, Japan 71
Yokohama Naval Air Group, at Butaritari Island 72
Yokosuka 6th Special Naval Landing Force 115
Yokosuka Naval Base, Japan 71
You Fook, Agnes 227
You Heedon, Korean construction worker 234
Yuan Lon Mei 226
Yugure, Japanese destroyer 103, 104
Yunagi, Japanese destroyer 57

Z

Zeke (Zero), Japanese fighter aircraft 131, 132
Zentsuji Prison Camp, Japan 71, 72